SPECIAL THANKS TO MY DAD. MY HERO.

HARBOR MOON

RYAN COLUCCI
WRITER, EDITOR, PRODUCER

DIKRAN ORNEKIAN
WRITER

PAWEL SAMBOR
ARTIST

KAROL WISNIEWSKI
ART DIRECTOR

NIKODEM CABALA
SUPPORTING ARTIST

BRIAN ANDERSON
STORY BY

ARCANA
www.arcana.com

CEO and Owner
Sean O'Reilly

VP of Operations
Mark Poulton

VP of Marketing
Tyler Nichol

VP of Special Projects
Nick Schley

Senior Editor
Mike Kalvoda

General Manager
Michelle Meyers

WWW.HARBOR-MOON.COM

Printed in Canada

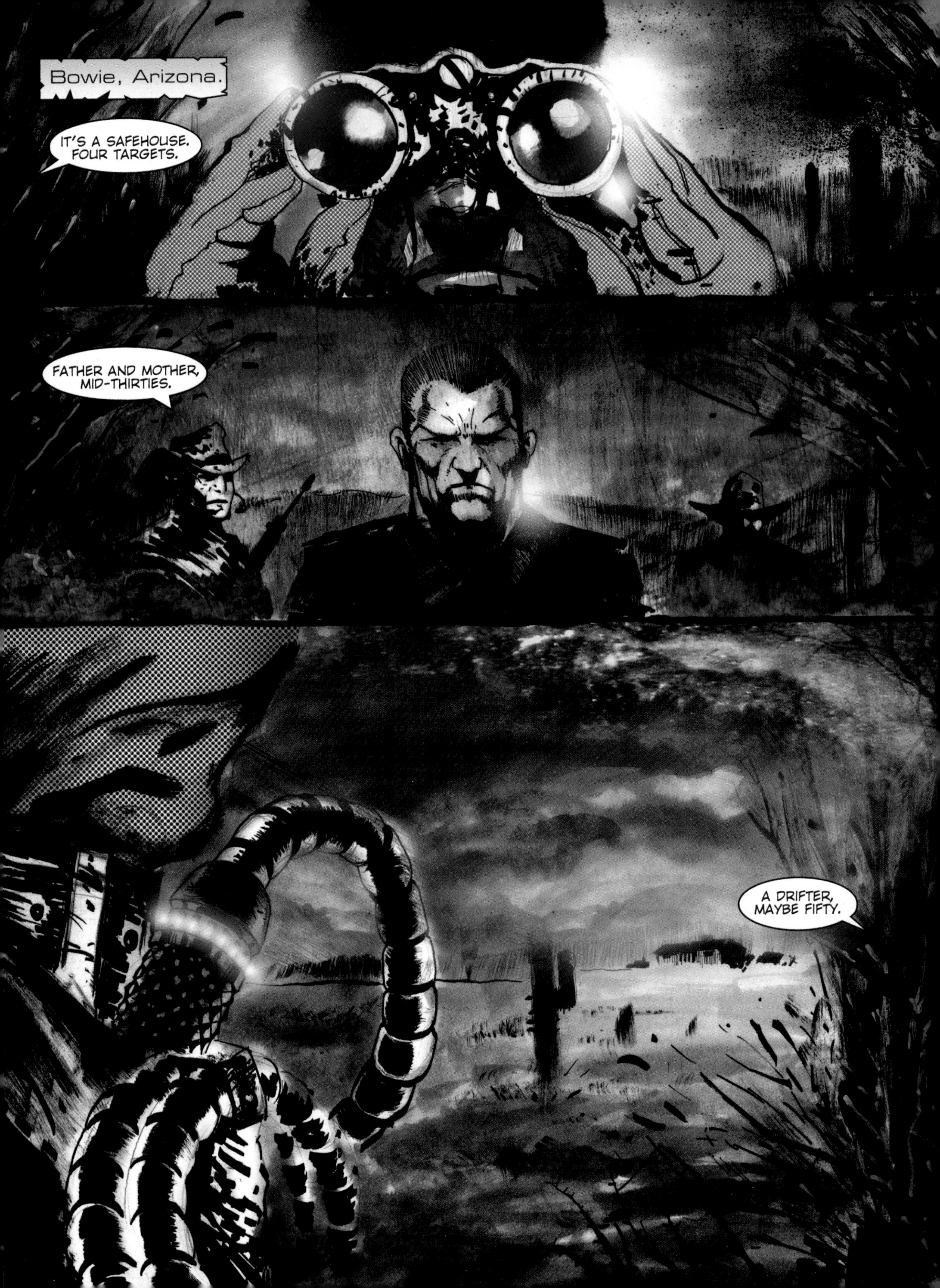
Bowie, Arizona.
IT'S A SAFEHOUSE. FOUR TARGETS.
FATHER AND MOTHER, MID-THIRTIES.
A DRIFTER, MAYBE FIFTY.

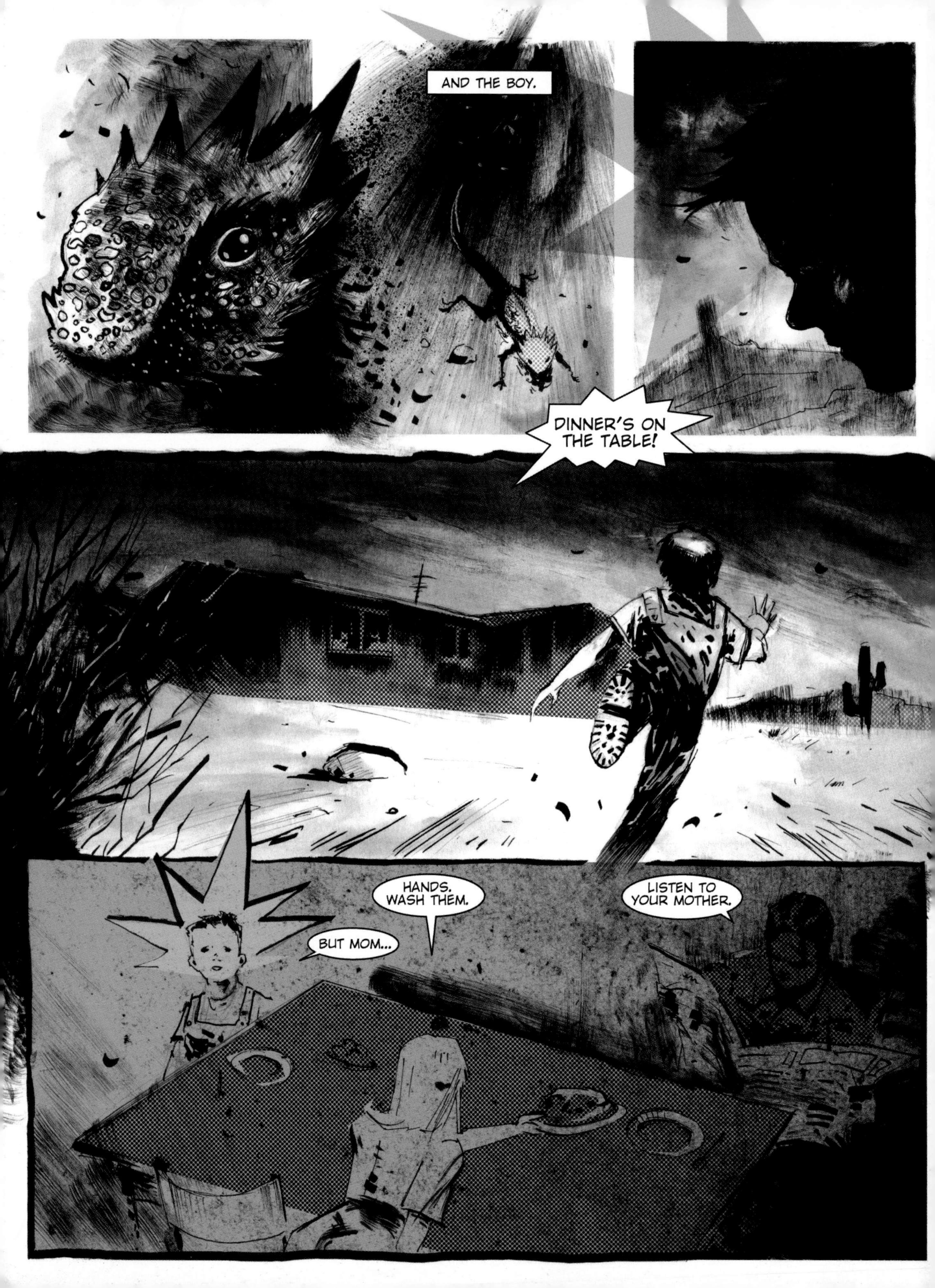
AND THE BOY.
DINNER'S ON THE TABLE!
HANDS. WASH THEM.
BUT MOM...
LISTEN TO YOUR MOTHER.

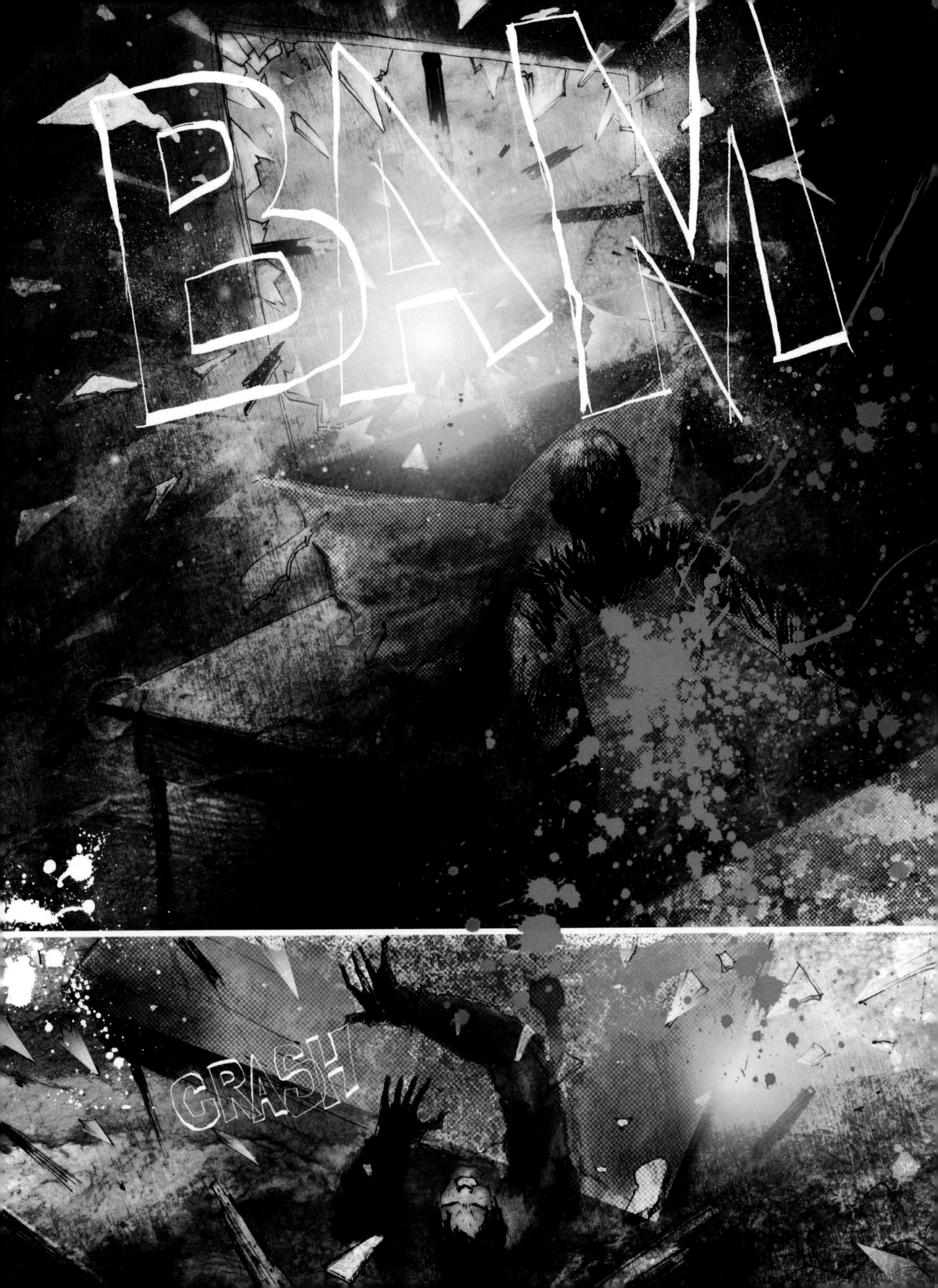
BAM
CRASH

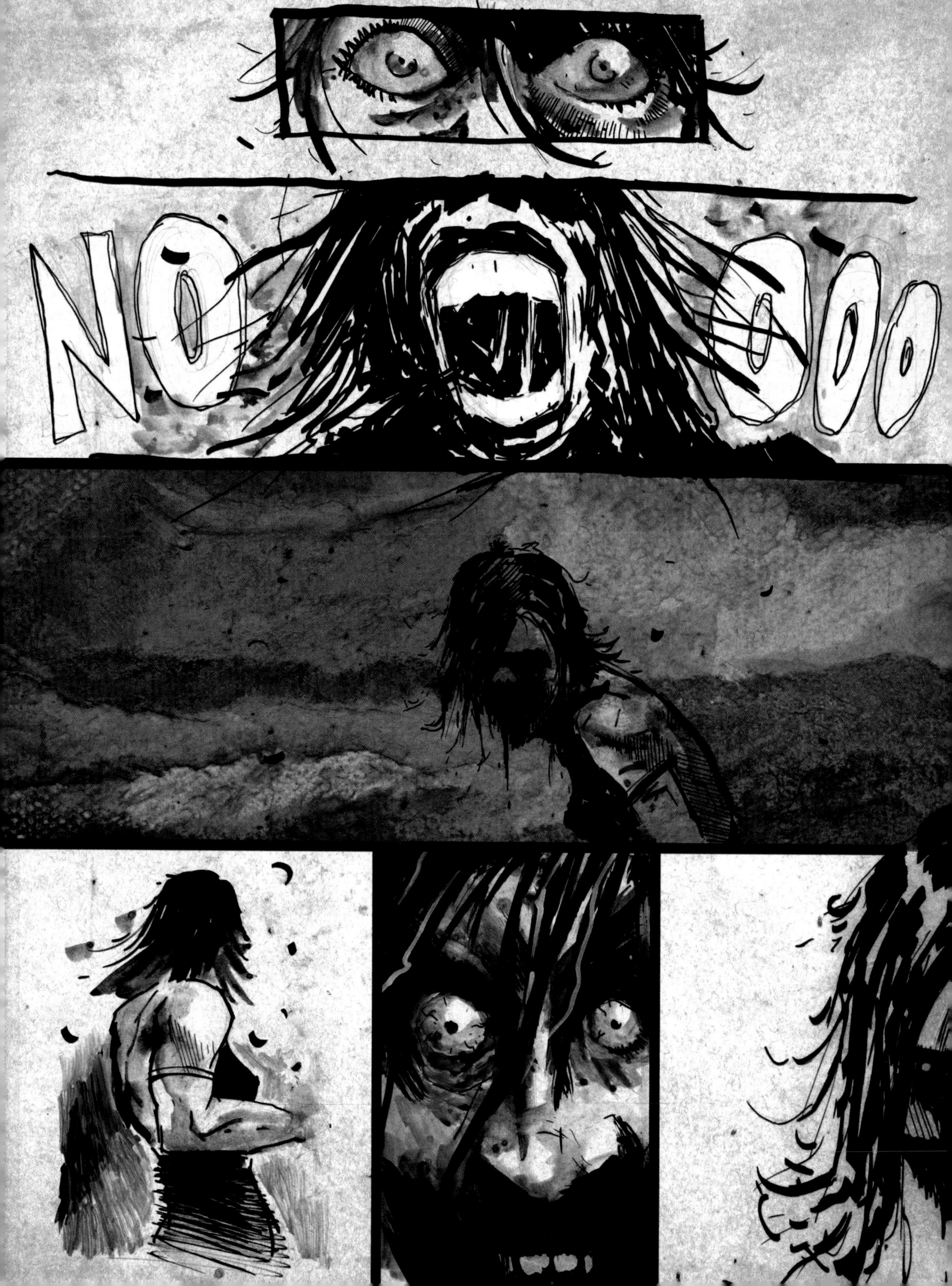
NOOOOO

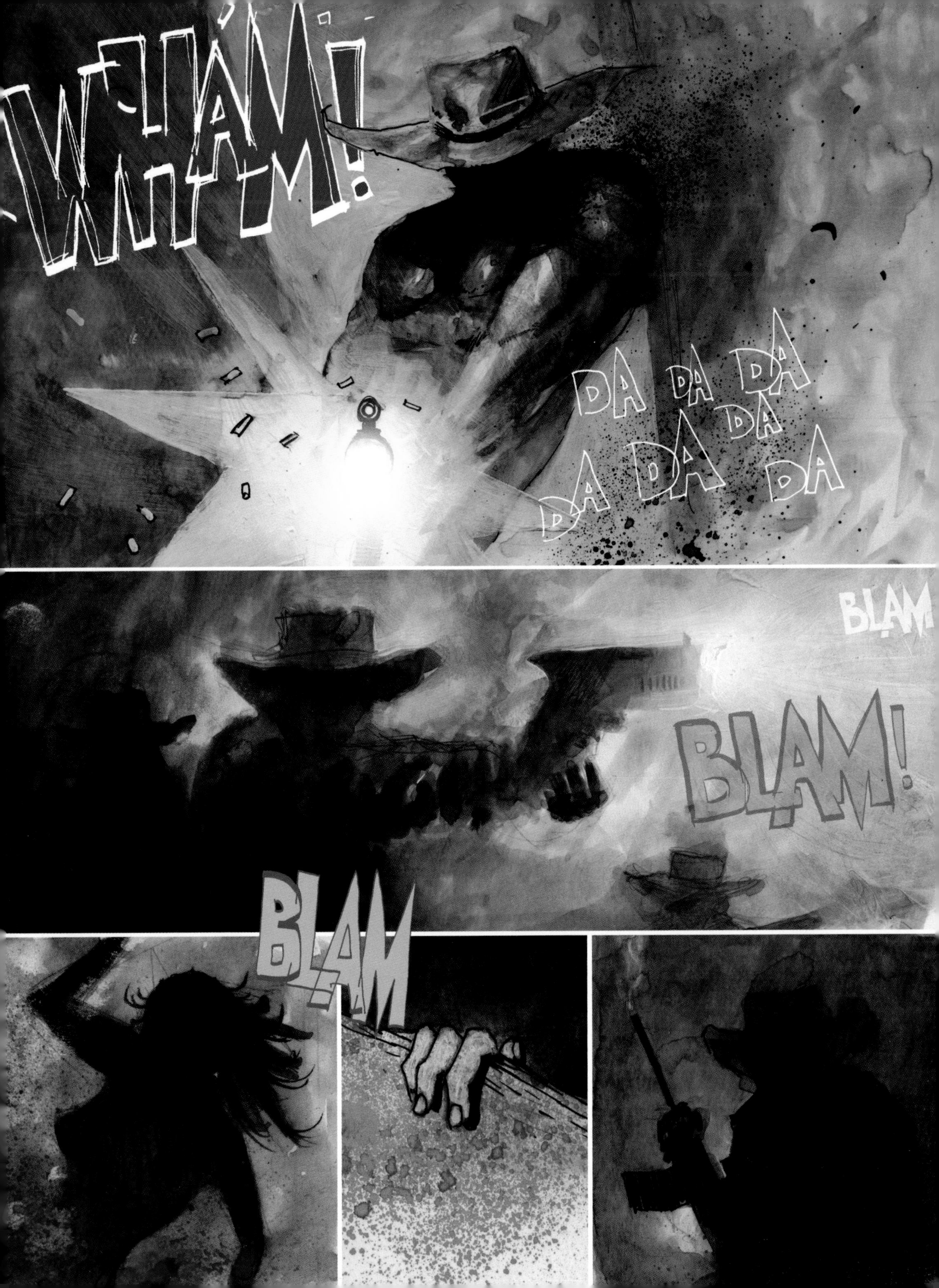
WHAM!
DA DA DA
DA
DA DA DA DA
BLAM
BLAM!
BLAM

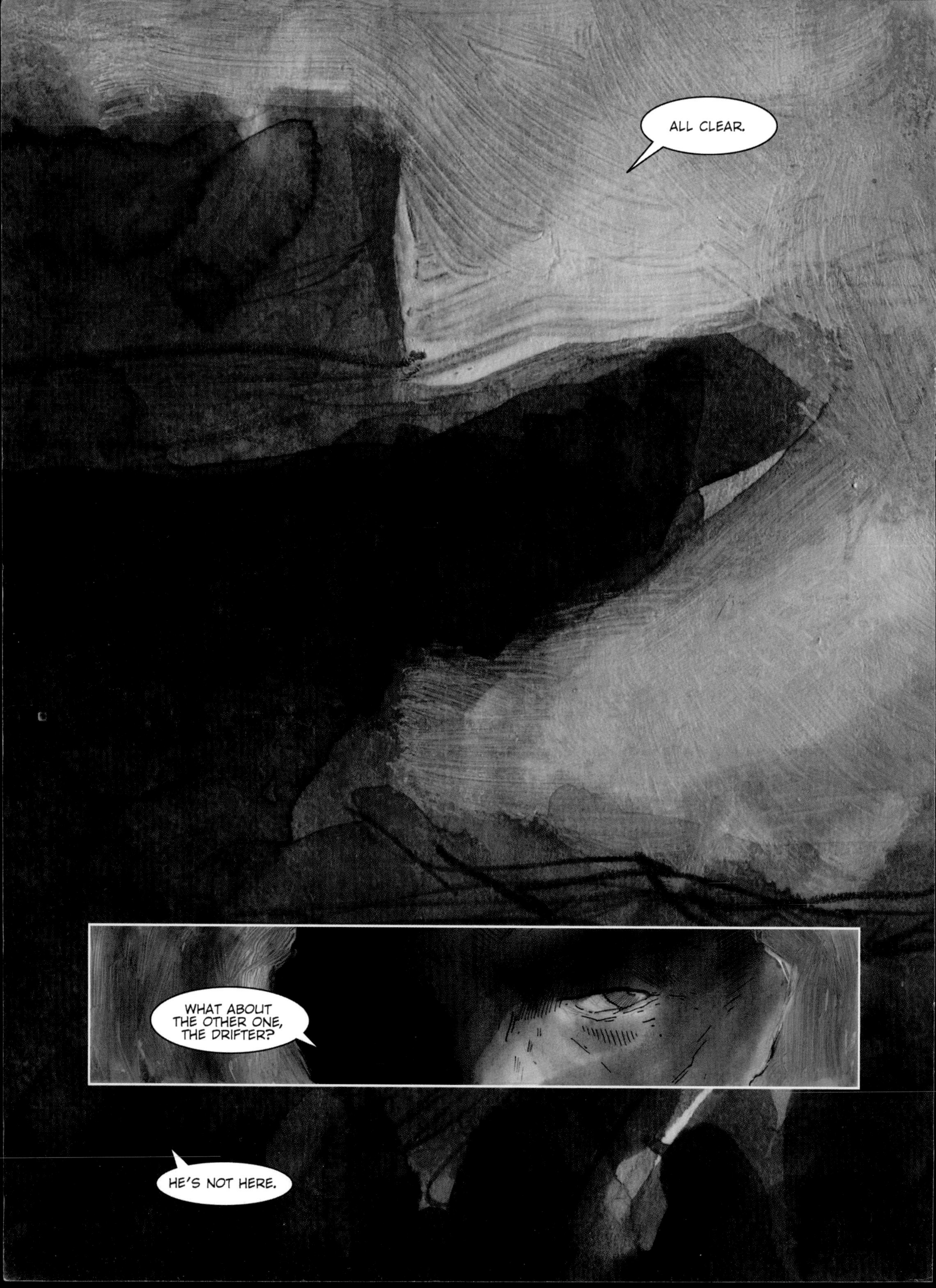
ALL CLEAR.
WHAT ABOUT THE OTHER ONE, THE DRIFTER?
HE'S NOT HERE.

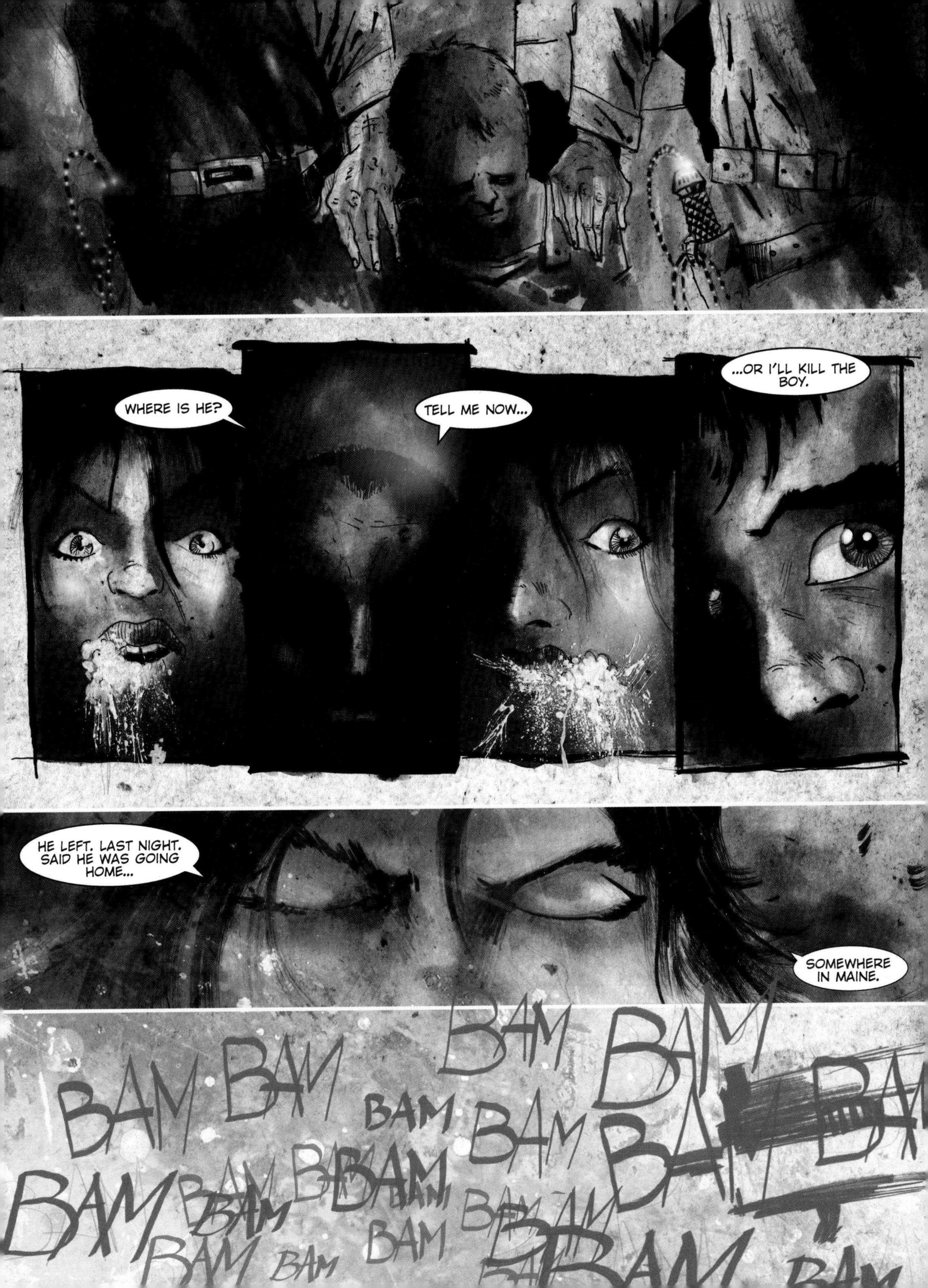
WHERE IS HE?
TELL ME NOW...
...OR I'LL KILL THE BOY.
HE LEFT. LAST NIGHT. SAID HE WAS GOING HOME...
SOMEWHERE IN MAINE.
BAM BAM BAM BAM BAM BAM BAM BAM BAM BAM BAM BAM BAM BAM BAM BAM BAM BAM

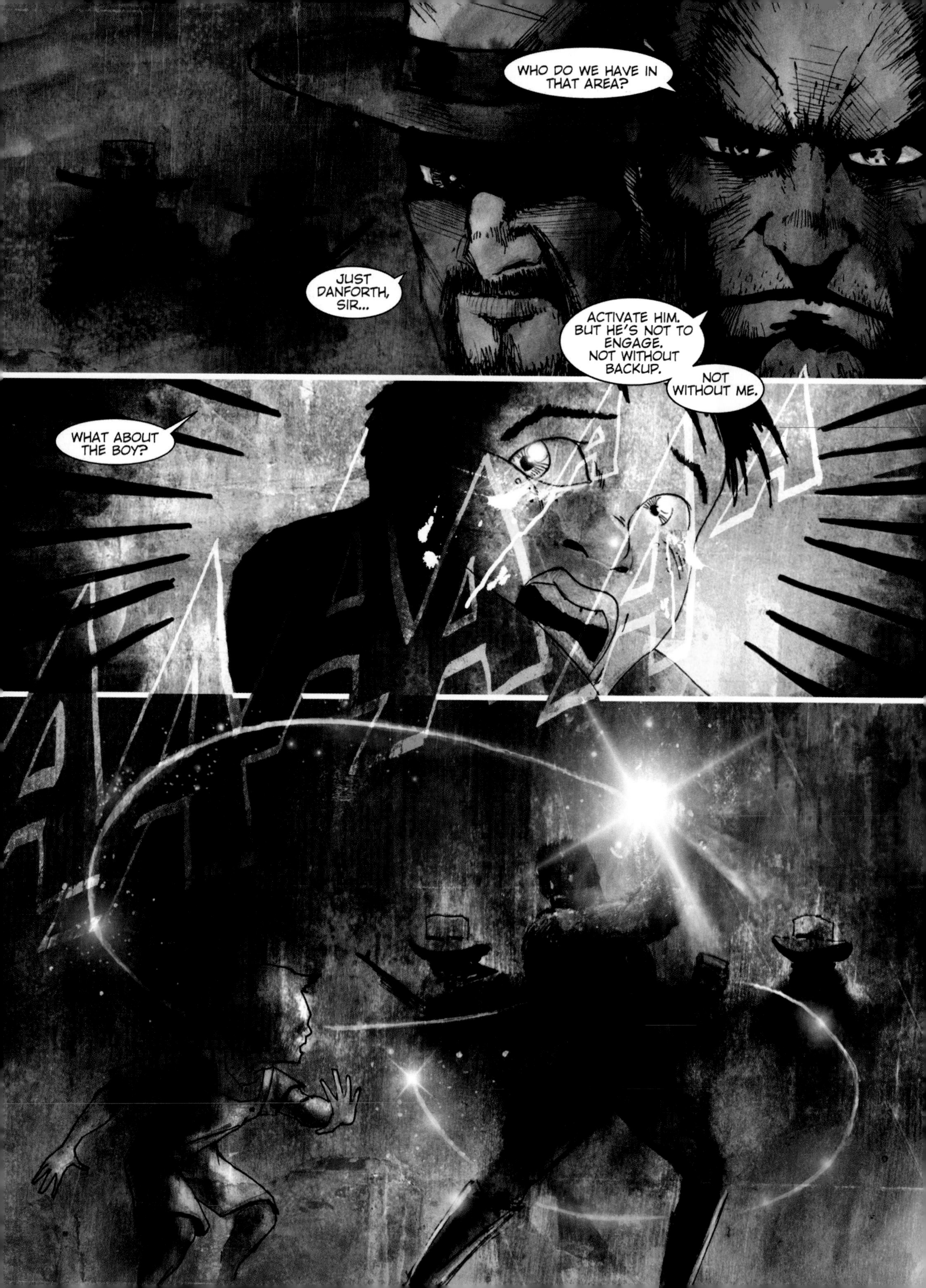
WHO DO WE HAVE IN THAT AREA?
JUST DANFORTH, SIR...
ACTIVATE HIM. BUT HE'S NOT TO ENGAGE. NOT WITHOUT BACKUP.
NOT WITHOUT ME.
WHAT ABOUT THE BOY?

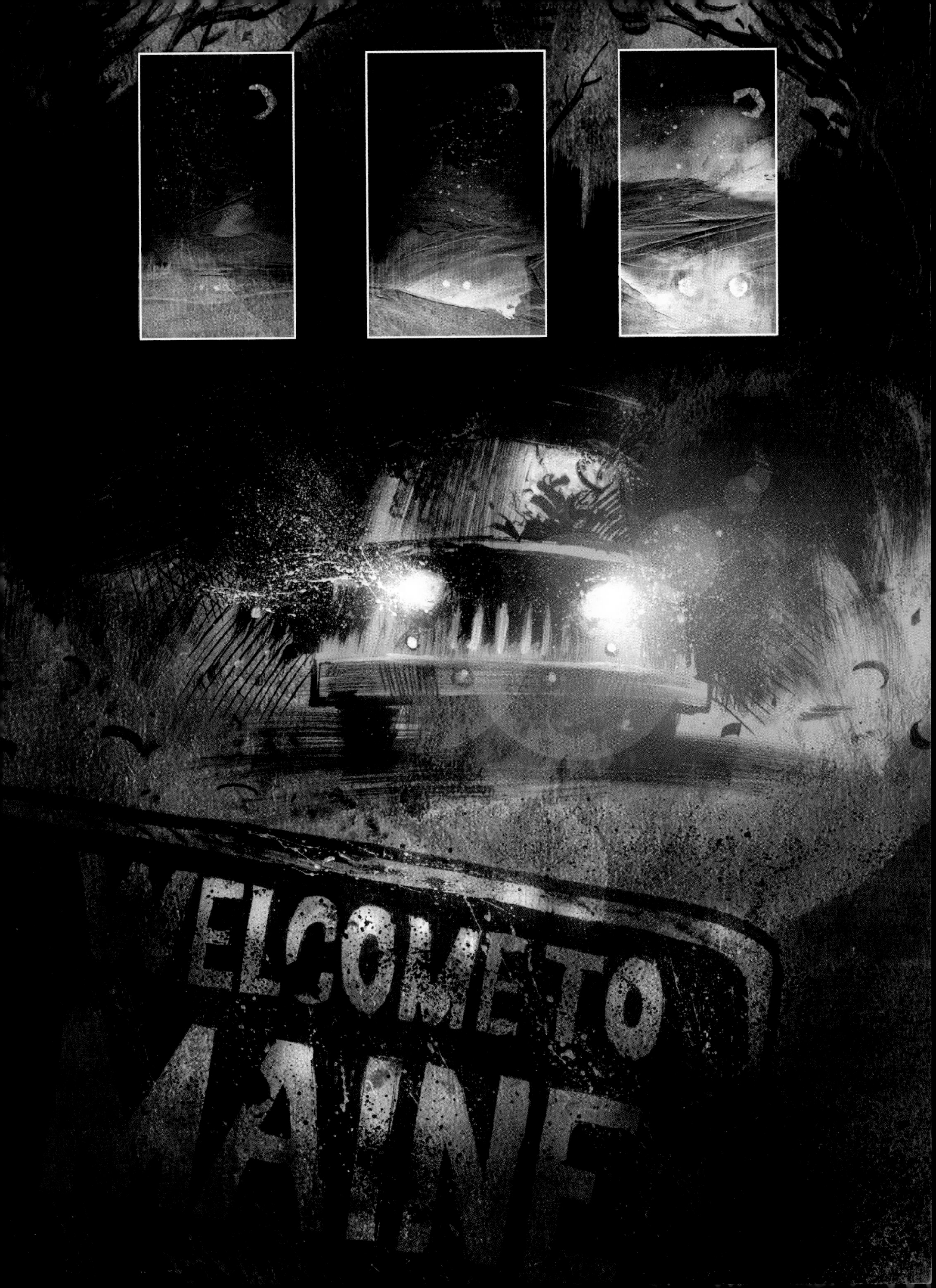
ELCOME TO
AINE

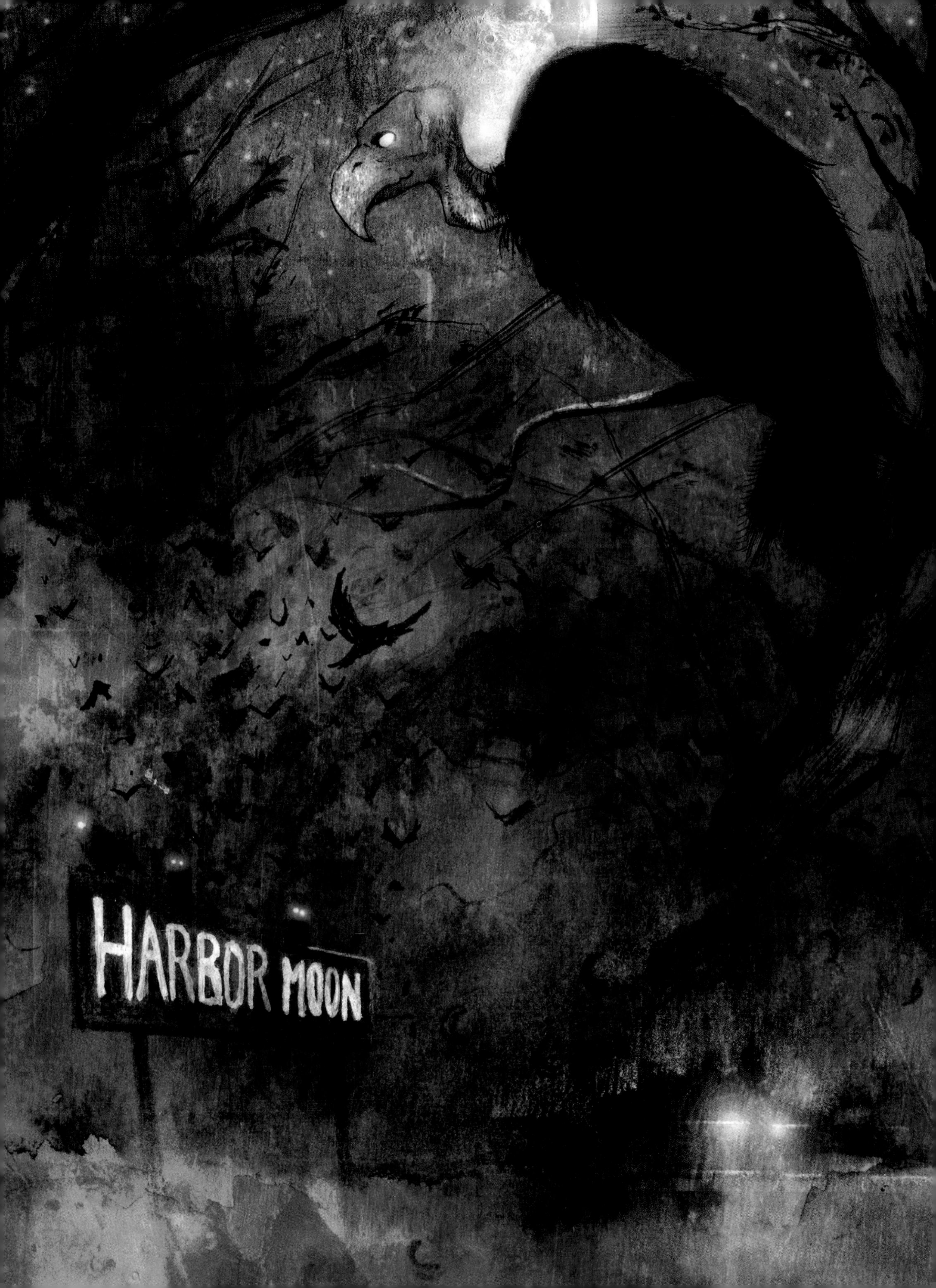
HARBOR MOON

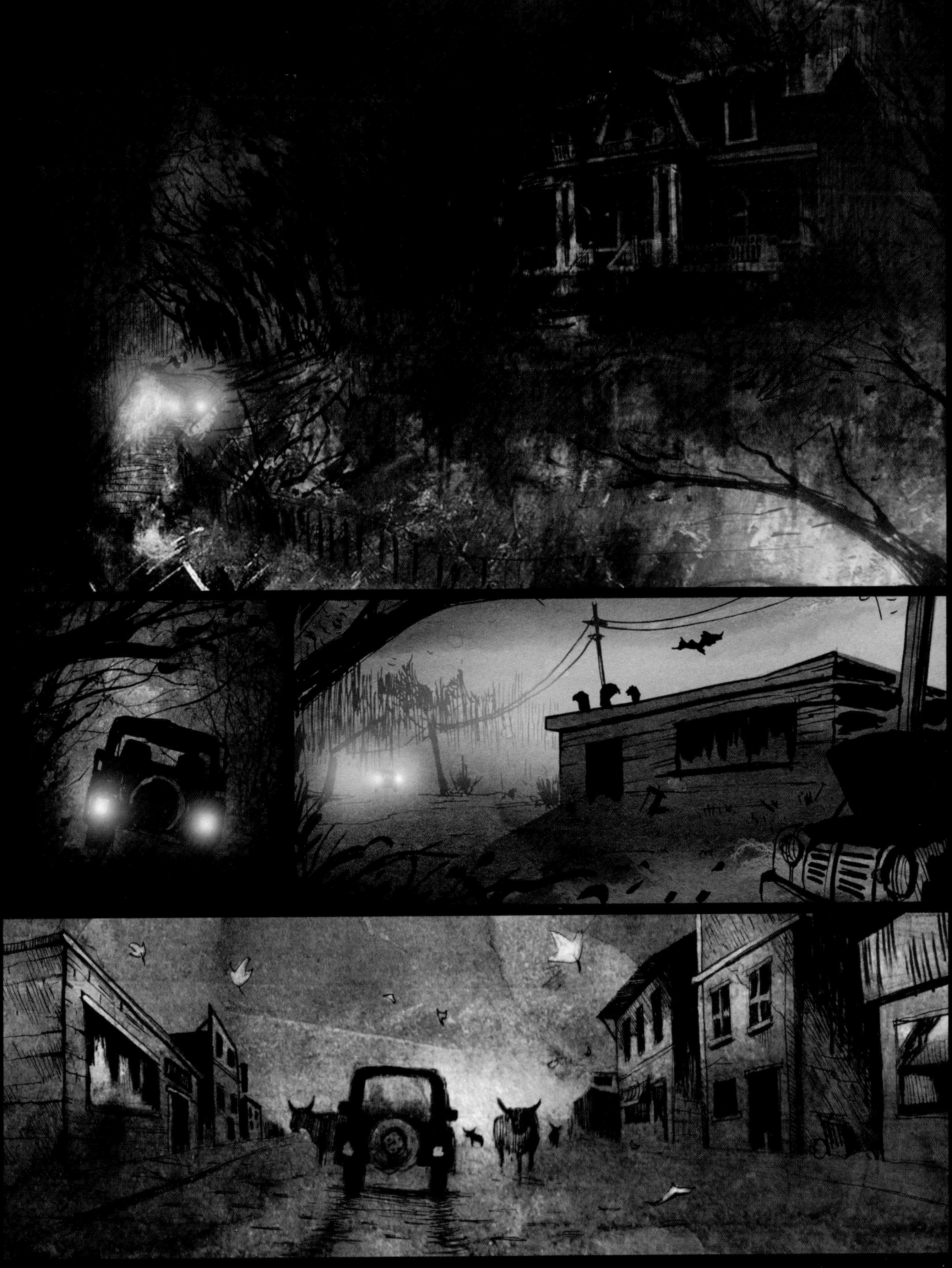

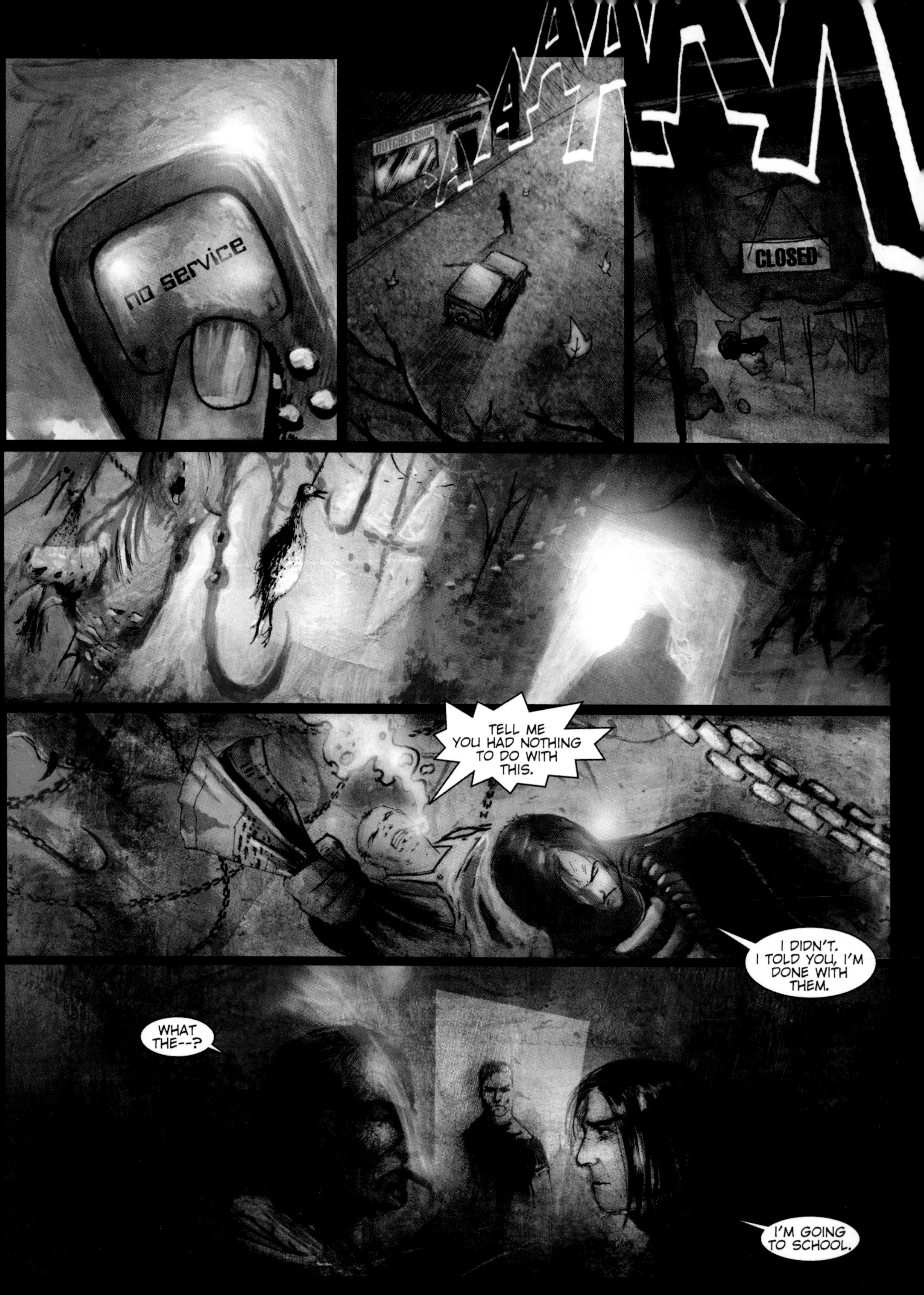
no service
BUTCHER SHOP
CLOSED
TELL ME YOU HAD NOTHING TO DO WITH THIS.
I DIDN'T. I TOLD YOU, I'M DONE WITH THEM.
WHAT THE--?
I'M GOING TO SCHOOL.

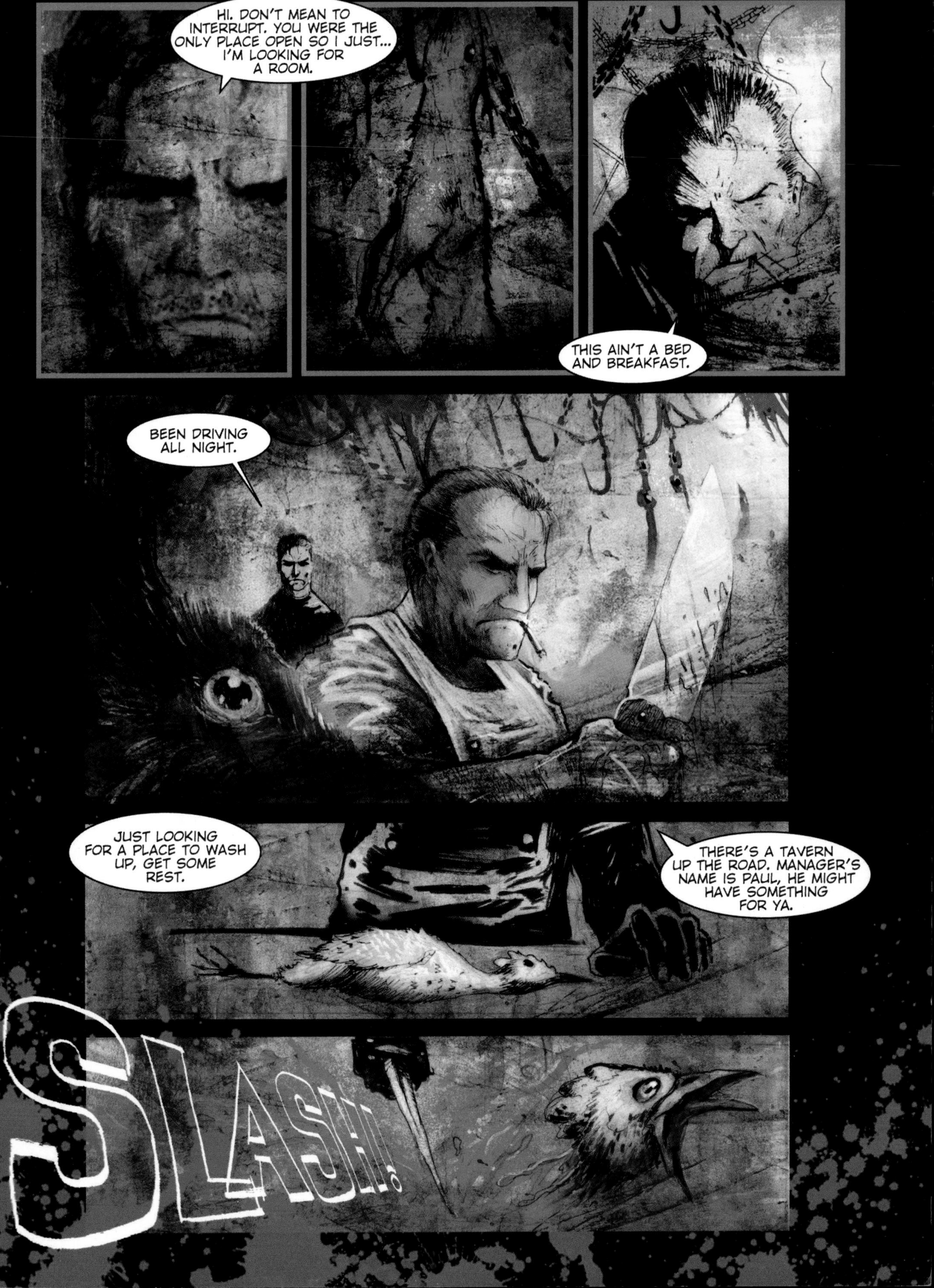
HI. DON'T MEAN TO INTERRUPT. YOU WERE THE ONLY PLACE OPEN SO I JUST... I'M LOOKING FOR A ROOM.
THIS AIN'T A BED AND BREAKFAST.
BEEN DRIVING ALL NIGHT.
JUST LOOKING FOR A PLACE TO WASH UP, GET SOME REST.
THERE'S A TAVERN UP THE ROAD. MANAGER'S NAME IS PAUL, HE MIGHT HAVE SOMETHING FOR YA.
SLASH!

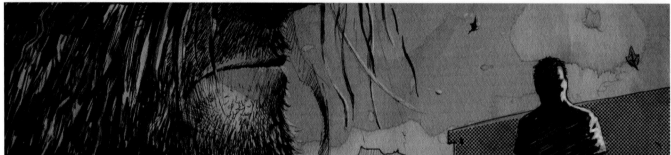

CAN I HELP YOU?

YOU WORK HERE?

NOPE.

THEN I GUESS NOT, THANKS.

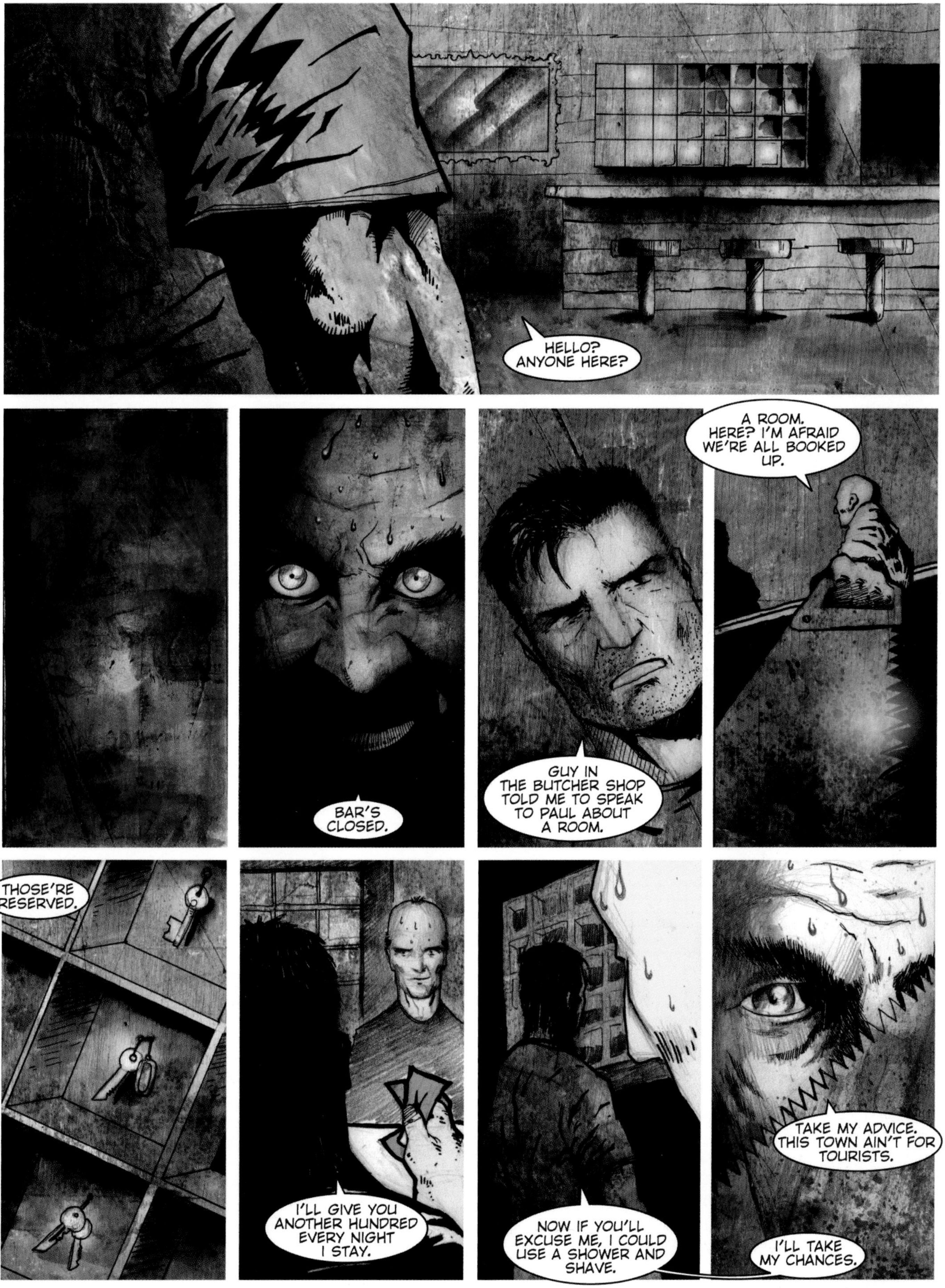
HELLO? ANYONE HERE?
BAR'S CLOSED.
GUY IN THE BUTCHER SHOP TOLD ME TO SPEAK TO PAUL ABOUT A ROOM.
A ROOM. HERE? I'M AFRAID WE'RE ALL BOOKED UP.
THOSE'RE RESERVED.
I'LL GIVE YOU ANOTHER HUNDRED EVERY NIGHT I STAY.
NOW IF YOU'LL EXCUSE ME, I COULD USE A SHOWER AND SHAVE.
TAKE MY ADVICE. THIS TOWN AIN'T FOR TOURISTS.
I'LL TAKE MY CHANCES.

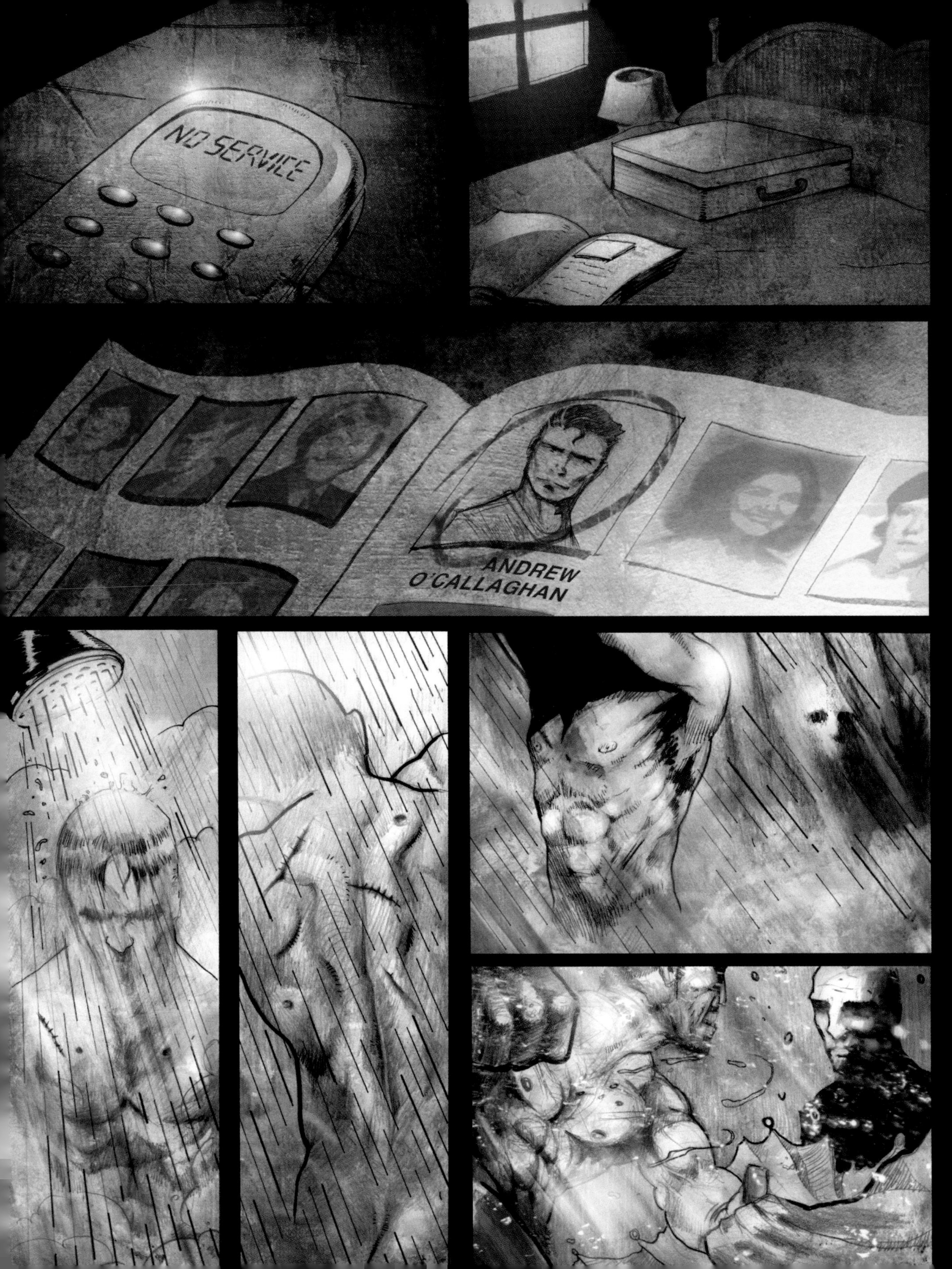
NO SERVICE
ANDREW O'CALLAGHAN

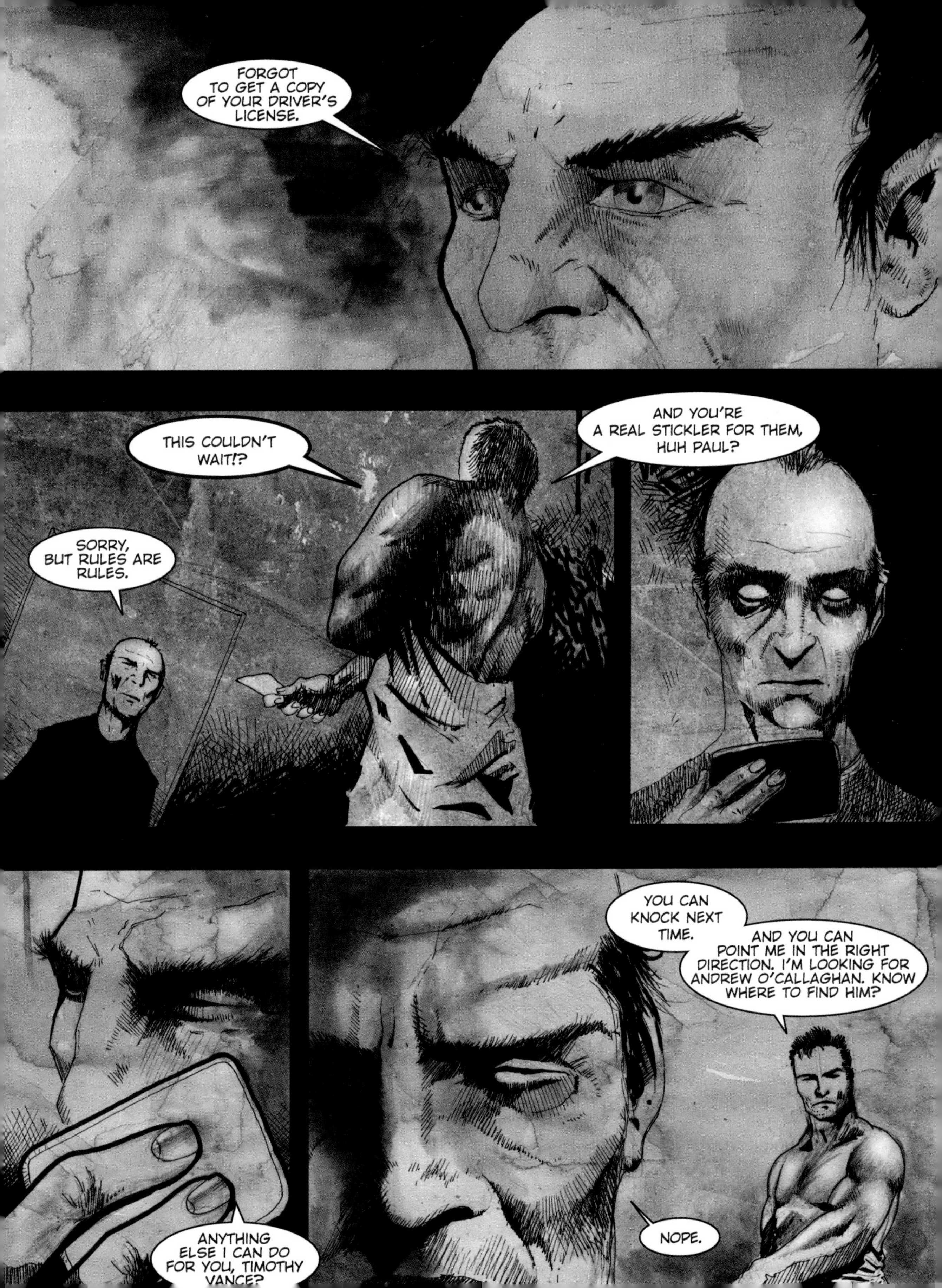
FORGOT TO GET A COPY OF YOUR DRIVER'S LICENSE.
THIS COULDN'T WAIT!?
SORRY, BUT RULES ARE RULES.
AND YOU'RE A REAL STICKLER FOR THEM, HUH PAUL?
ANYTHING ELSE I CAN DO FOR YOU, TIMOTHY VANCE?
YOU CAN KNOCK NEXT TIME.
AND YOU CAN POINT ME IN THE RIGHT DIRECTION. I'M LOOKING FOR ANDREW O'CALLAGHAN. KNOW WHERE TO FIND HIM?
NOPE.

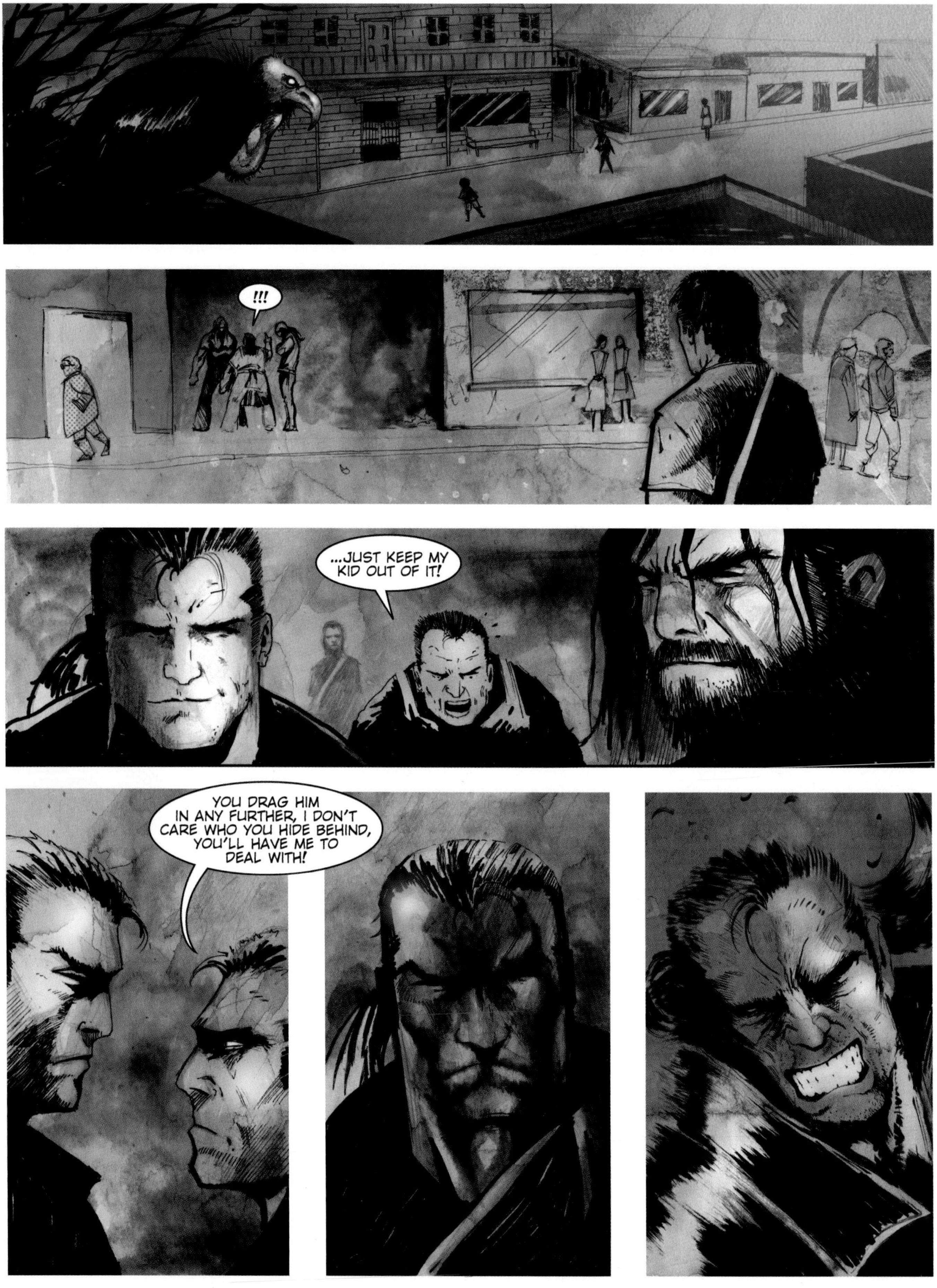
!!!
...JUST KEEP MY KID OUT OF IT!
YOU DRAG HIM IN ANY FURTHER, I DON'T CARE WHO YOU HIDE BEHIND, YOU'LL HAVE ME TO DEAL WITH!

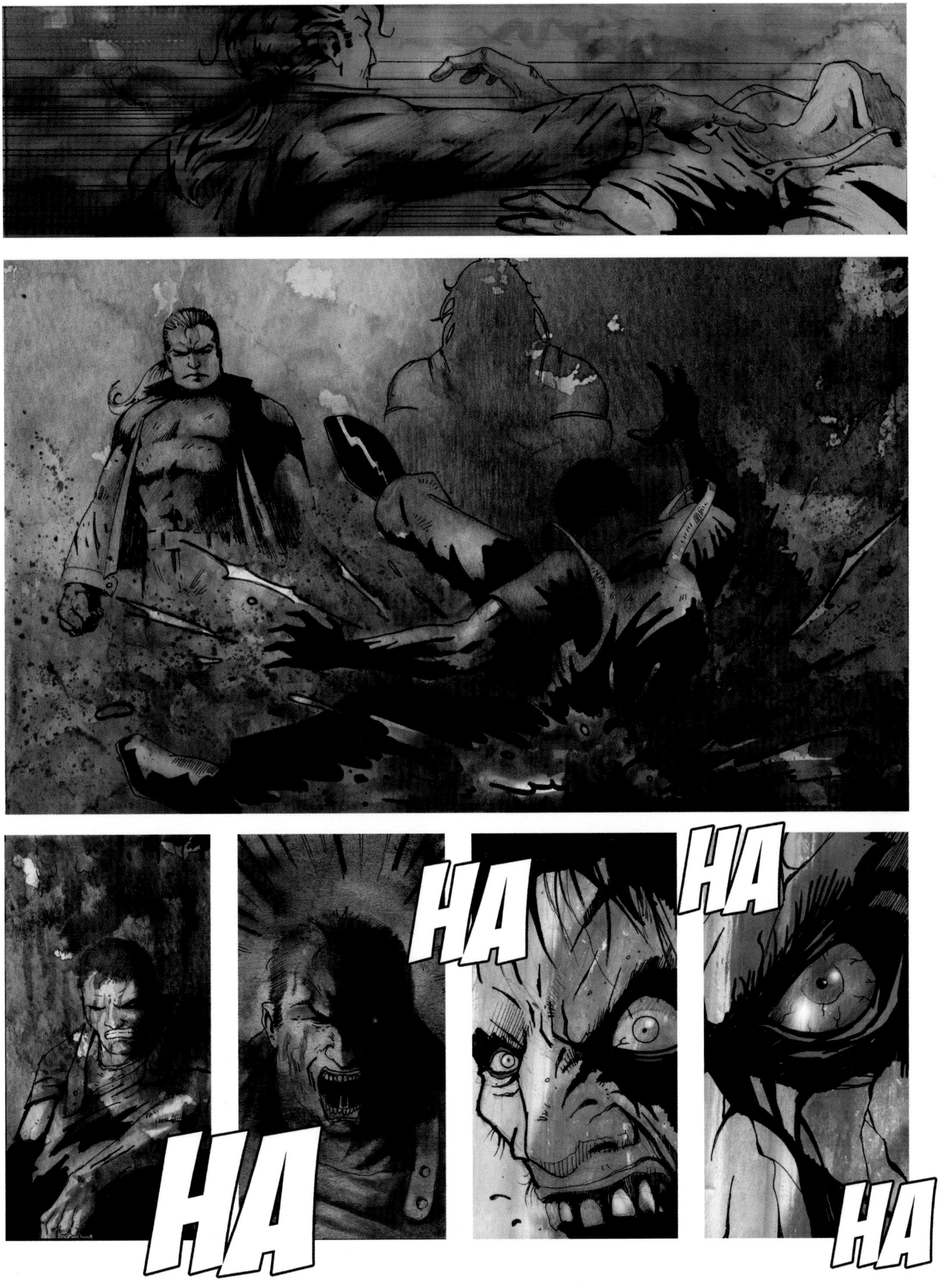
HA
HA
HA
HA

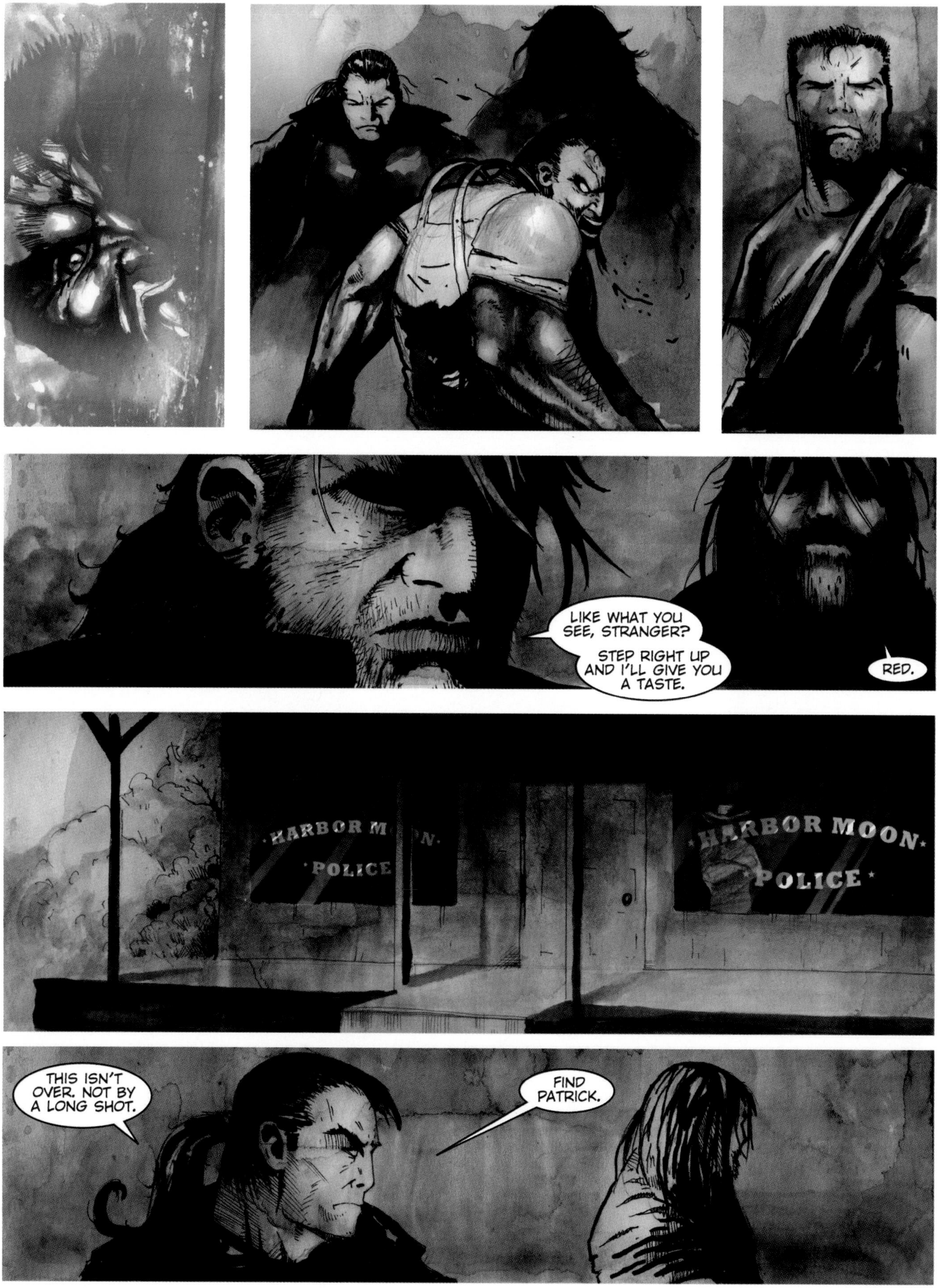
LIKE WHAT YOU SEE, STRANGER?
STEP RIGHT UP AND I'LL GIVE YOU A TASTE.
RED.
HARBOR MOON POLICE
HARBOR MOON POLICE
THIS ISN'T OVER. NOT BY A LONG SHOT.
FIND PATRICK.

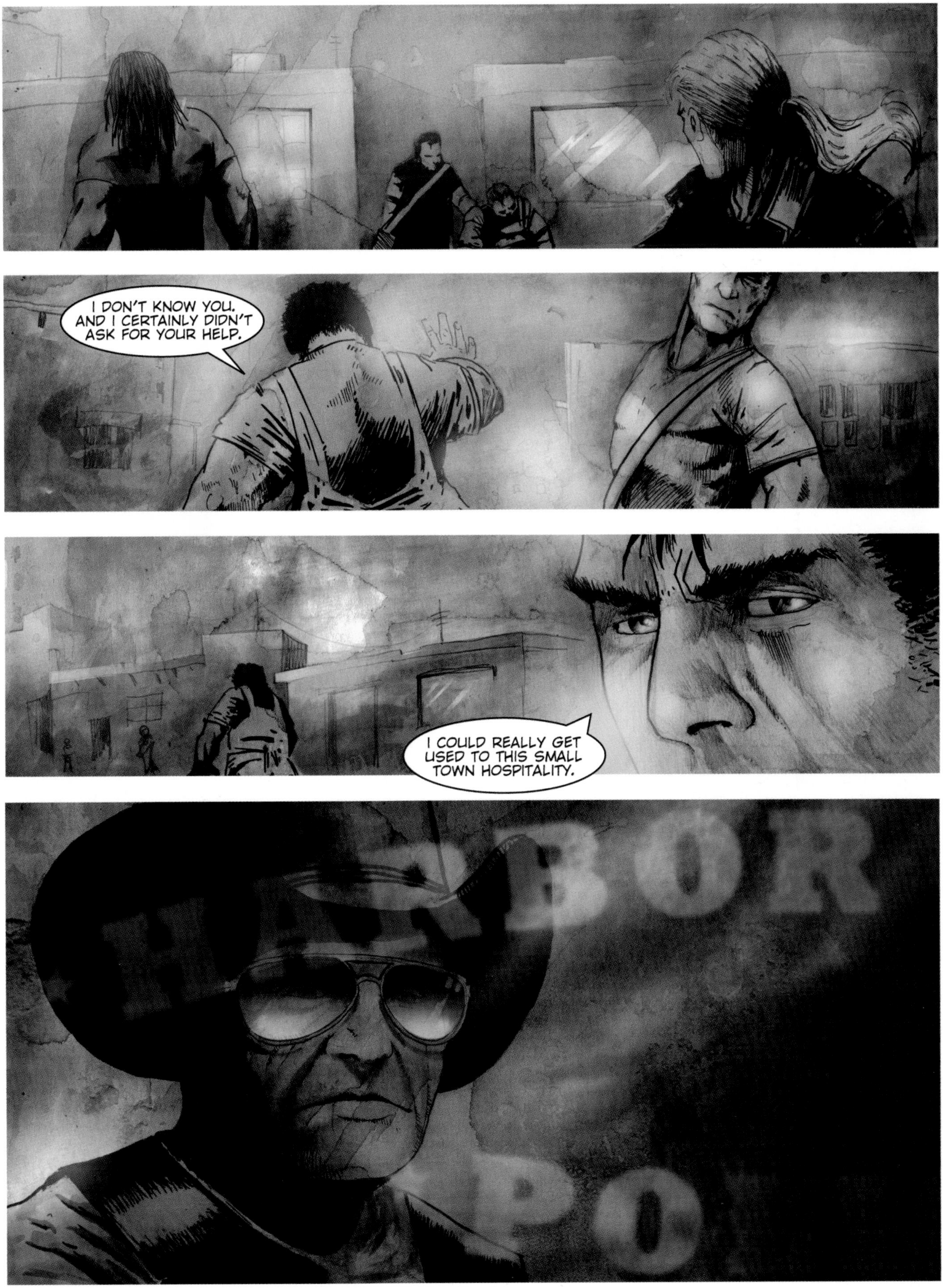
I DON'T KNOW YOU. AND I CERTAINLY DIDN'T ASK FOR YOUR HELP.
I COULD REALLY GET USED TO THIS SMALL TOWN HOSPITALITY.

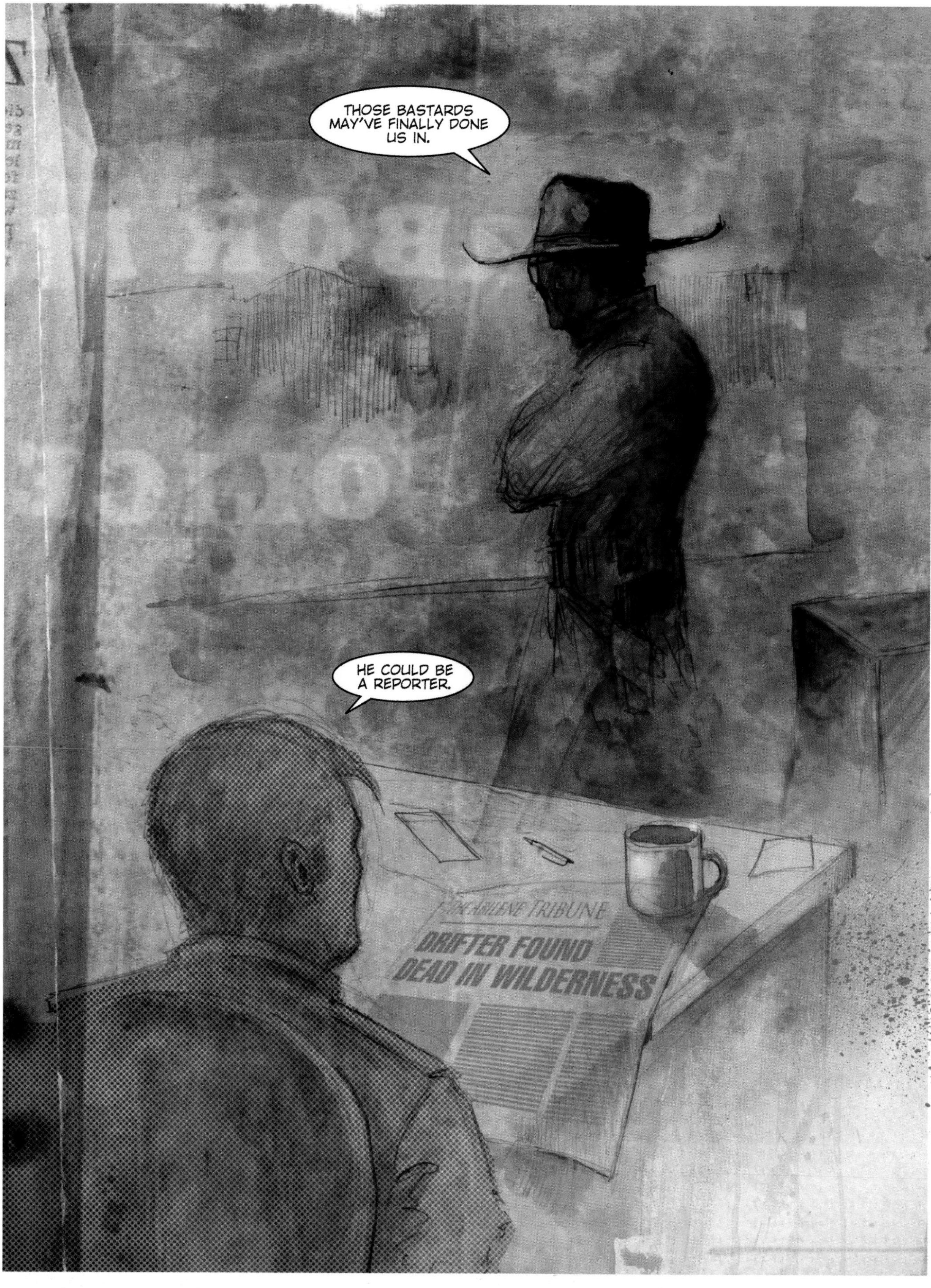
THOSE BASTARDS MAY'VE FINALLY DONE US IN.
HE COULD BE A REPORTER.
THE ABILENE TRIBUNE
DRIFTER FOUND DEAD IN WILDERNESS

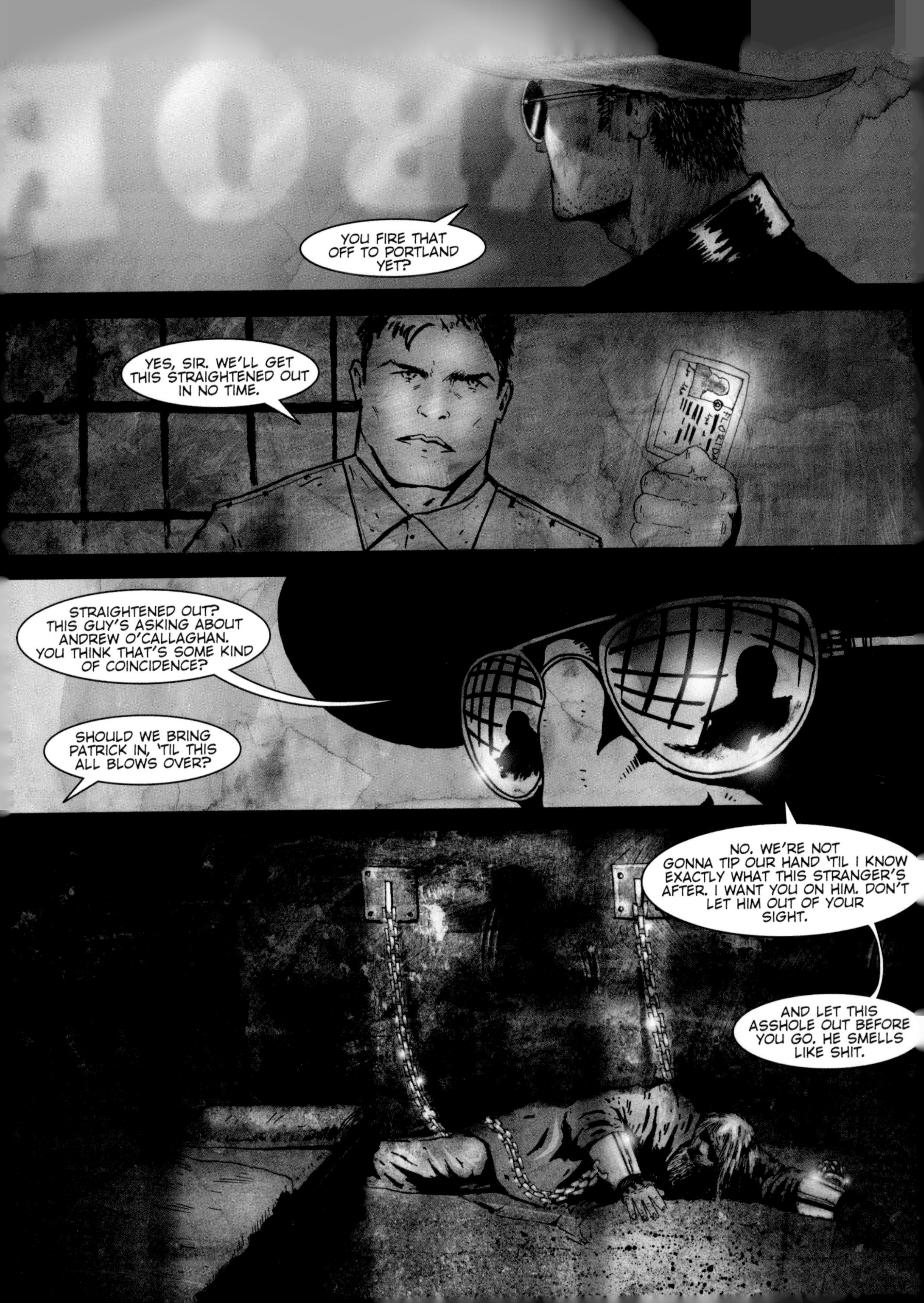
YOU FIRE THAT OFF TO PORTLAND YET?
YES, SIR. WE'LL GET THIS STRAIGHTENED OUT IN NO TIME.
STRAIGHTENED OUT? THIS GUY'S ASKING ABOUT ANDREW O'CALLAGHAN. YOU THINK THAT'S SOME KIND OF COINCIDENCE?
SHOULD WE BRING PATRICK IN, 'TIL THIS ALL BLOWS OVER?
NO. WE'RE NOT GONNA TIP OUR HAND 'TIL I KNOW EXACTLY WHAT THIS STRANGER'S AFTER. I WANT YOU ON HIM. DON'T LET HIM OUT OF YOUR SIGHT.
AND LET THIS ASSHOLE OUT BEFORE YOU GO. HE SMELLS LIKE SHIT.

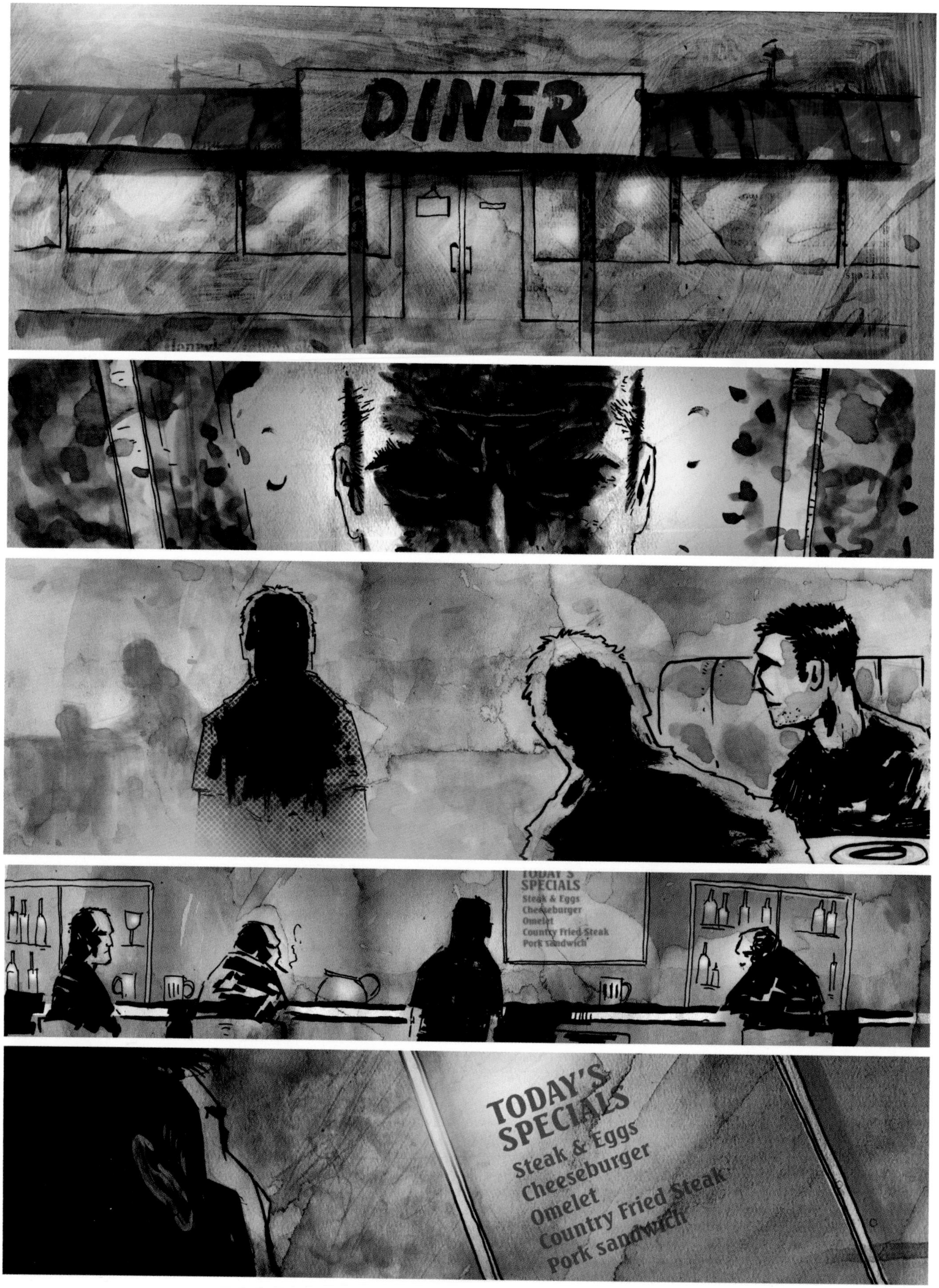
DINER
TODAY'S SPECIALS
Steak & Eggs
Cheeseburger
Omelet
Country Fried Steak
Pork sandwich
TODAY'S SPECIALS
Steak & Eggs
Cheeseburger
Omelet
Country Fried Steak
Pork sandwich

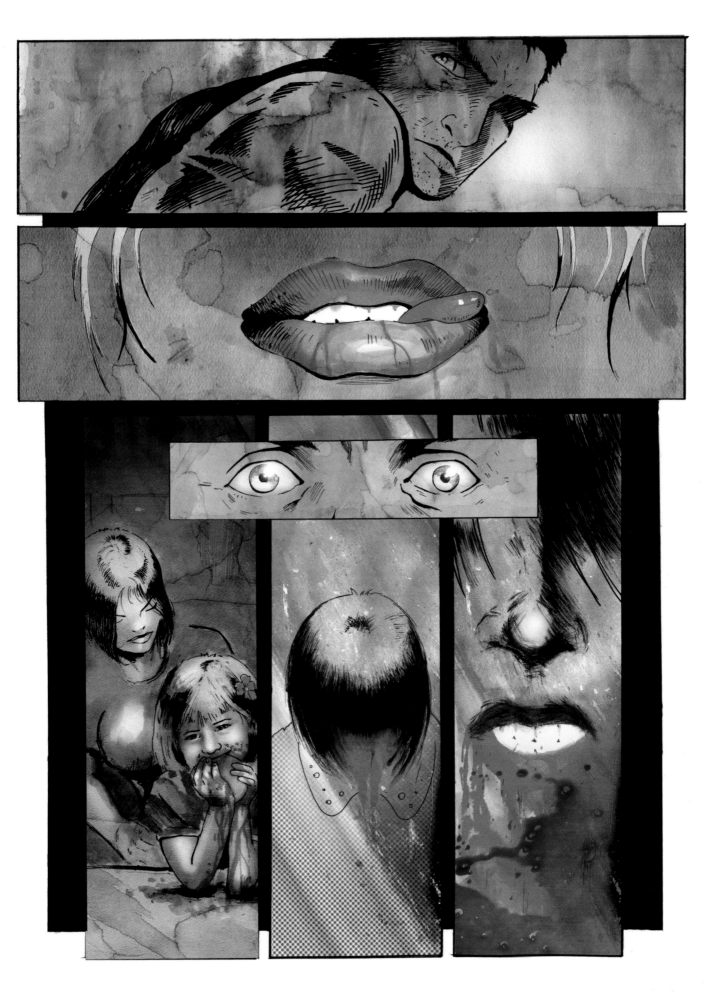

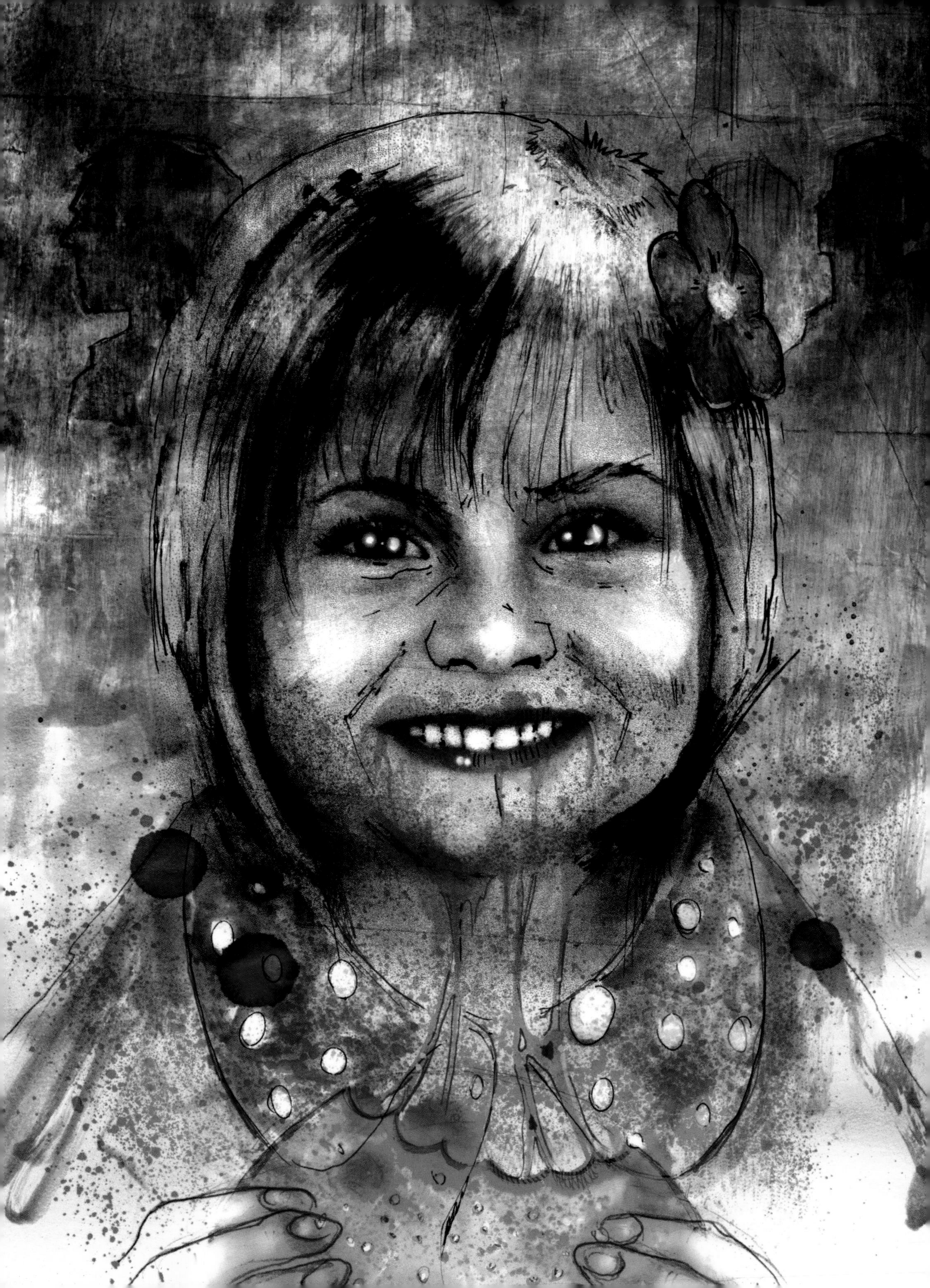

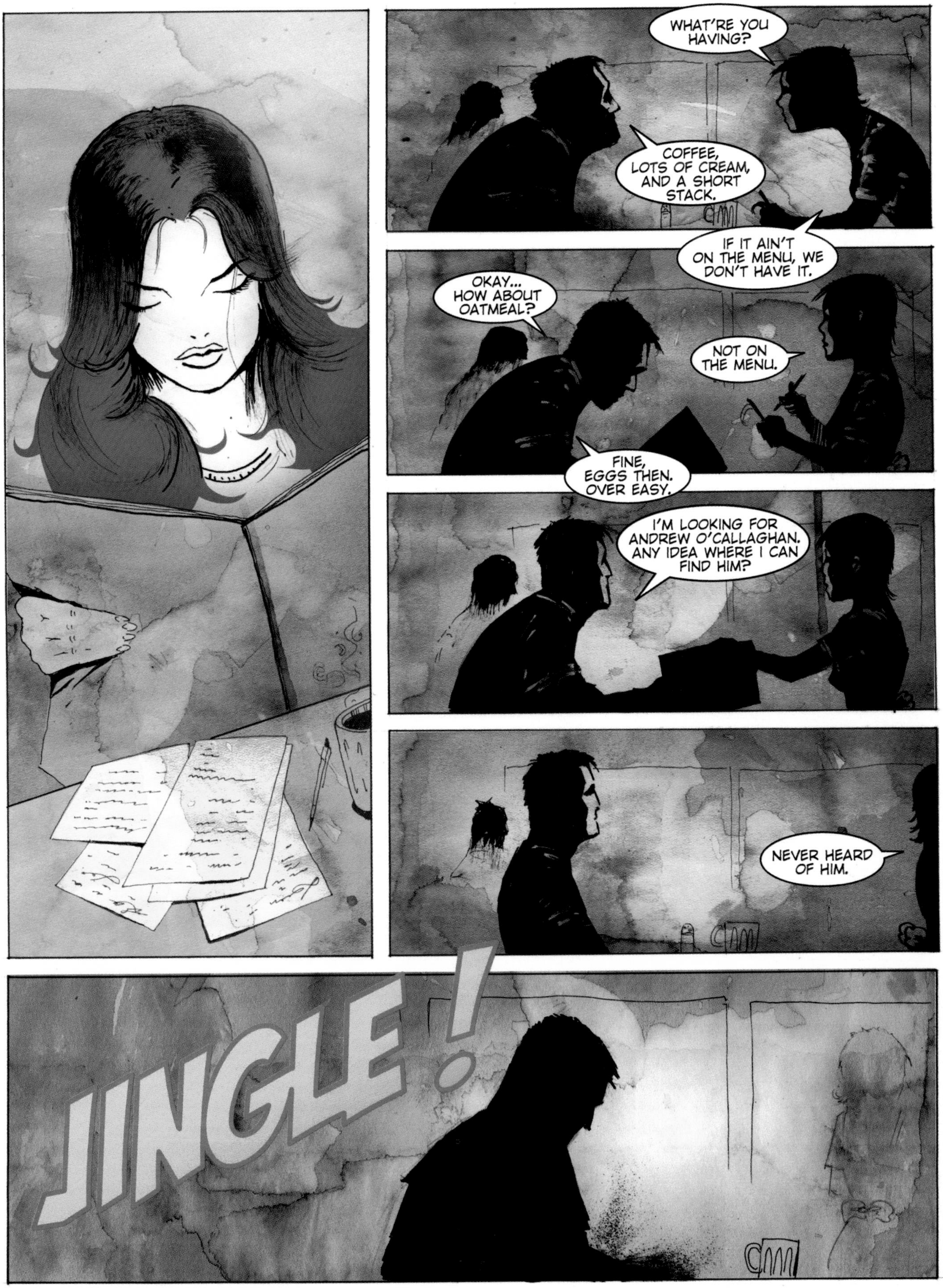
WHAT'RE YOU HAVING?
COFFEE, LOTS OF CREAM, AND A SHORT STACK.
IF IT AIN'T ON THE MENU, WE DON'T HAVE IT.
OKAY... HOW ABOUT OATMEAL?
NOT ON THE MENU.
FINE, EGGS THEN. OVER EASY.
I'M LOOKING FOR ANDREW O'CALLAGHAN. ANY IDEA WHERE I CAN FIND HIM?
NEVER HEARD OF HIM.
JINGLE!

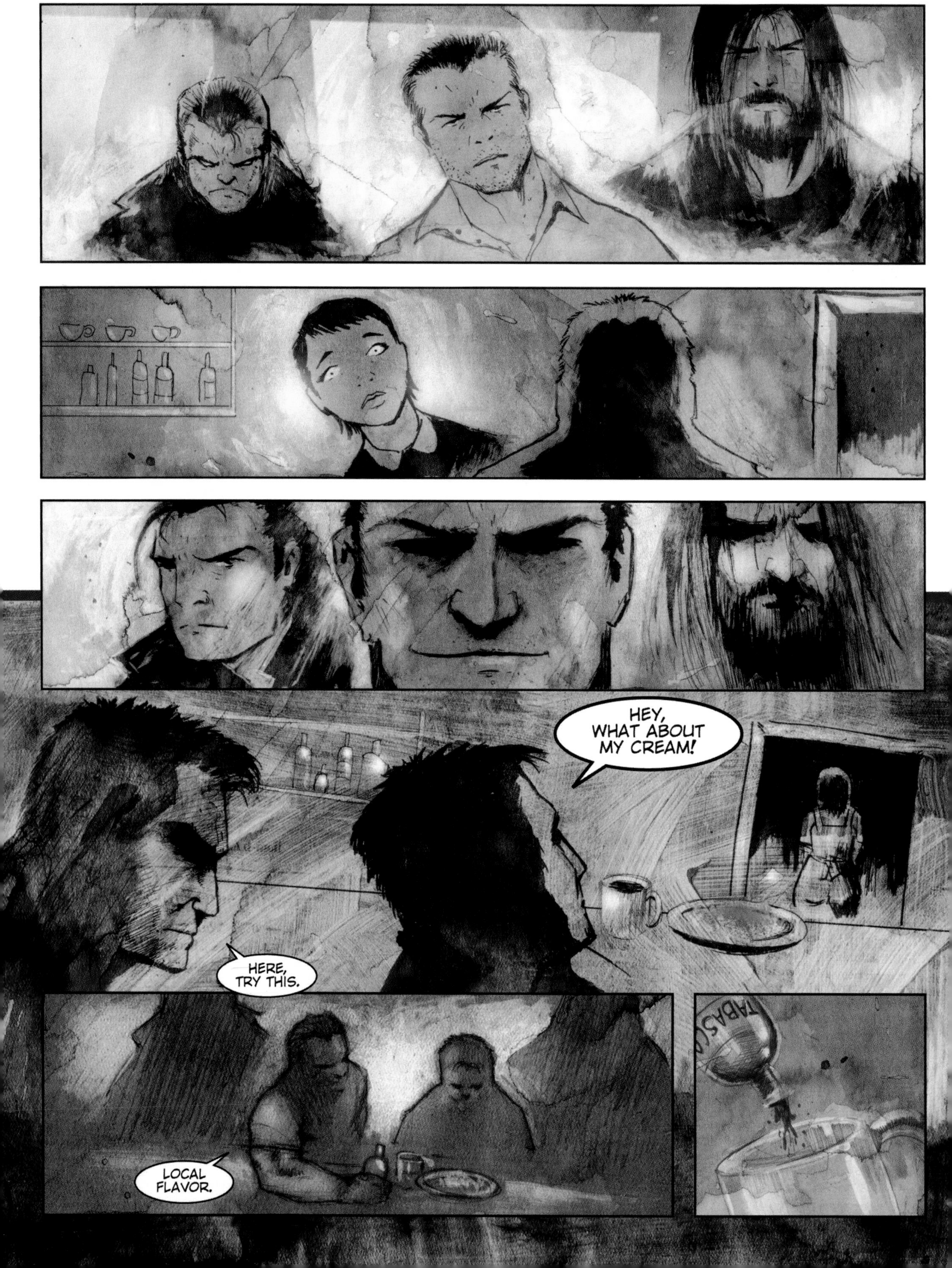
HEY, WHAT ABOUT MY CREAM!
HERE, TRY THIS.
LOCAL FLAVOR.
TABASCO

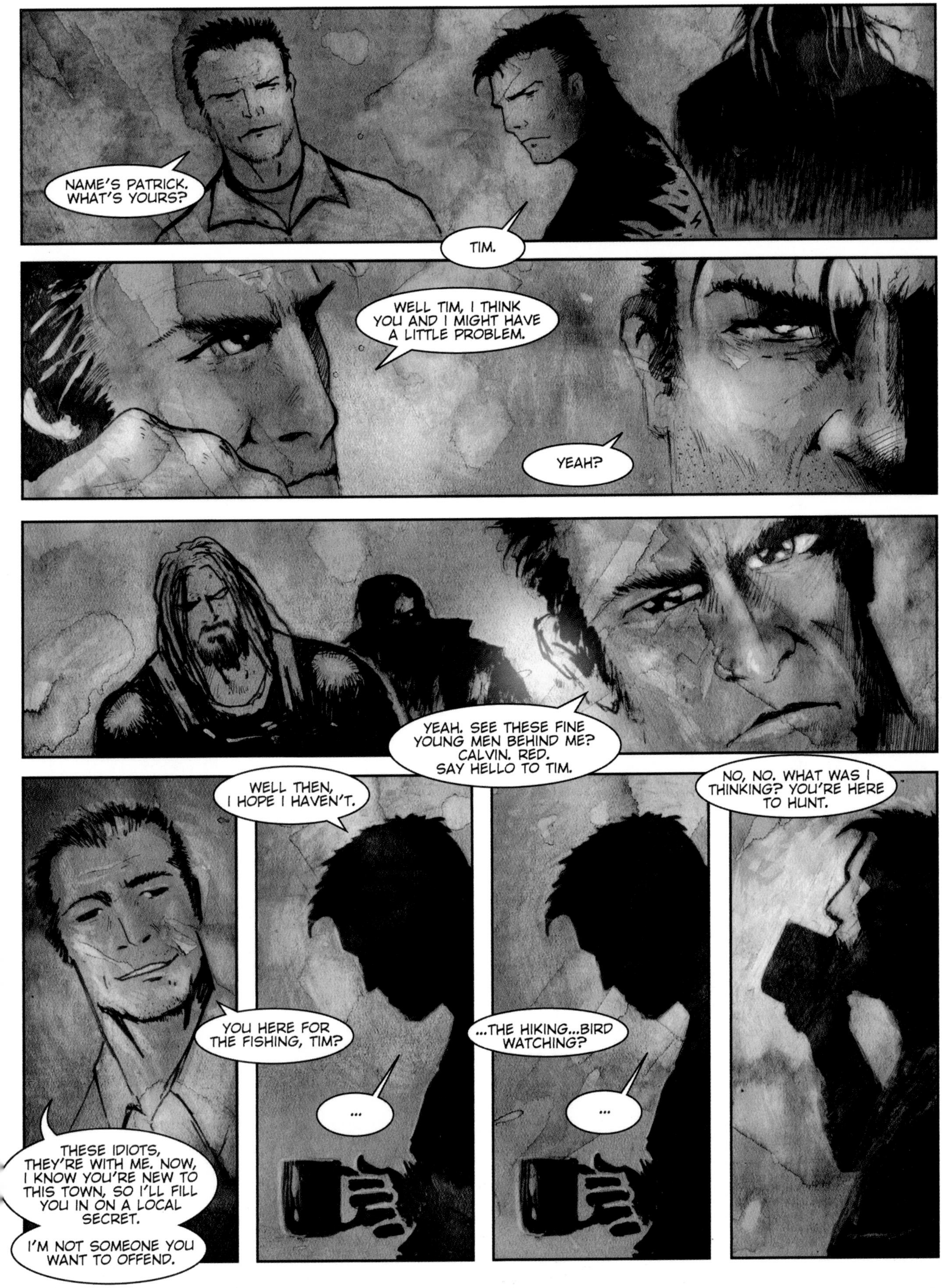
NAME'S PATRICK. WHAT'S YOURS?
TIM.
WELL TIM, I THINK YOU AND I MIGHT HAVE A LITTLE PROBLEM.
YEAH?
YEAH. SEE THESE FINE YOUNG MEN BEHIND ME? CALVIN. RED. SAY HELLO TO TIM.
THESE IDIOTS, THEY'RE WITH ME. NOW, I KNOW YOU'RE NEW TO THIS TOWN, SO I'LL FILL YOU IN ON A LOCAL SECRET.
I'M NOT SOMEONE YOU WANT TO OFFEND.
WELL THEN, I HOPE I HAVEN'T.
YOU HERE FOR THE FISHING, TIM?
...
...THE HIKING...BIRD WATCHING?
...
NO, NO. WHAT WAS I THINKING? YOU'RE HERE TO HUNT.

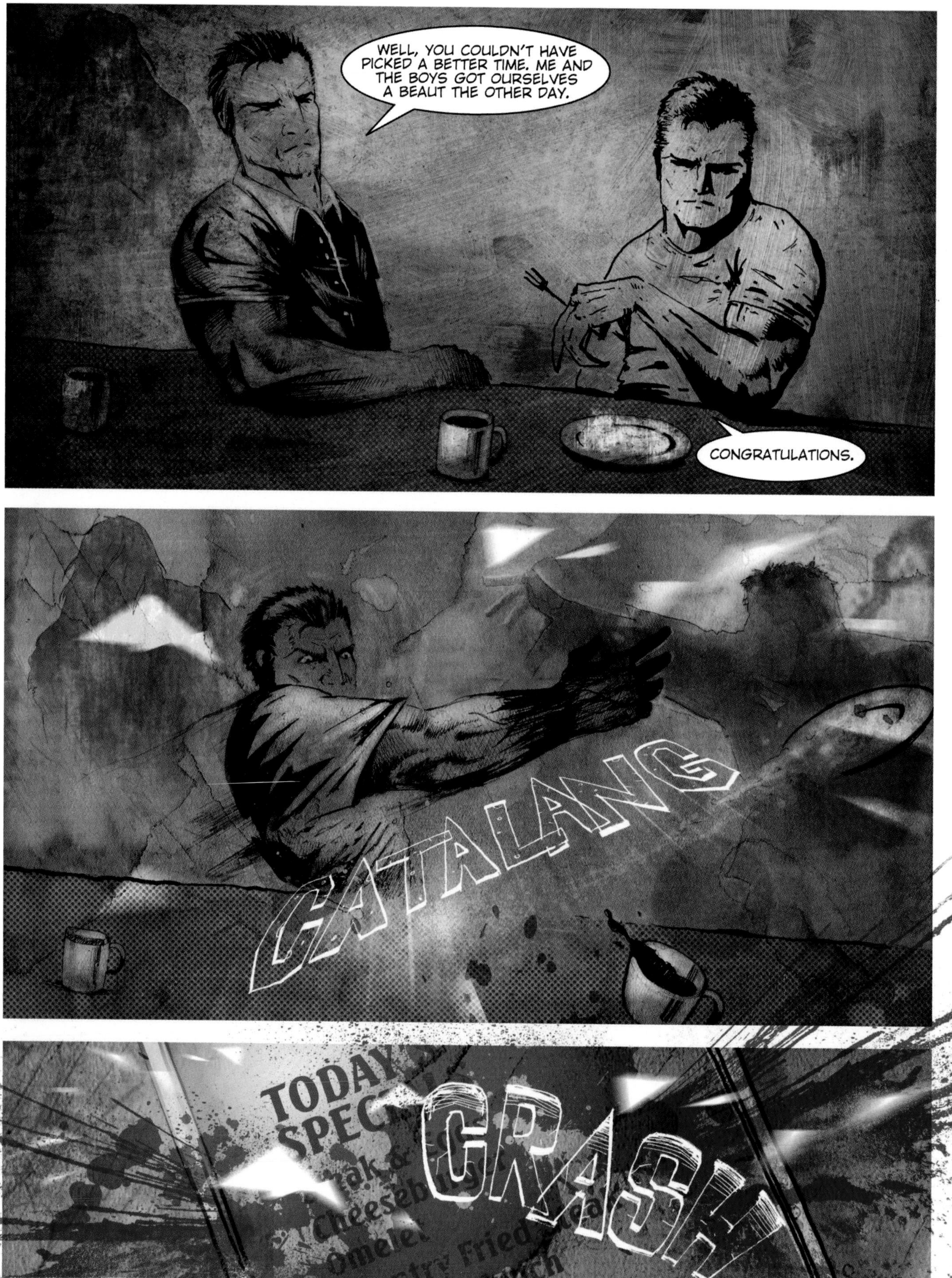
WELL, YOU COULDN'T HAVE PICKED A BETTER TIME. ME AND THE BOYS GOT OURSELVES A BEAUT THE OTHER DAY.
CONGRATULATIONS.
CATALANG
CRASH

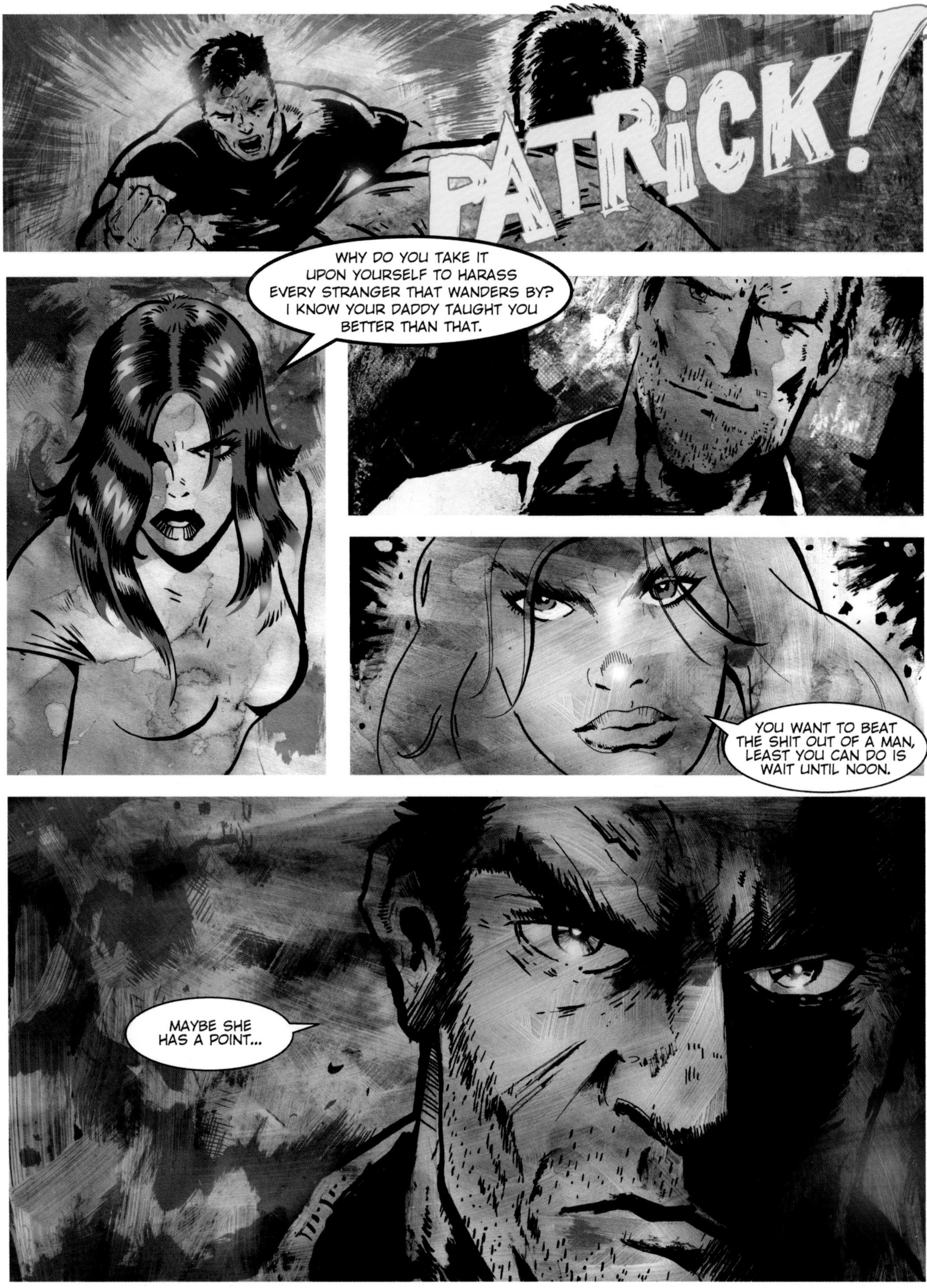
PATRICK!
WHY DO YOU TAKE IT UPON YOURSELF TO HARASS EVERY STRANGER THAT WANDERS BY? I KNOW YOUR DADDY TAUGHT YOU BETTER THAN THAT.
YOU WANT TO BEAT THE SHIT OUT OF A MAN, LEAST YOU CAN DO IS WAIT UNTIL NOON.
MAYBE SHE HAS A POINT...

COME BY LATER!

I'LL SHOW 'YA HOW WE HUNT AROUND HERE.

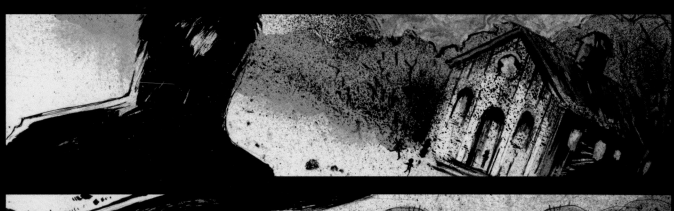

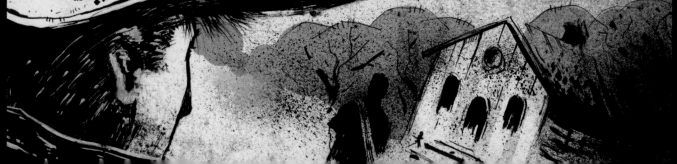

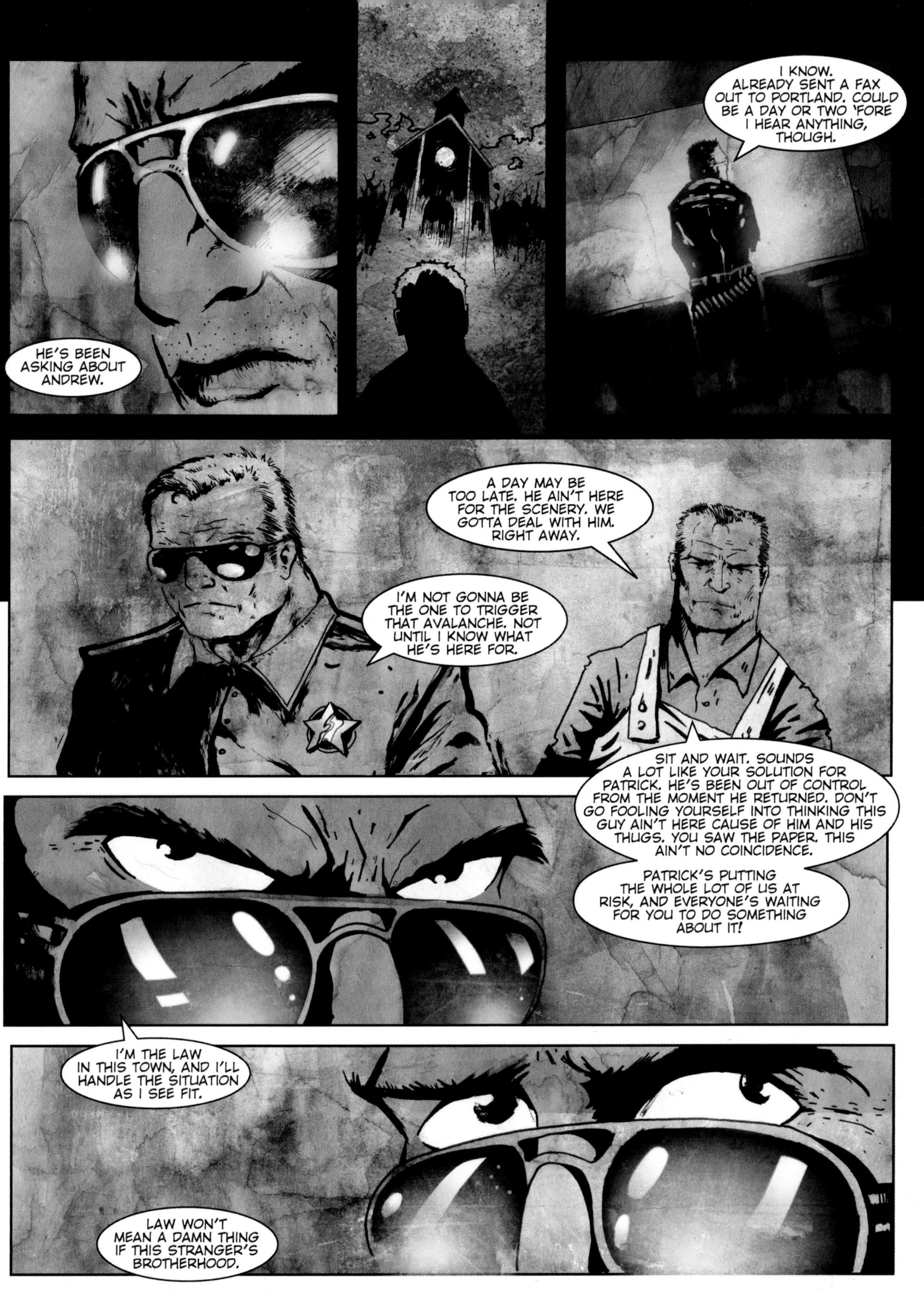

HE'S BEEN ASKING ABOUT ANDREW.
I KNOW. ALREADY SENT A FAX OUT TO PORTLAND. COULD BE A DAY OR TWO 'FORE I HEAR ANYTHING, THOUGH.
A DAY MAY BE TOO LATE. HE AIN'T HERE FOR THE SCENERY. WE GOTTA DEAL WITH HIM. RIGHT AWAY.
I'M NOT GONNA BE THE ONE TO TRIGGER THAT AVALANCHE. NOT UNTIL I KNOW WHAT HE'S HERE FOR.
SIT AND WAIT. SOUNDS A LOT LIKE YOUR SOLUTION FOR PATRICK. HE'S BEEN OUT OF CONTROL FROM THE MOMENT HE RETURNED. DON'T GO FOOLING YOURSELF INTO THINKING THIS GUY AIN'T HERE CAUSE OF HIM AND HIS THUGS. YOU SAW THE PAPER. THIS AIN'T NO COINCIDENCE.
PATRICK'S PUTTING THE WHOLE LOT OF US AT RISK, AND EVERYONE'S WAITING FOR YOU TO DO SOMETHING ABOUT IT!
I'M THE LAW IN THIS TOWN, AND I'LL HANDLE THE SITUATION AS I SEE FIT.
LAW WON'T MEAN A DAMN THING IF THIS STRANGER'S BROTHERHOOD.

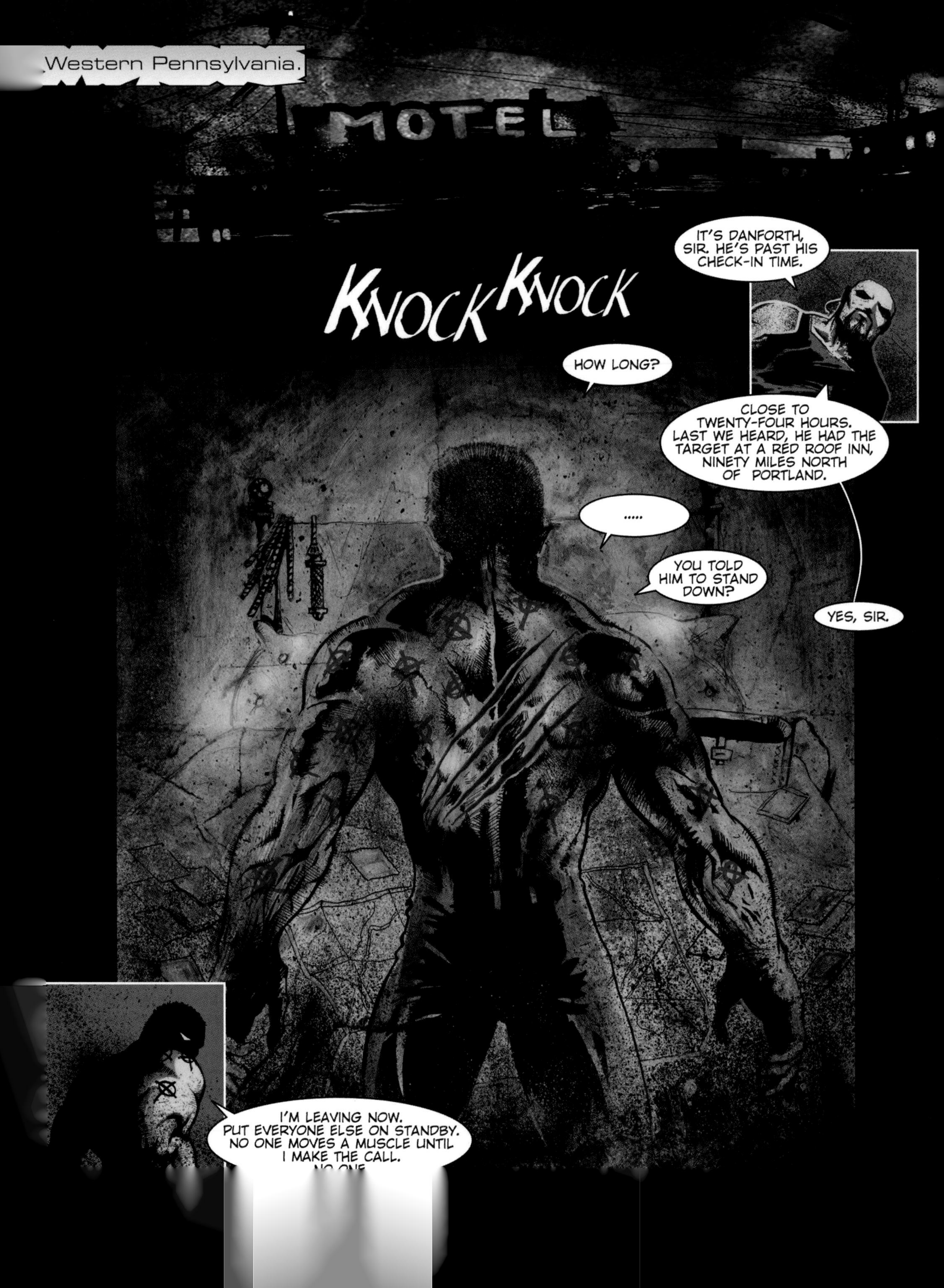

Western Pennsylvania.
MOTEL
KNOCK KNOCK
IT'S DANFORTH, SIR. HE'S PAST HIS CHECK-IN TIME.
HOW LONG?
CLOSE TO TWENTY-FOUR HOURS. LAST WE HEARD, HE HAD THE TARGET AT A RED ROOF INN, NINETY MILES NORTH OF PORTLAND.
.....
YOU TOLD HIM TO STAND DOWN?
YES, SIR.
I'M LEAVING NOW. PUT EVERYONE ELSE ON STANDBY. NO ONE MOVES A MUSCLE UNTIL I MAKE THE CALL.

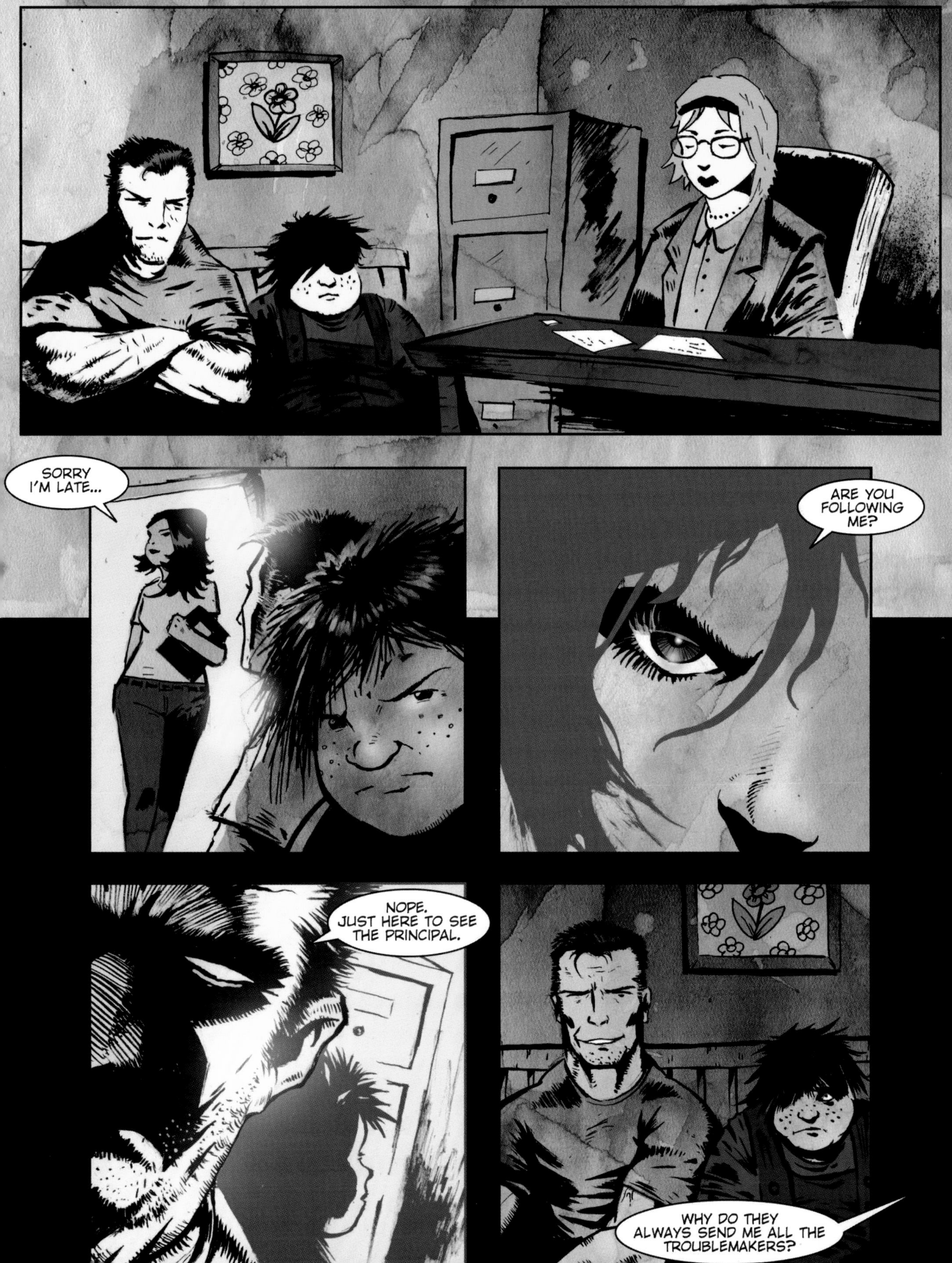
SORRY I'M LATE...
ARE YOU FOLLOWING ME?
NOPE. JUST HERE TO SEE THE PRINCIPAL.
WHY DO THEY ALWAYS SEND ME ALL THE TROUBLEMAKERS?

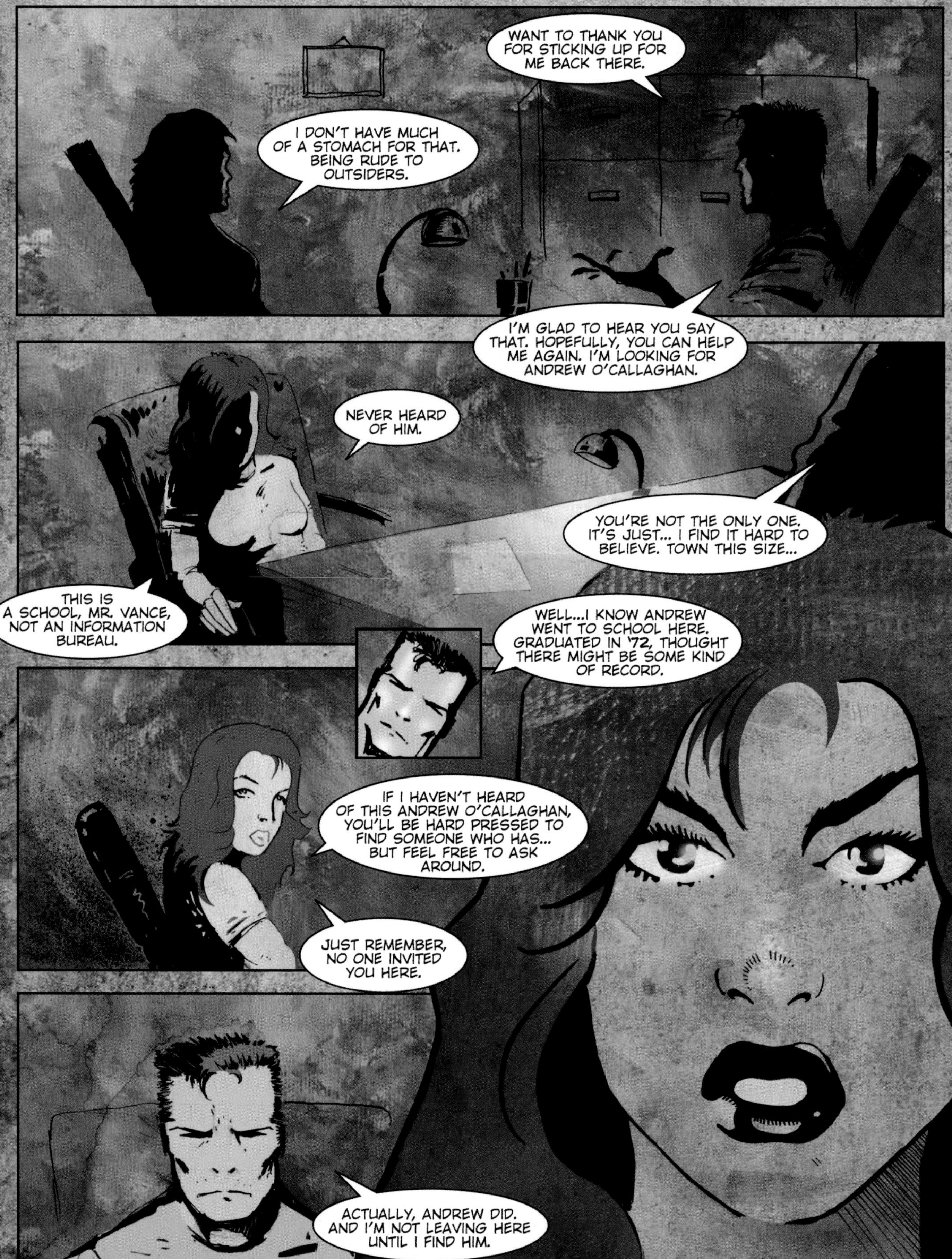
WANT TO THANK YOU FOR STICKING UP FOR ME BACK THERE.
I DON'T HAVE MUCH OF A STOMACH FOR THAT. BEING RUDE TO OUTSIDERS.
I'M GLAD TO HEAR YOU SAY THAT. HOPEFULLY, YOU CAN HELP ME AGAIN. I'M LOOKING FOR ANDREW O'CALLAGHAN.
NEVER HEARD OF HIM.
YOU'RE NOT THE ONLY ONE. IT'S JUST... I FIND IT HARD TO BELIEVE. TOWN THIS SIZE...
THIS IS A SCHOOL, MR. VANCE, NOT AN INFORMATION BUREAU.
WELL...I KNOW ANDREW WENT TO SCHOOL HERE. GRADUATED IN '72, THOUGHT THERE MIGHT BE SOME KIND OF RECORD.
IF I HAVEN'T HEARD OF THIS ANDREW O'CALLAGHAN, YOU'LL BE HARD PRESSED TO FIND SOMEONE WHO HAS... BUT FEEL FREE TO ASK AROUND.
JUST REMEMBER, NO ONE INVITED YOU HERE.
ACTUALLY, ANDREW DID. AND I'M NOT LEAVING HERE UNTIL I FIND HIM.

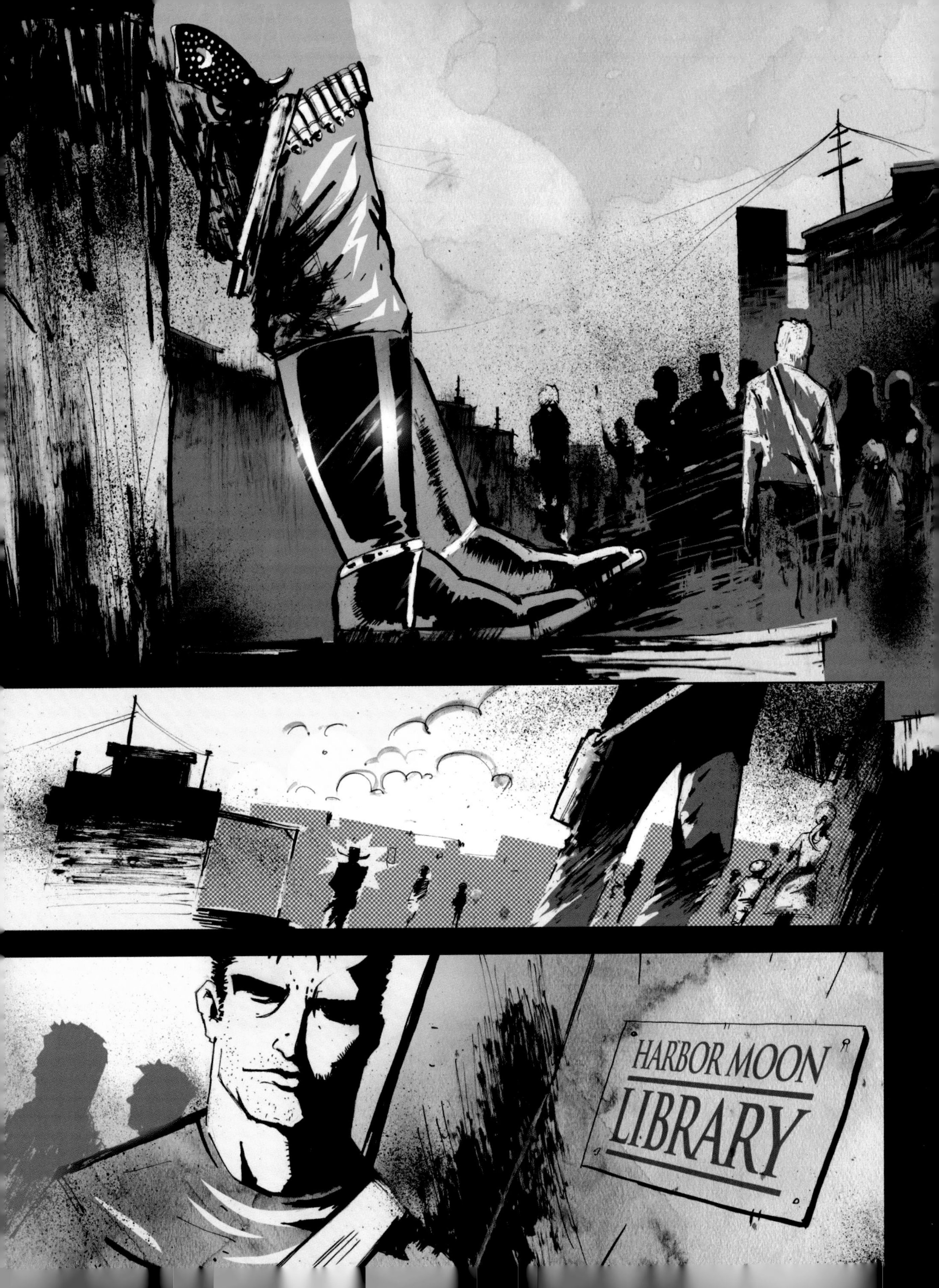
HARBOR MOON
LIBRARY

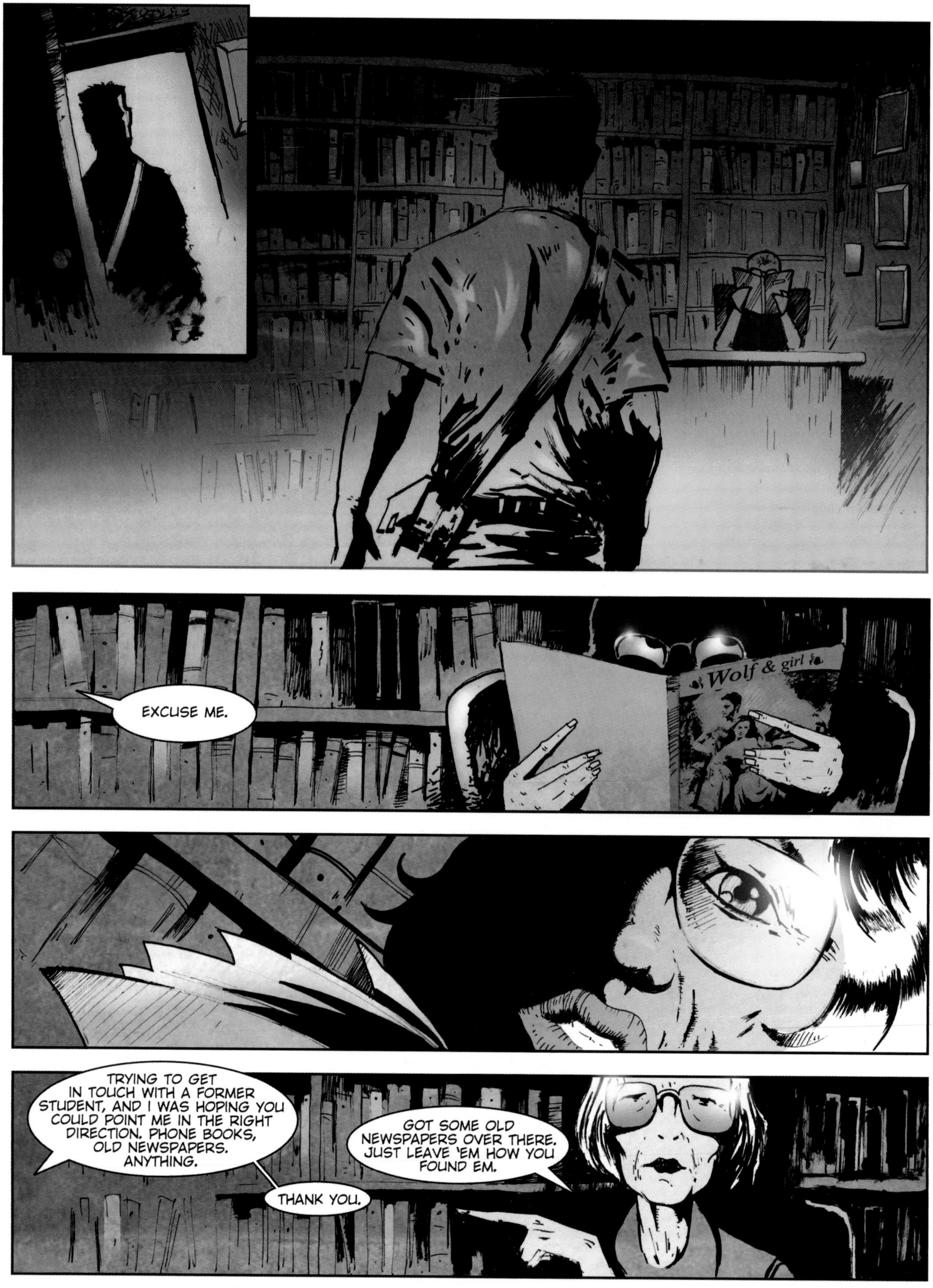
Wolf & girl
EXCUSE ME.
TRYING TO GET IN TOUCH WITH A FORMER STUDENT, AND I WAS HOPING YOU COULD POINT ME IN THE RIGHT DIRECTION. PHONE BOOKS, OLD NEWSPAPERS. ANYTHING.
GOT SOME OLD NEWSPAPERS OVER THERE. JUST LEAVE 'EM HOW YOU FOUND EM.
THANK YOU.

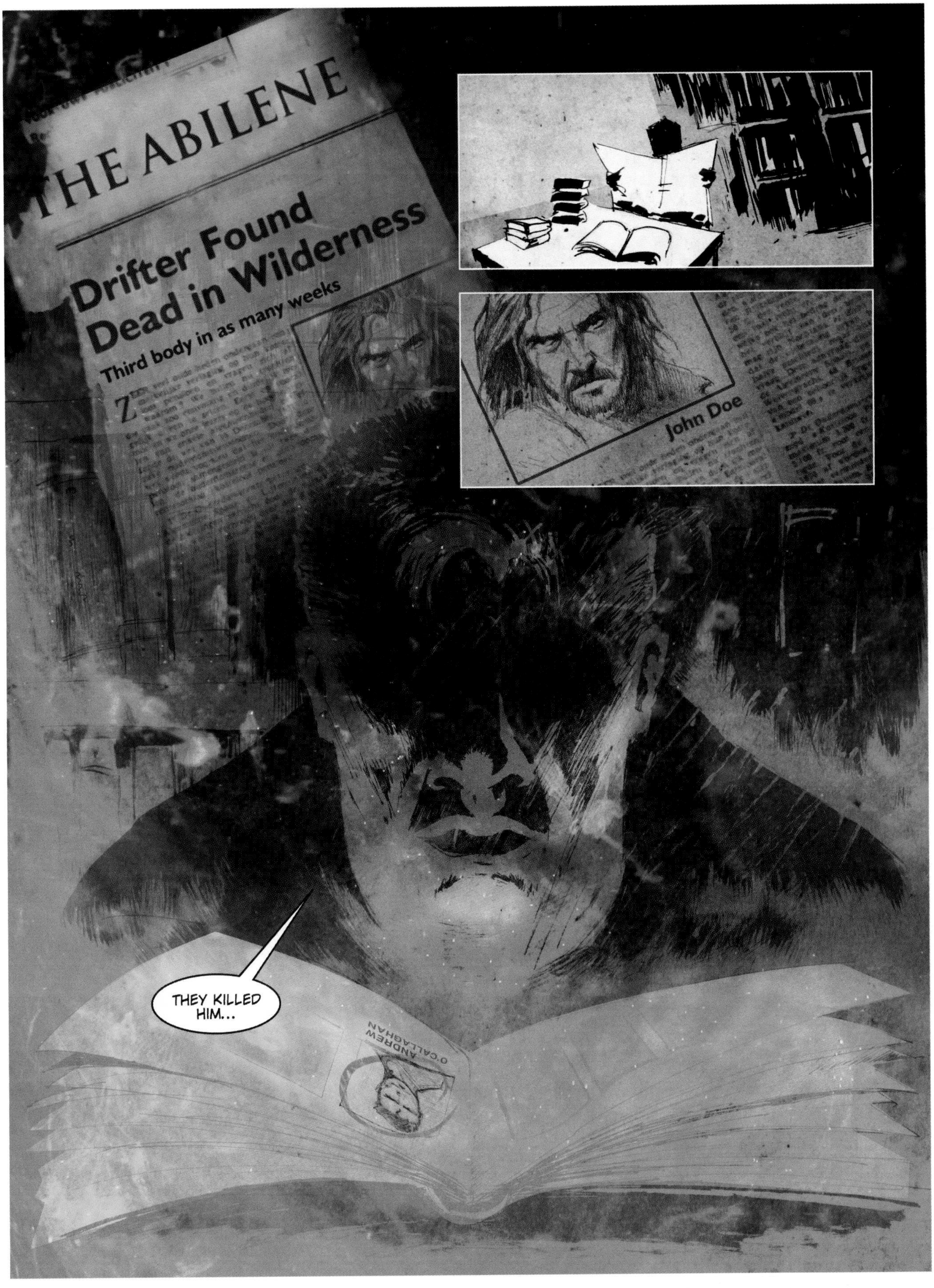
THE ABILENE
Drifter Found Dead in Wilderness
Third body in as many weeks
John Doe
THEY KILLED HIM...
ANDREW O'CALLAGHAN

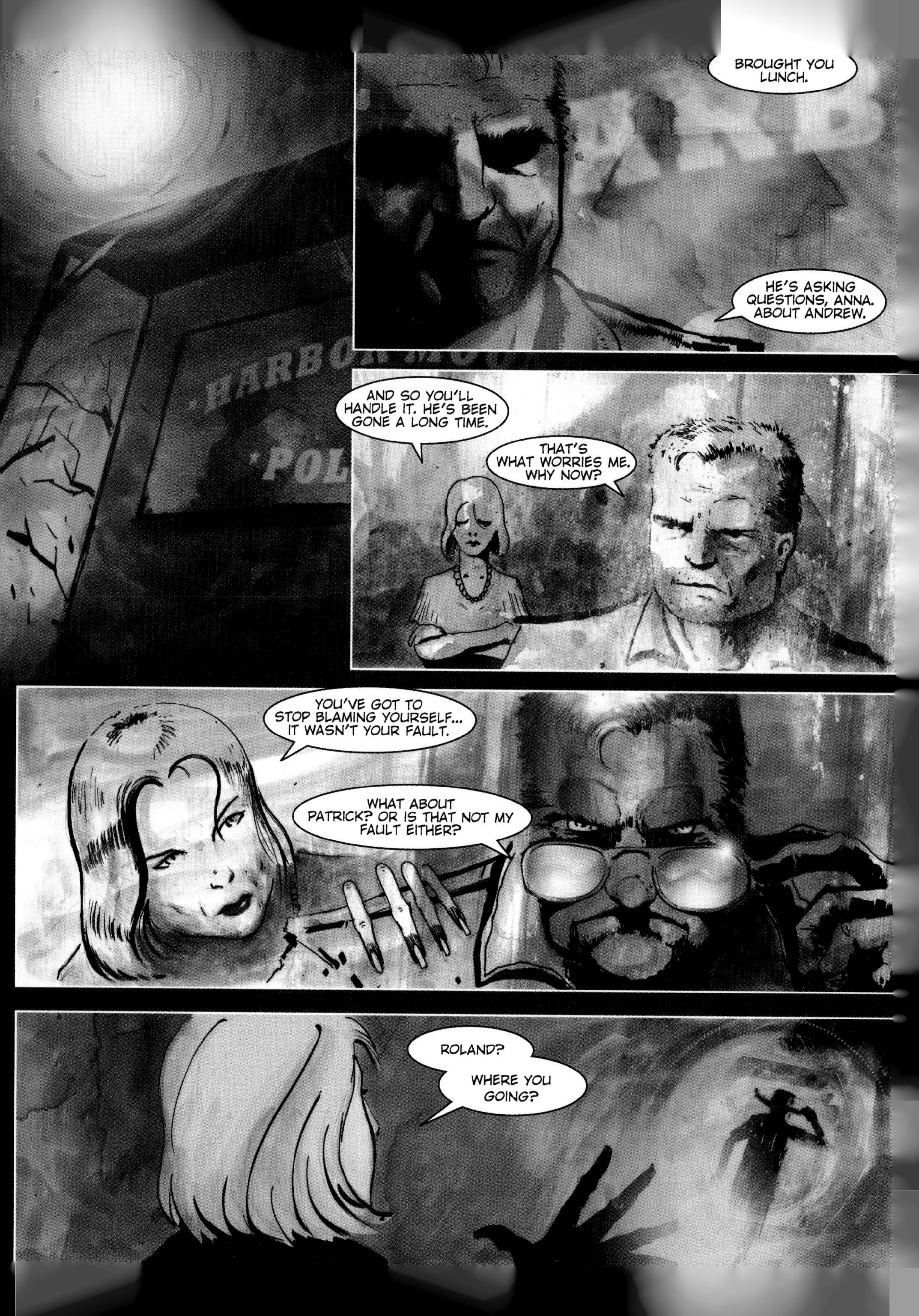
BROUGHT YOU LUNCH.
HE'S ASKING QUESTIONS, ANNA. ABOUT ANDREW.
AND SO YOU'LL HANDLE IT. HE'S BEEN GONE A LONG TIME.
THAT'S WHAT WORRIES ME. WHY NOW?
YOU'VE GOT TO STOP BLAMING YOURSELF... IT WASN'T YOUR FAULT.
WHAT ABOUT PATRICK? OR IS THAT NOT MY FAULT EITHER?
ROLAND?
WHERE YOU GOING?

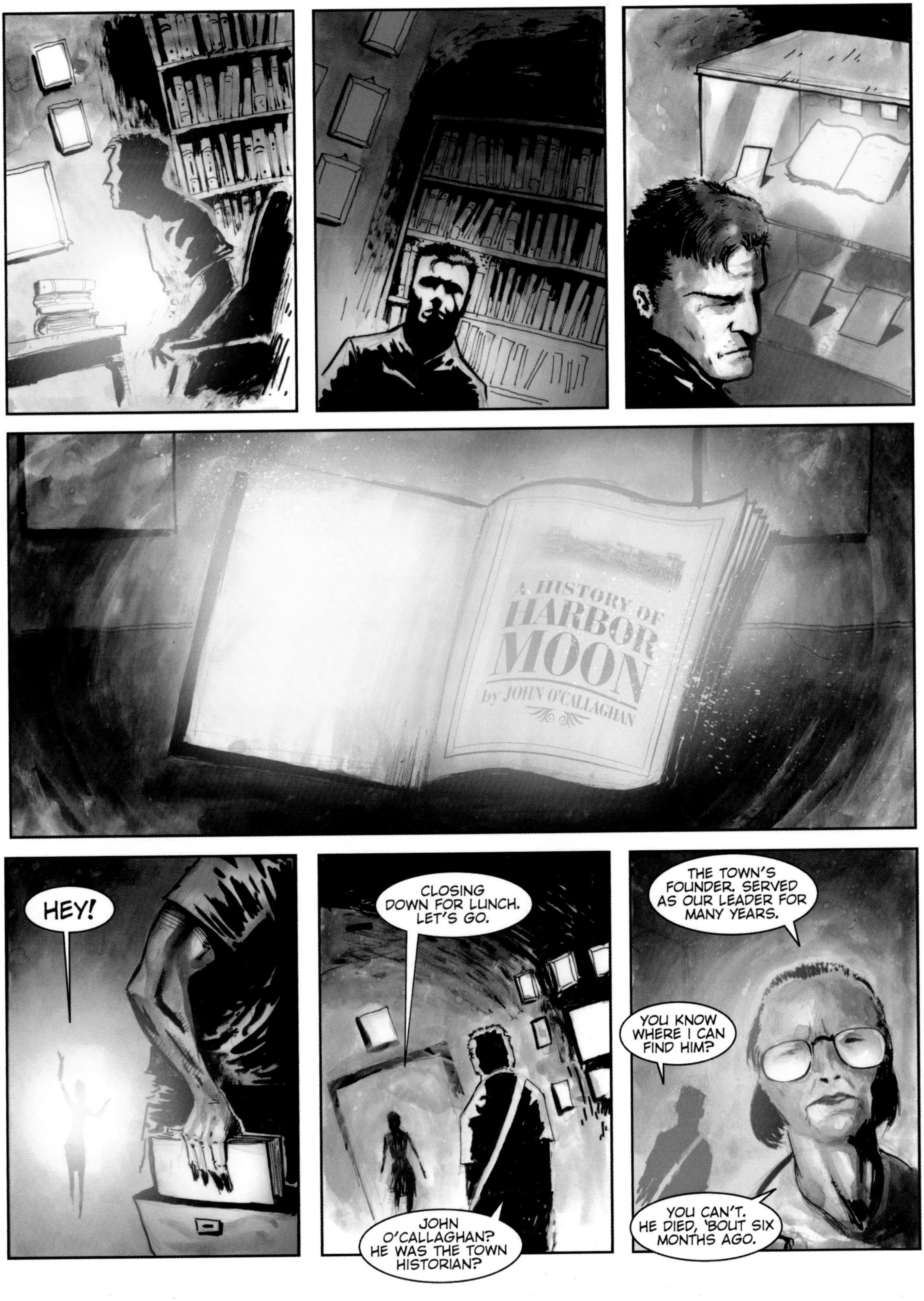
A HISTORY OF
HARBOR
MOON
by JOHN O'CALLAGHAN
HEY!
CLOSING DOWN FOR LUNCH. LET'S GO.
JOHN O'CALLAGHAN? HE WAS THE TOWN HISTORIAN?
THE TOWN'S FOUNDER. SERVED AS OUR LEADER FOR MANY YEARS.
YOU KNOW WHERE I CAN FIND HIM?
YOU CAN'T. HE DIED, 'BOUT SIX MONTHS AGO.

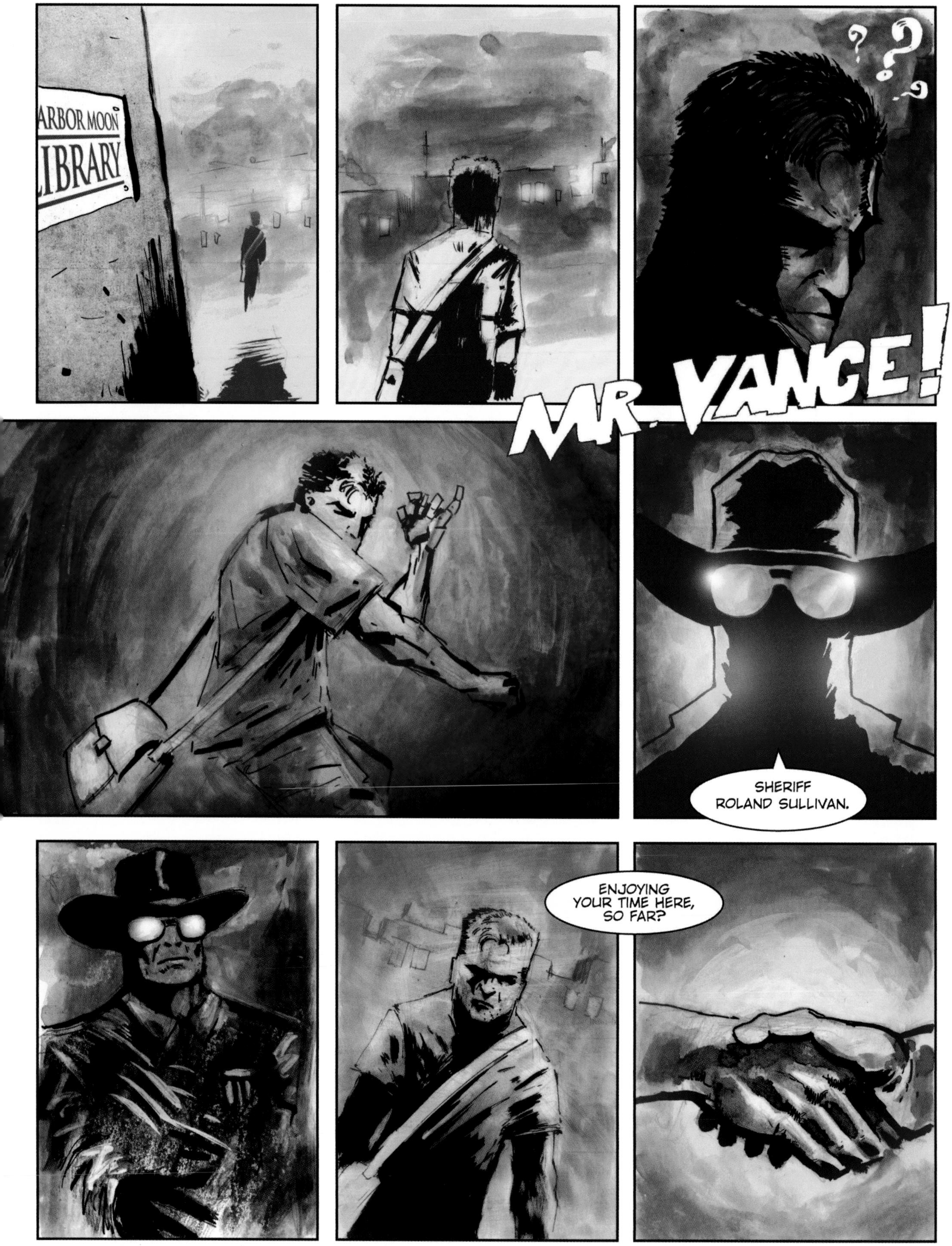
ARBOR MOON
LIBRARY
?
?
?
MR. VANCE!
SHERIFF ROLAND SULLIVAN.
ENJOYING YOUR TIME HERE, SO FAR?

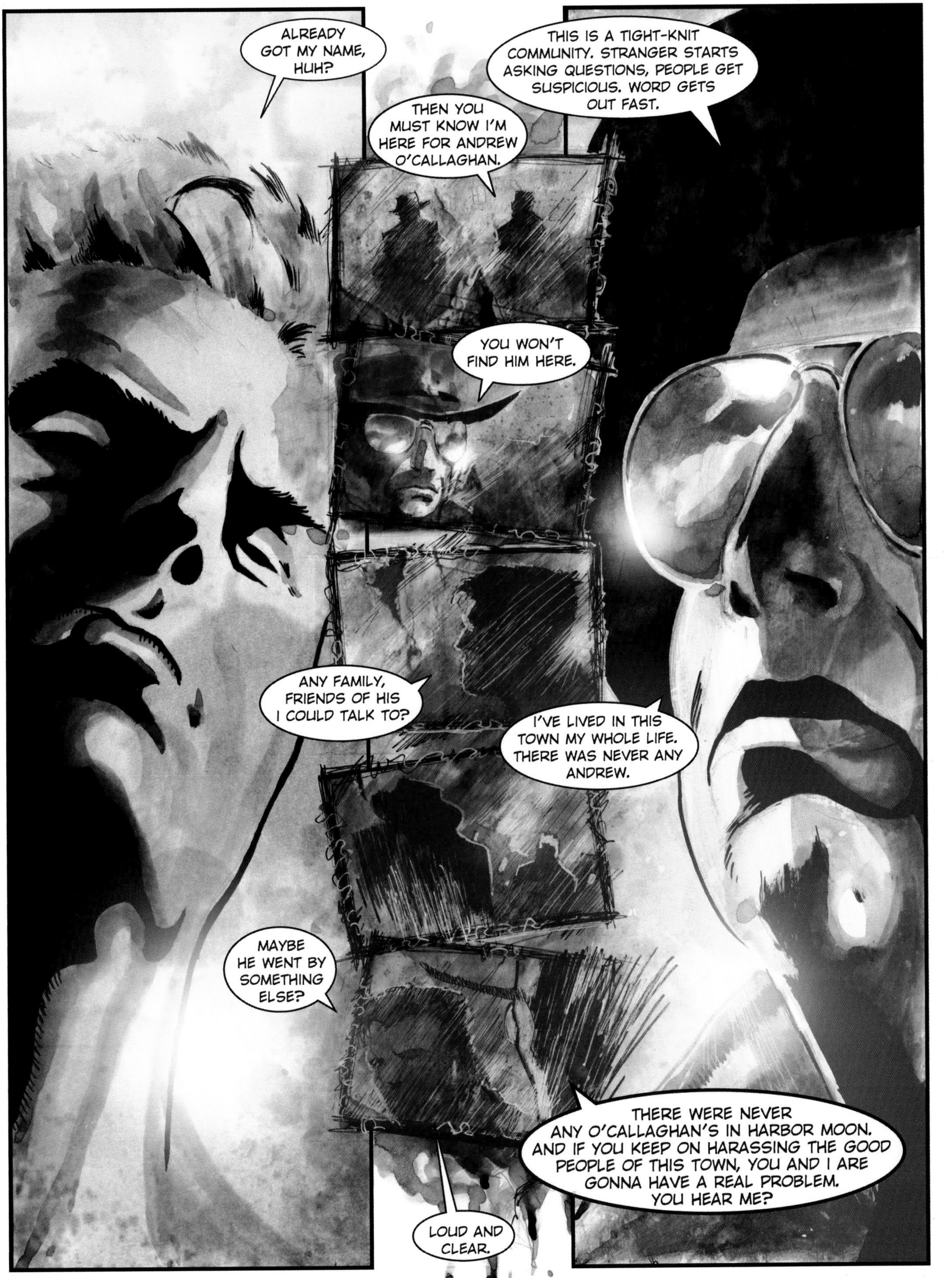
ALREADY GOT MY NAME, HUH?
THIS IS A TIGHT-KNIT COMMUNITY. STRANGER STARTS ASKING QUESTIONS, PEOPLE GET SUSPICIOUS. WORD GETS OUT FAST.
THEN YOU MUST KNOW I'M HERE FOR ANDREW O'CALLAGHAN.
YOU WON'T FIND HIM HERE.
ANY FAMILY, FRIENDS OF HIS I COULD TALK TO?
I'VE LIVED IN THIS TOWN MY WHOLE LIFE. THERE WAS NEVER ANY ANDREW.
MAYBE HE WENT BY SOMETHING ELSE?
THERE WERE NEVER ANY O'CALLAGHAN'S IN HARBOR MOON. AND IF YOU KEEP ON HARASSING THE GOOD PEOPLE OF THIS TOWN, YOU AND I ARE GONNA HAVE A REAL PROBLEM. YOU HEAR ME?
LOUD AND CLEAR.

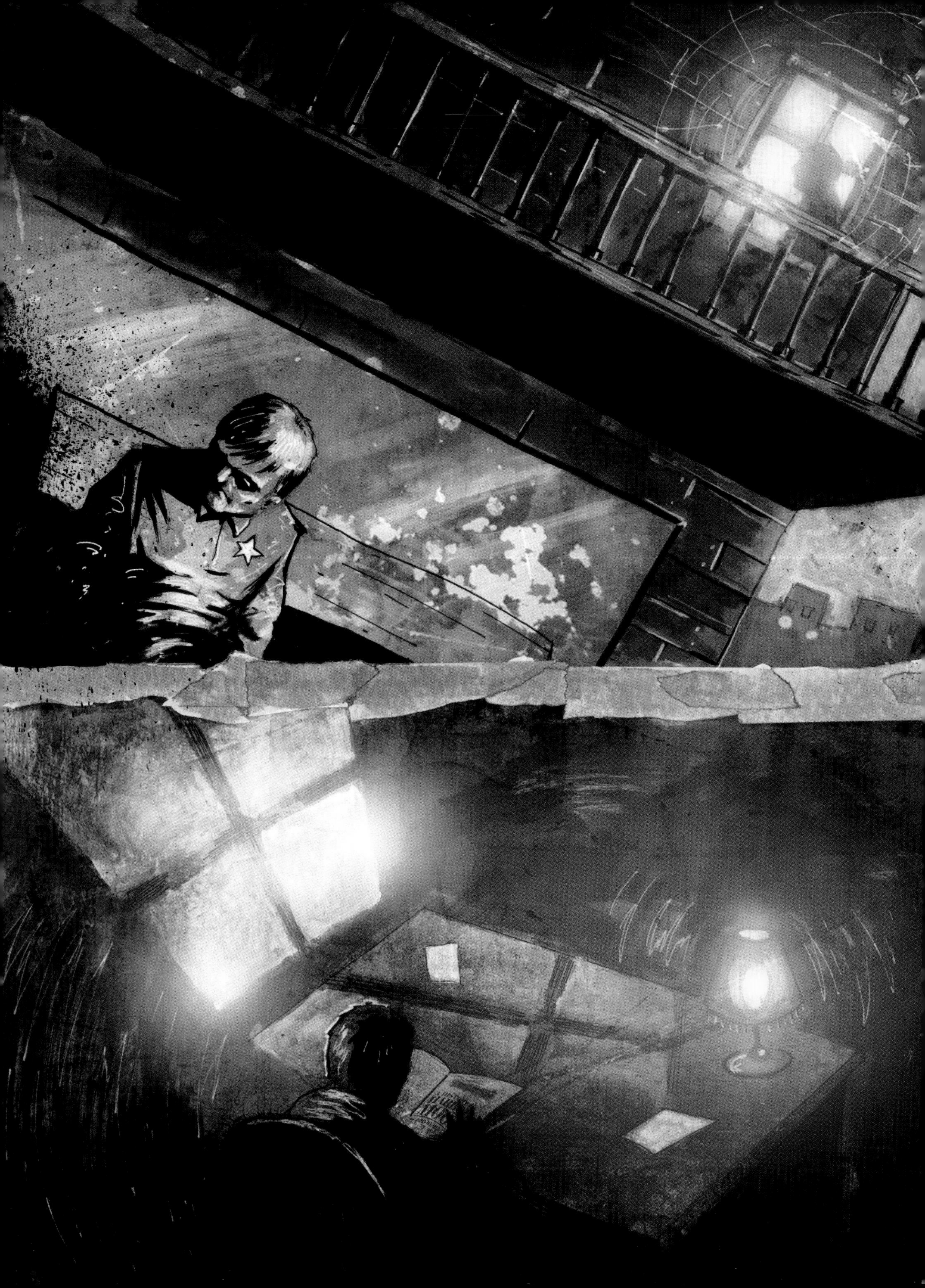

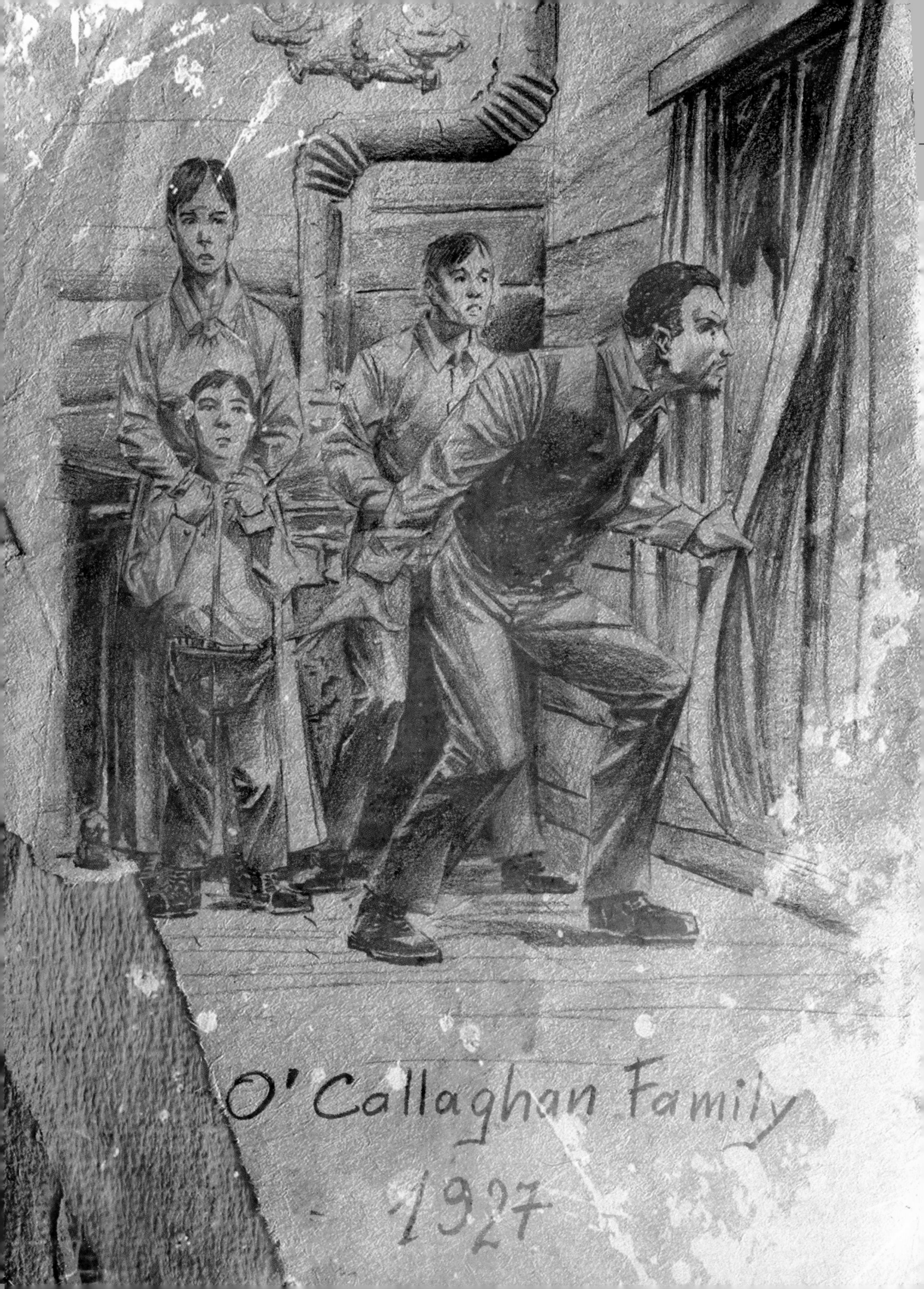
O'Callaghan Family
1927

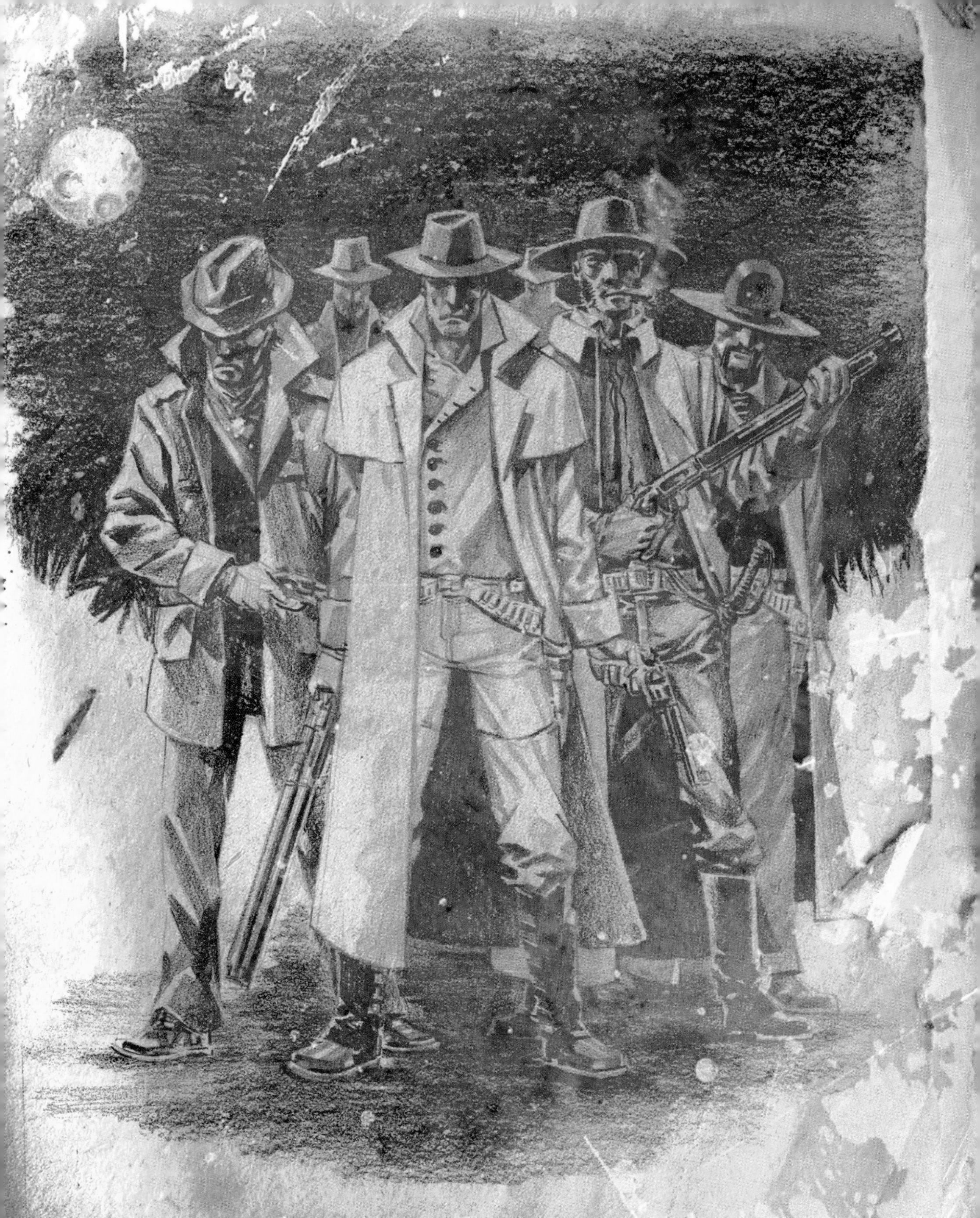

The Brotherhood of the Moon

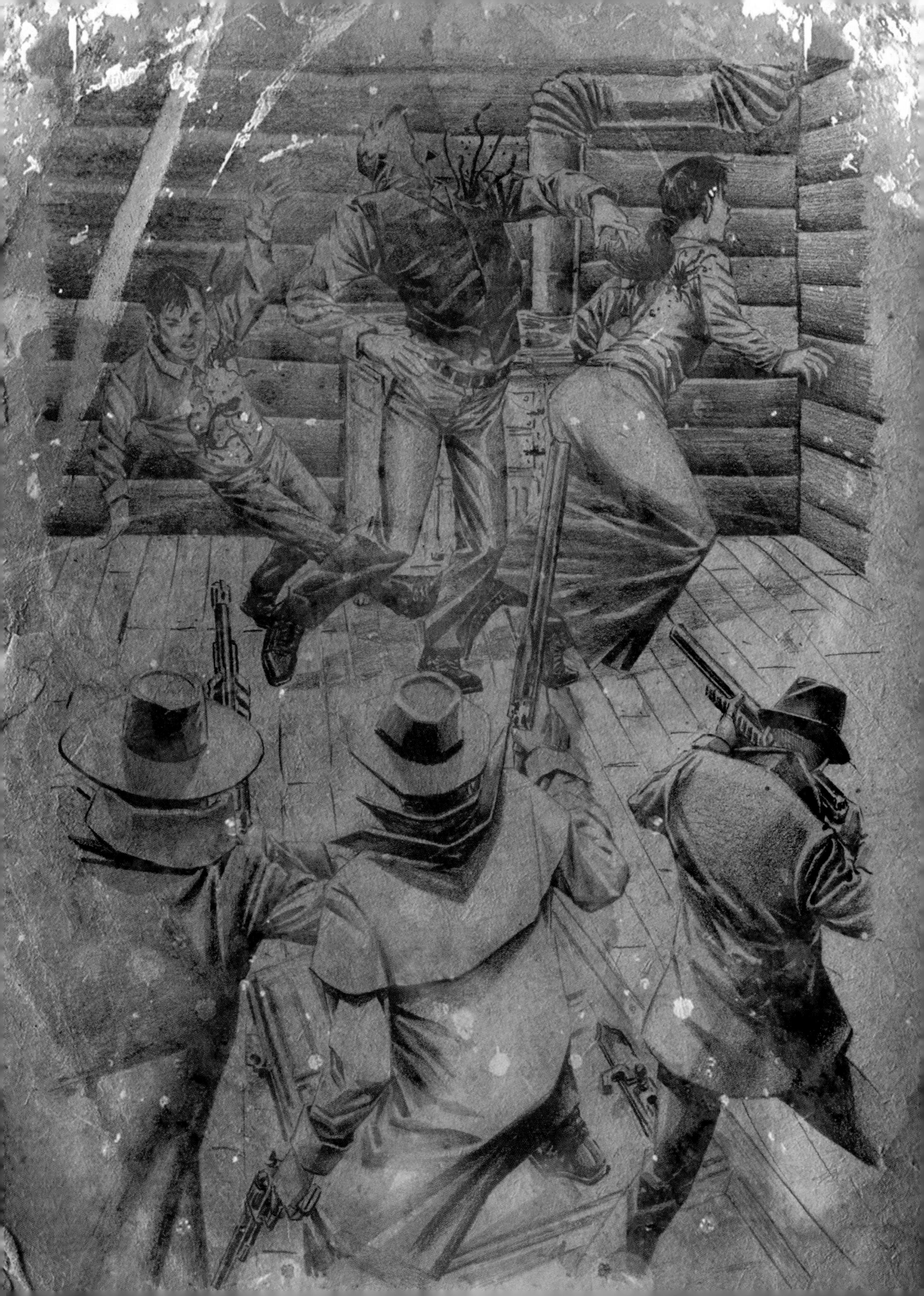

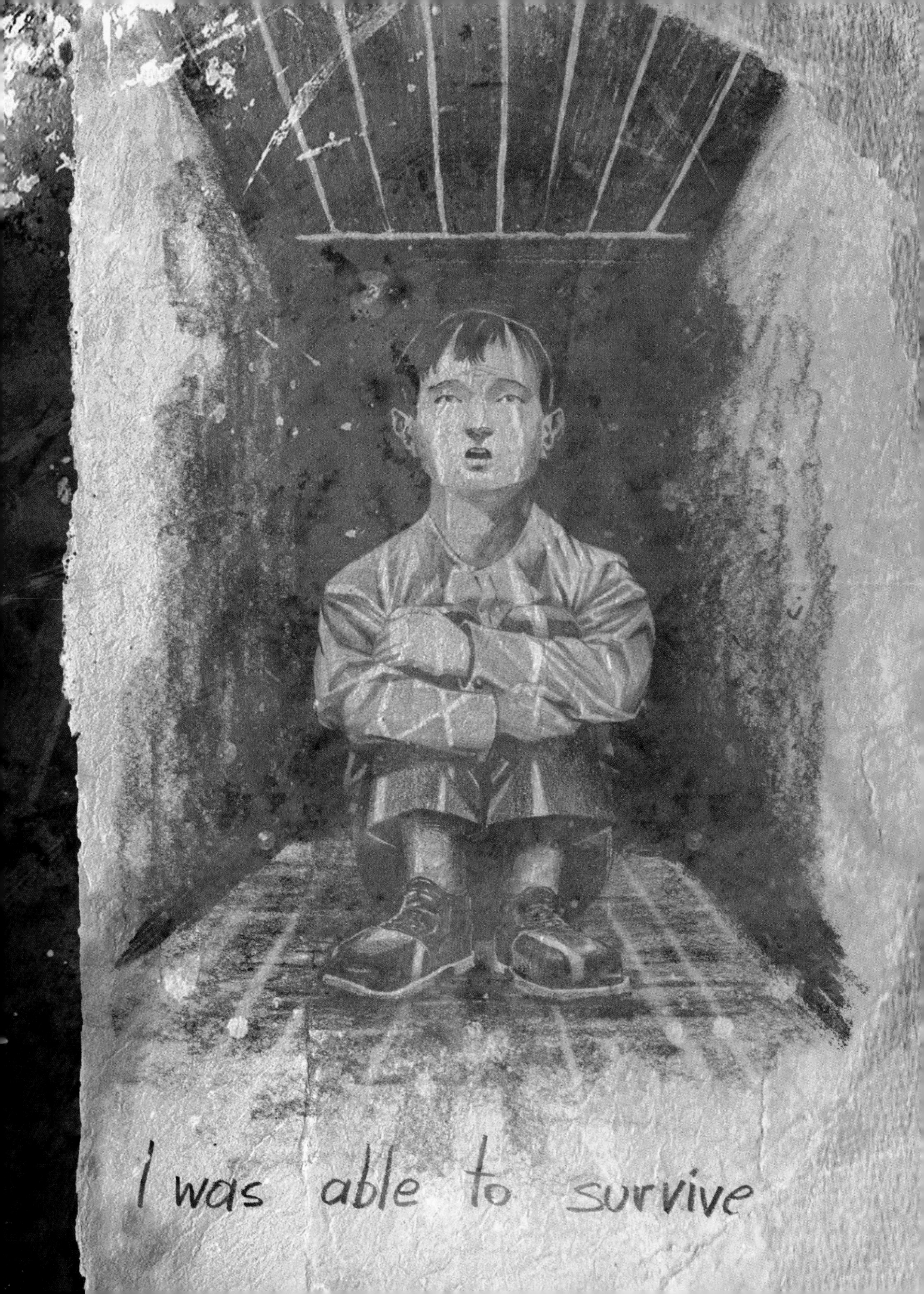

I was able to survive

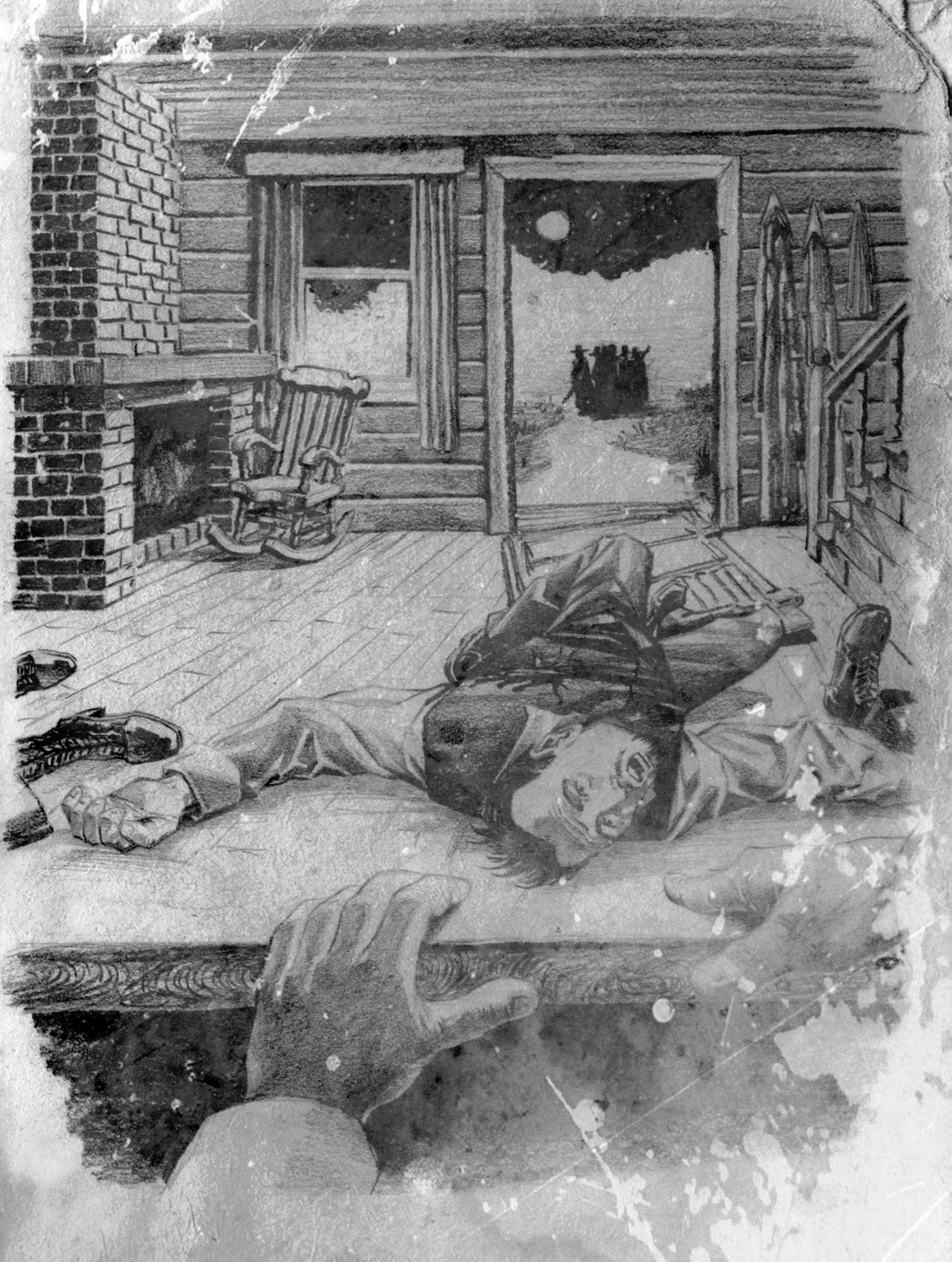

Integration impossible.

Tru

A large, self-sustaining community

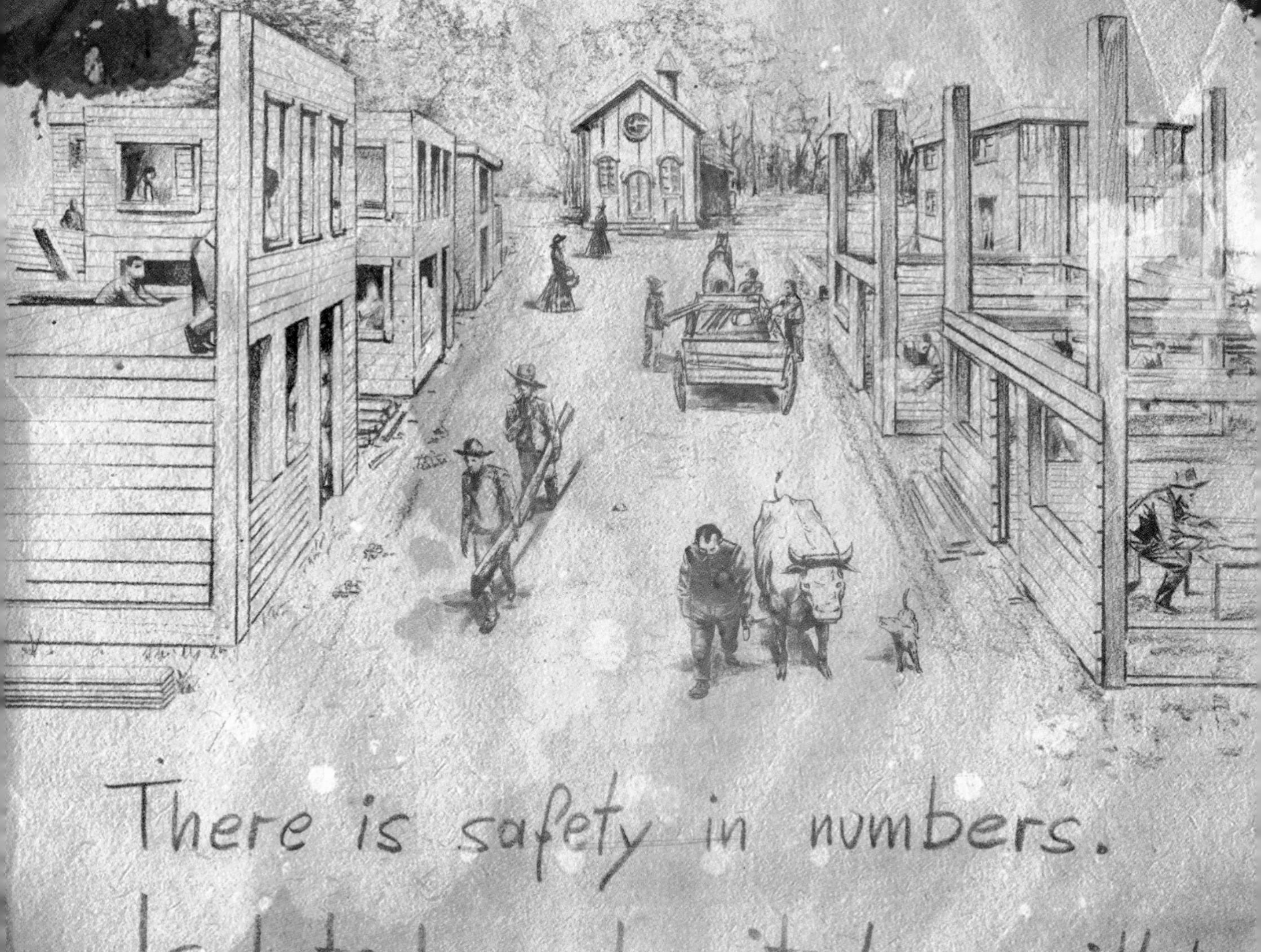

There is safety in numbers.
Isolated and united, we will be protected.

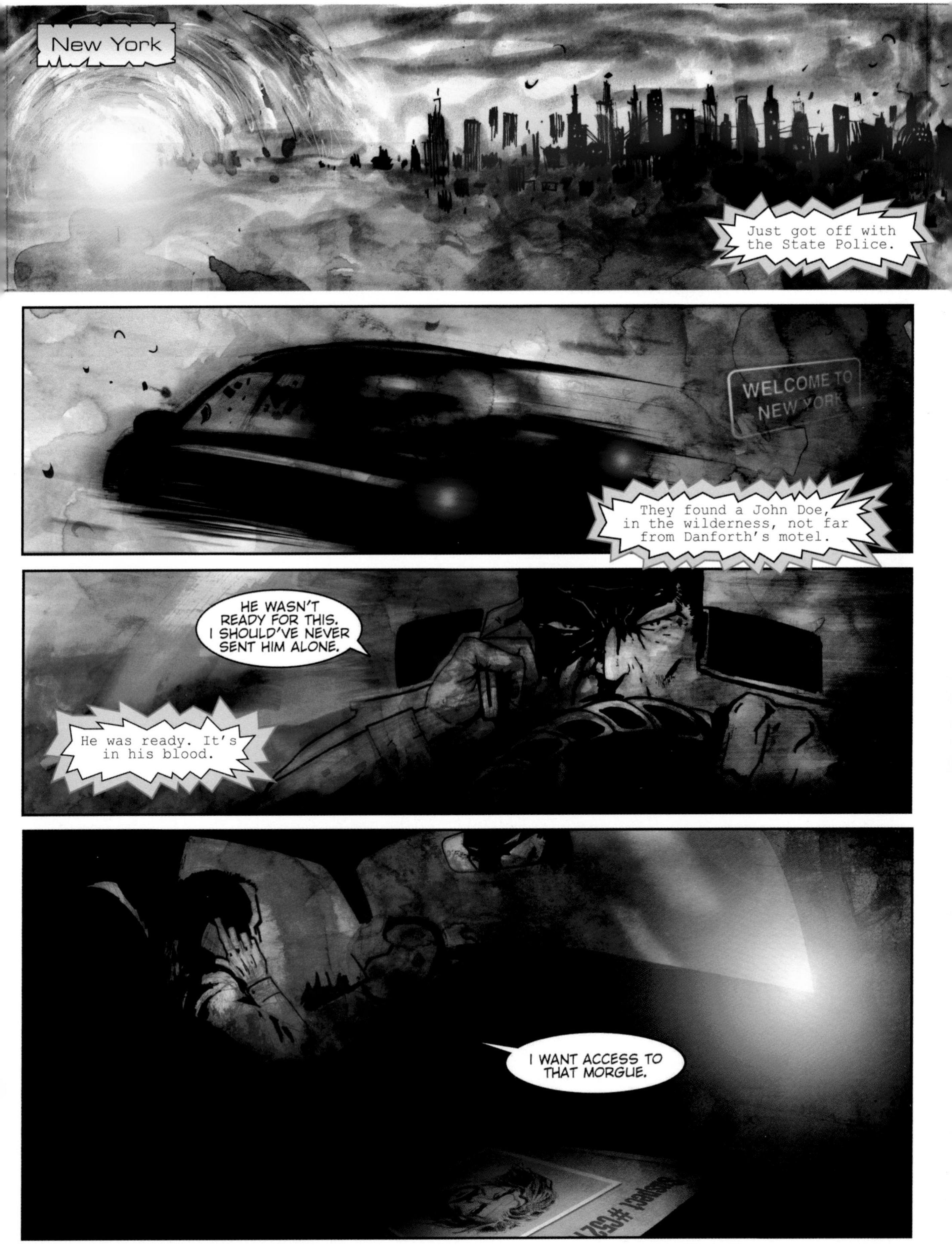
New York
Just got off with the State Police.
WELCOME TO NEW YORK
They found a John Doe, in the wilderness, not far from Danforth's motel.
HE WASN'T READY FOR THIS. I SHOULD'VE NEVER SENT HIM ALONE.
He was ready. It's in his blood.
I WANT ACCESS TO THAT MORGUE.

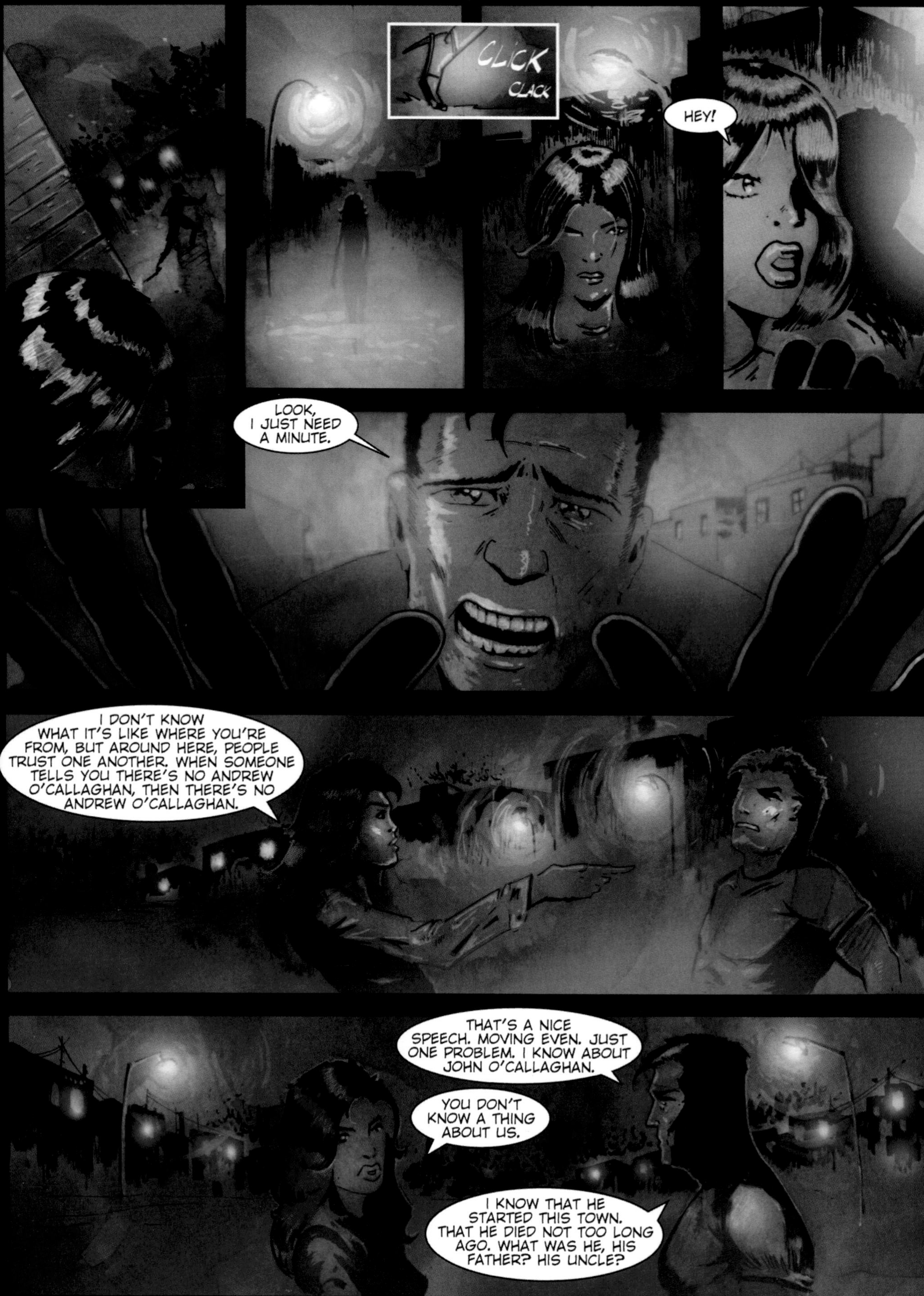
CLICK
CLACK
HEY!
LOOK, I JUST NEED A MINUTE.
I DON'T KNOW WHAT IT'S LIKE WHERE YOU'RE FROM, BUT AROUND HERE, PEOPLE TRUST ONE ANOTHER. WHEN SOMEONE TELLS YOU THERE'S NO ANDREW O'CALLAGHAN, THEN THERE'S NO ANDREW O'CALLAGHAN.
THAT'S A NICE SPEECH. MOVING EVEN. JUST ONE PROBLEM. I KNOW ABOUT JOHN O'CALLAGHAN.
YOU DON'T KNOW A THING ABOUT US.
I KNOW THAT HE STARTED THIS TOWN. THAT HE DIED NOT TOO LONG AGO. WHAT WAS HE, HIS FATHER? HIS UNCLE?

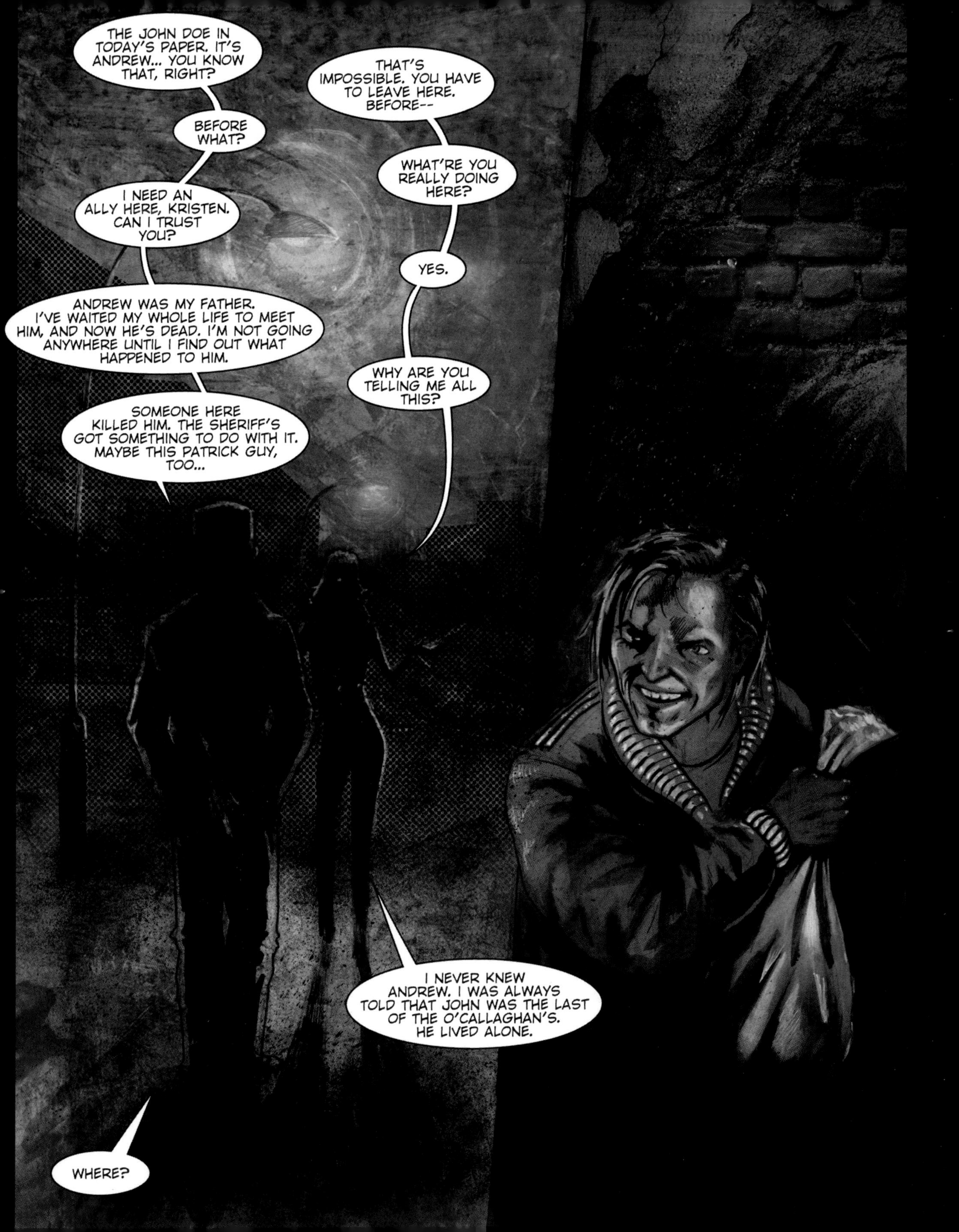
THE JOHN DOE IN TODAY'S PAPER. IT'S ANDREW... YOU KNOW THAT, RIGHT?
THAT'S IMPOSSIBLE. YOU HAVE TO LEAVE HERE. BEFORE--
BEFORE WHAT?
WHAT'RE YOU REALLY DOING HERE?
I NEED AN ALLY HERE, KRISTEN. CAN I TRUST YOU?
YES.
ANDREW WAS MY FATHER. I'VE WAITED MY WHOLE LIFE TO MEET HIM, AND NOW HE'S DEAD. I'M NOT GOING ANYWHERE UNTIL I FIND OUT WHAT HAPPENED TO HIM.
WHY ARE YOU TELLING ME ALL THIS?
SOMEONE HERE KILLED HIM. THE SHERIFF'S GOT SOMETHING TO DO WITH IT. MAYBE THIS PATRICK GUY, TOO...
I NEVER KNEW ANDREW. I WAS ALWAYS TOLD THAT JOHN WAS THE LAST OF THE O'CALLAGHAN'S. HE LIVED ALONE.
WHERE?

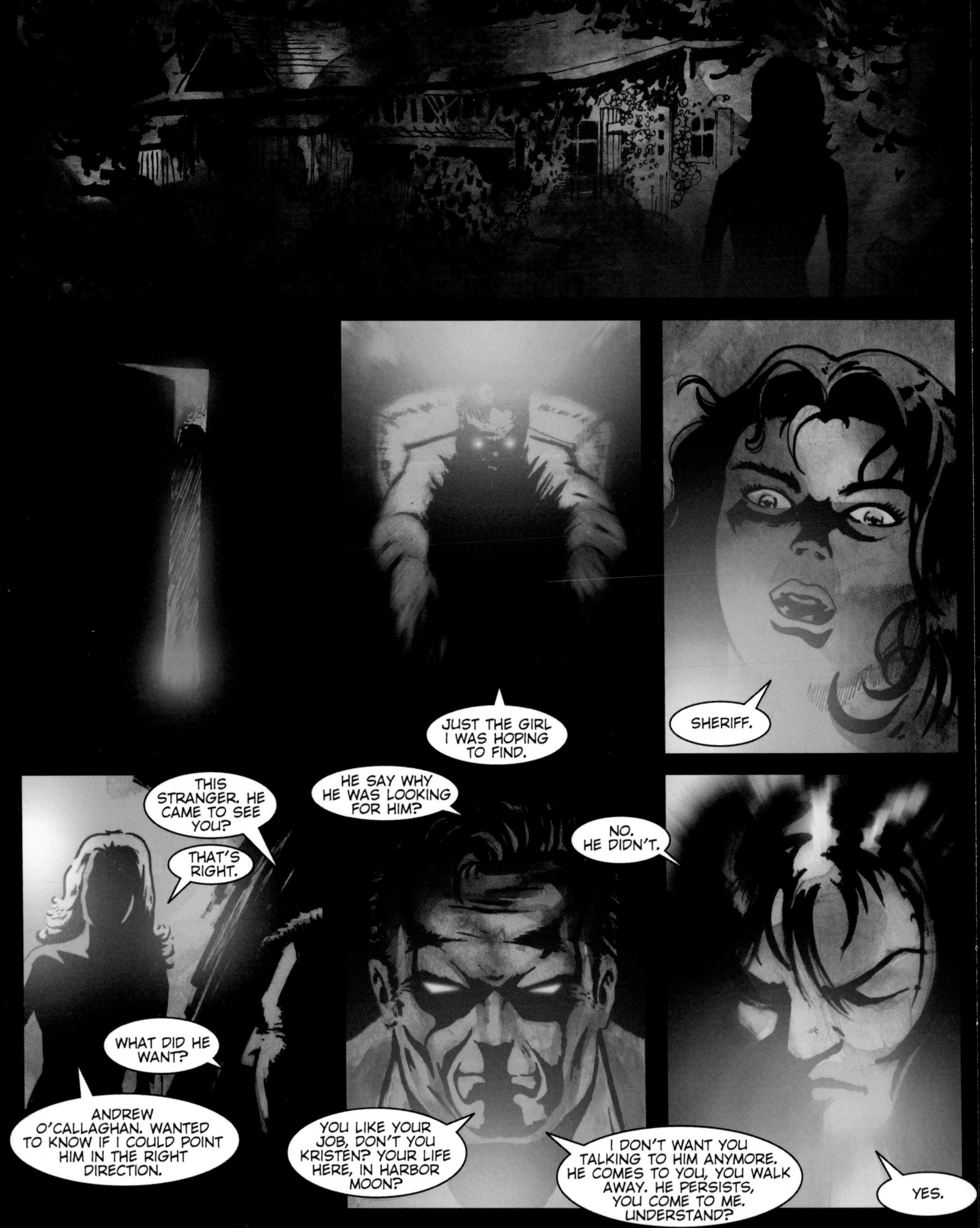
JUST THE GIRL I WAS HOPING TO FIND.
SHERIFF.
THIS STRANGER. HE CAME TO SEE YOU?
THAT'S RIGHT.
WHAT DID HE WANT?
ANDREW O'CALLAGHAN. WANTED TO KNOW IF I COULD POINT HIM IN THE RIGHT DIRECTION.
HE SAY WHY HE WAS LOOKING FOR HIM?
NO. HE DIDN'T.
YOU LIKE YOUR JOB, DON'T YOU KRISTEN? YOUR LIFE HERE, IN HARBOR MOON?
I DON'T WANT YOU TALKING TO HIM ANYMORE. HE COMES TO YOU, YOU WALK AWAY. HE PERSISTS, YOU COME TO ME. UNDERSTAND?
YES.

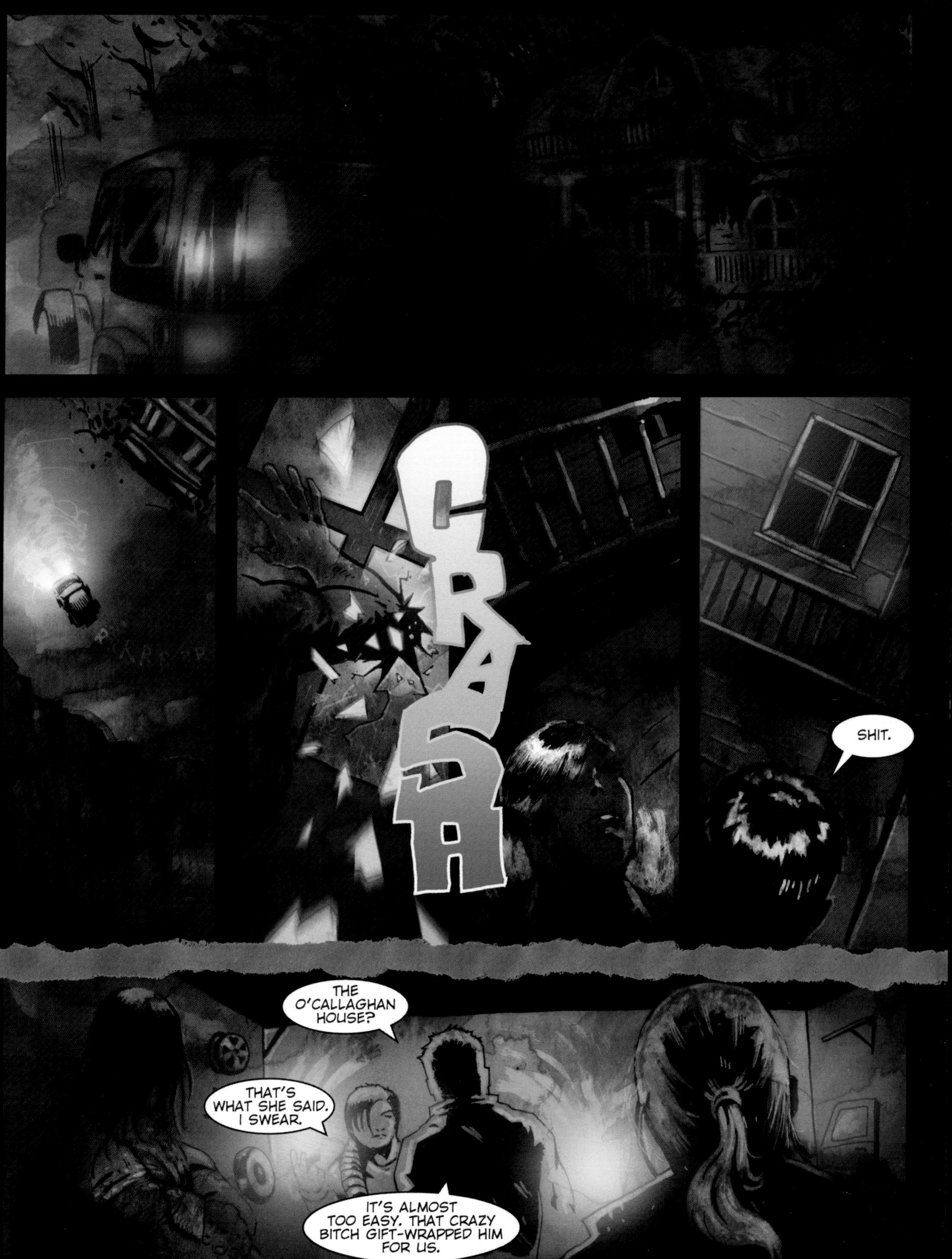
CRASH
SHIT.
THE O'CALLAGHAN HOUSE?
THAT'S WHAT SHE SAID. I SWEAR.
IT'S ALMOST TOO EASY. THAT CRAZY BITCH GIFT-WRAPPED HIM FOR US.

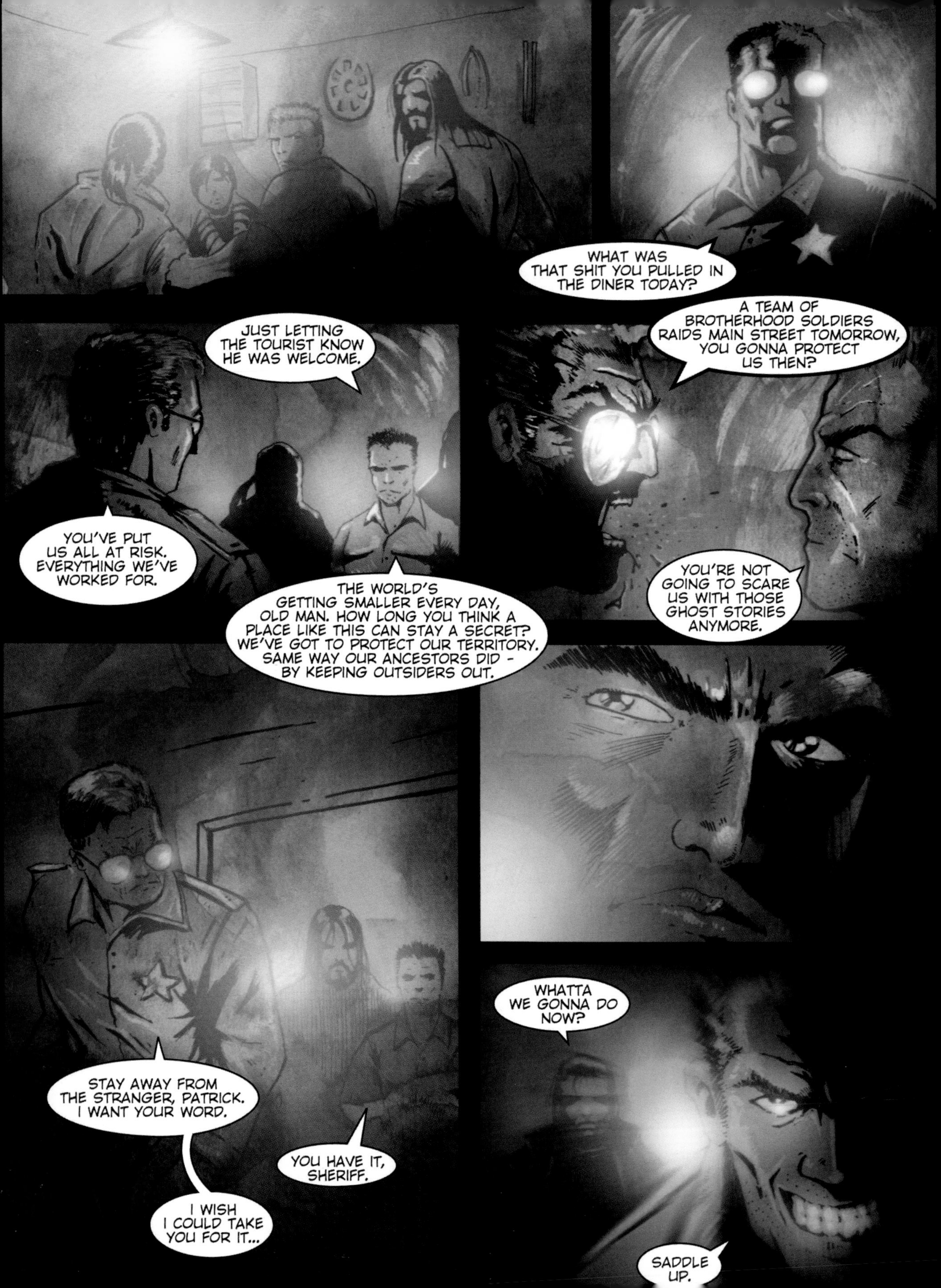
WHAT WAS THAT SHIT YOU PULLED IN THE DINER TODAY?
JUST LETTING THE TOURIST KNOW HE WAS WELCOME.
YOU'VE PUT US ALL AT RISK. EVERYTHING WE'VE WORKED FOR.
A TEAM OF BROTHERHOOD SOLDIERS RAIDS MAIN STREET TOMORROW, YOU GONNA PROTECT US THEN?
YOU'RE NOT GOING TO SCARE US WITH THOSE GHOST STORIES ANYMORE.
THE WORLD'S GETTING SMALLER EVERY DAY, OLD MAN. HOW LONG YOU THINK A PLACE LIKE THIS CAN STAY A SECRET? WE'VE GOT TO PROTECT OUR TERRITORY. SAME WAY OUR ANCESTORS DID - BY KEEPING OUTSIDERS OUT.
STAY AWAY FROM THE STRANGER, PATRICK. I WANT YOUR WORD.
YOU HAVE IT, SHERIFF.
I WISH I COULD TAKE YOU FOR IT...
WHATTA WE GONNA DO NOW?
SADDLE UP.

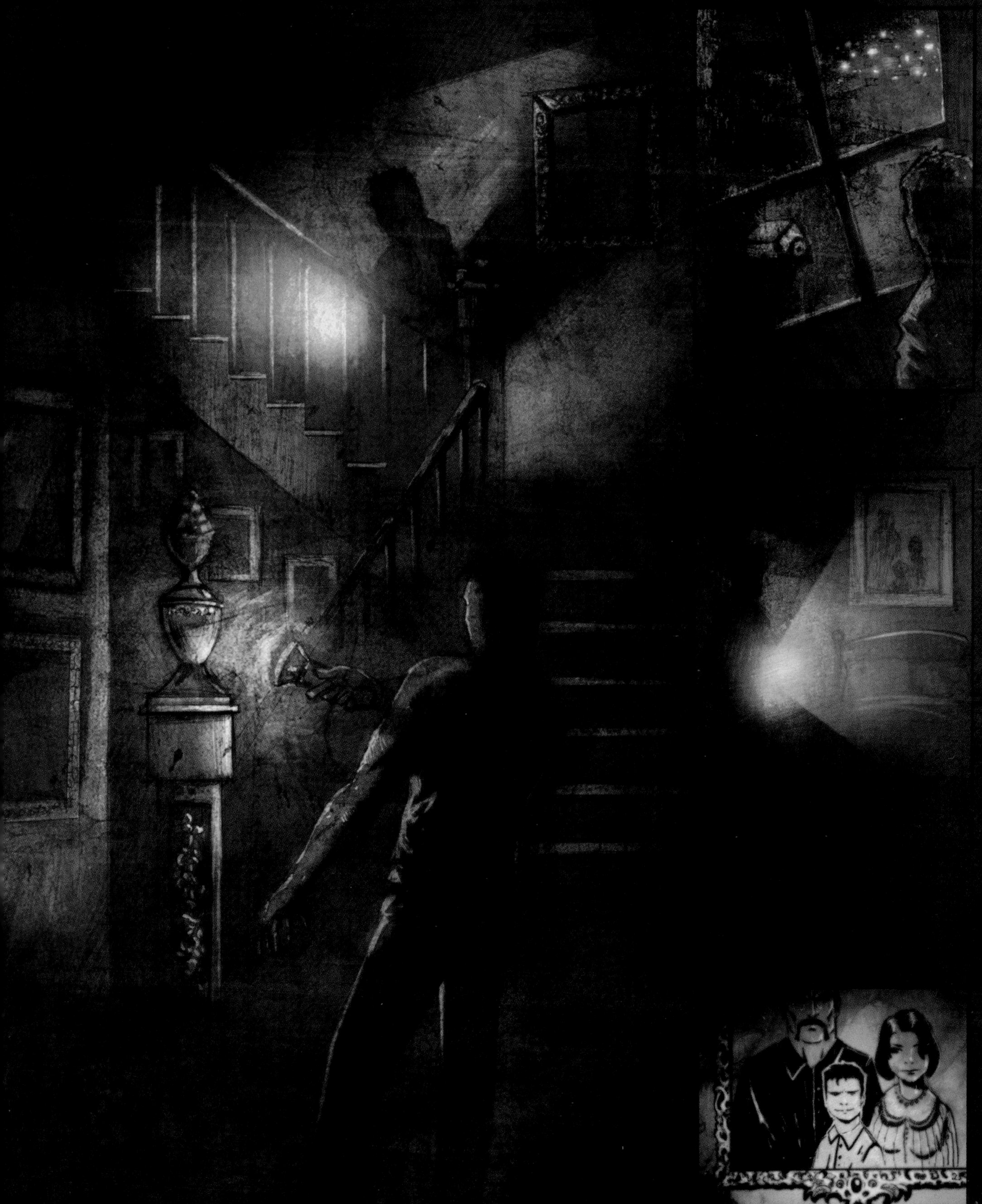

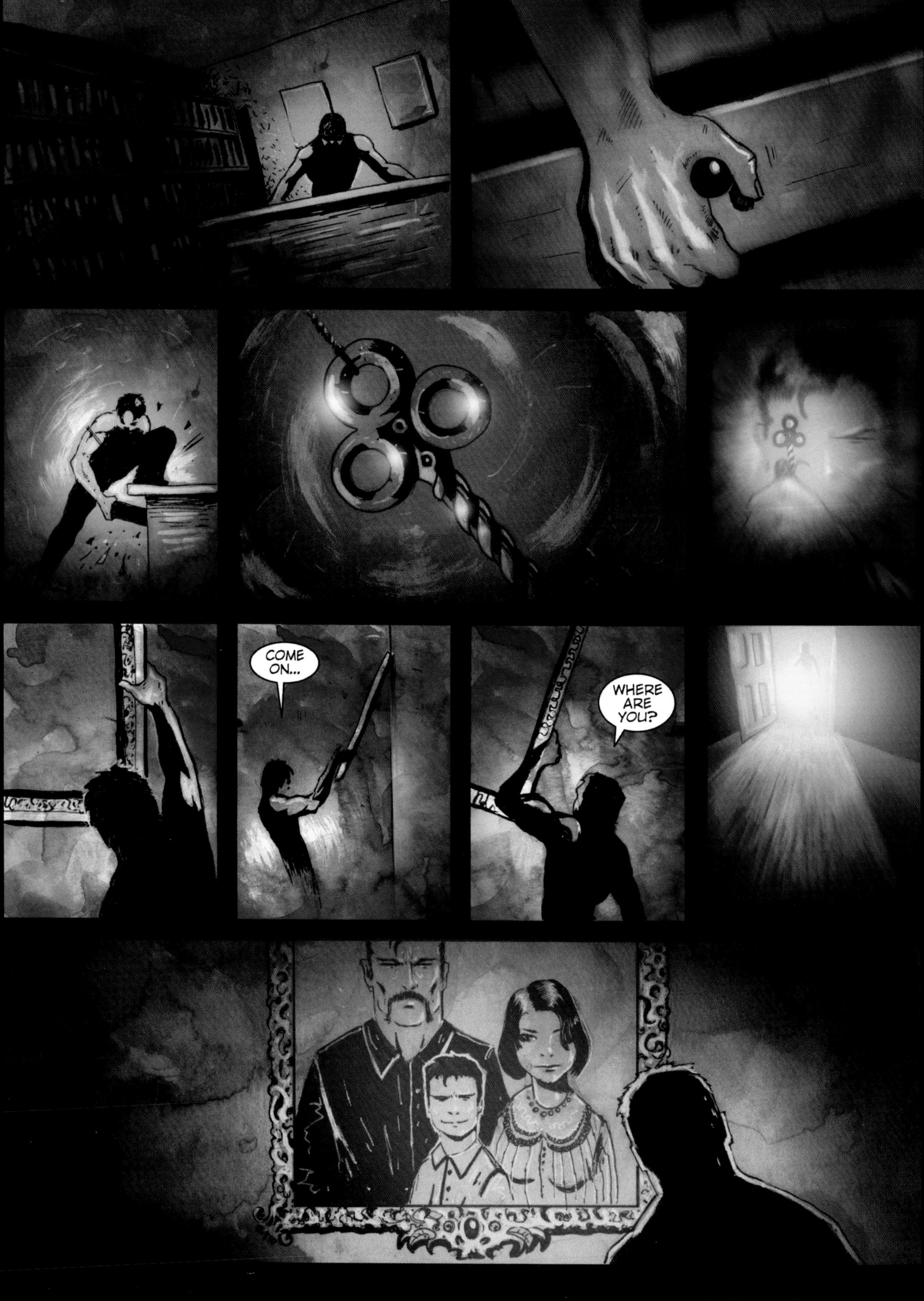
COME ON...
WHERE ARE YOU?

CLICK

CLICK

CLICK

CIGARETTES

Port Lucie High Alum Saves Platoon from Taliban Ambush

by Timothy Vance

"I just heard 'em coming..."

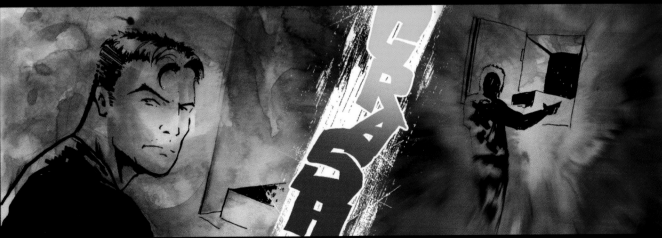

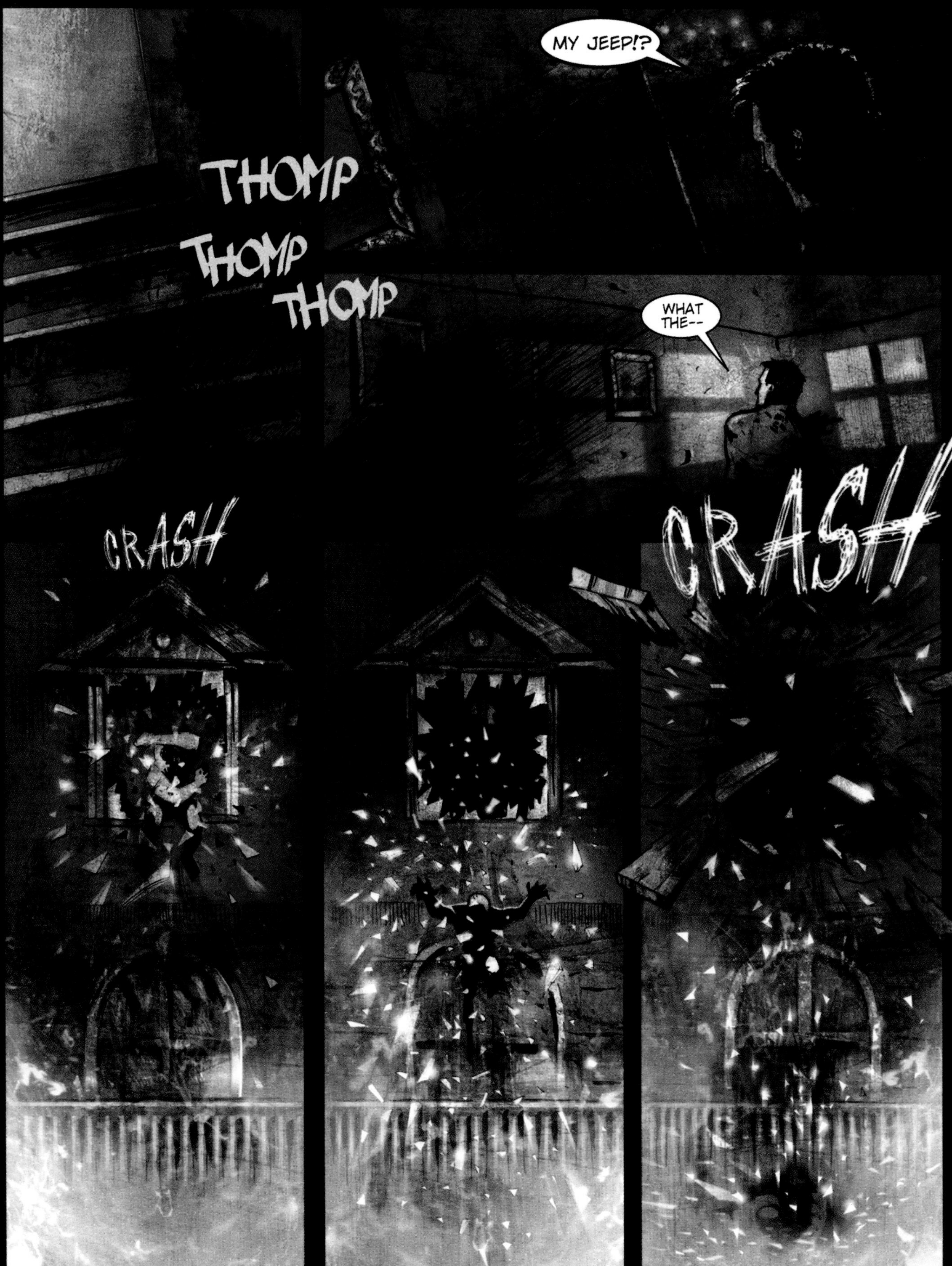
MY JEEP!?
THOMP
THOMP
THOMP
WHAT THE--
CRASH
CRASH

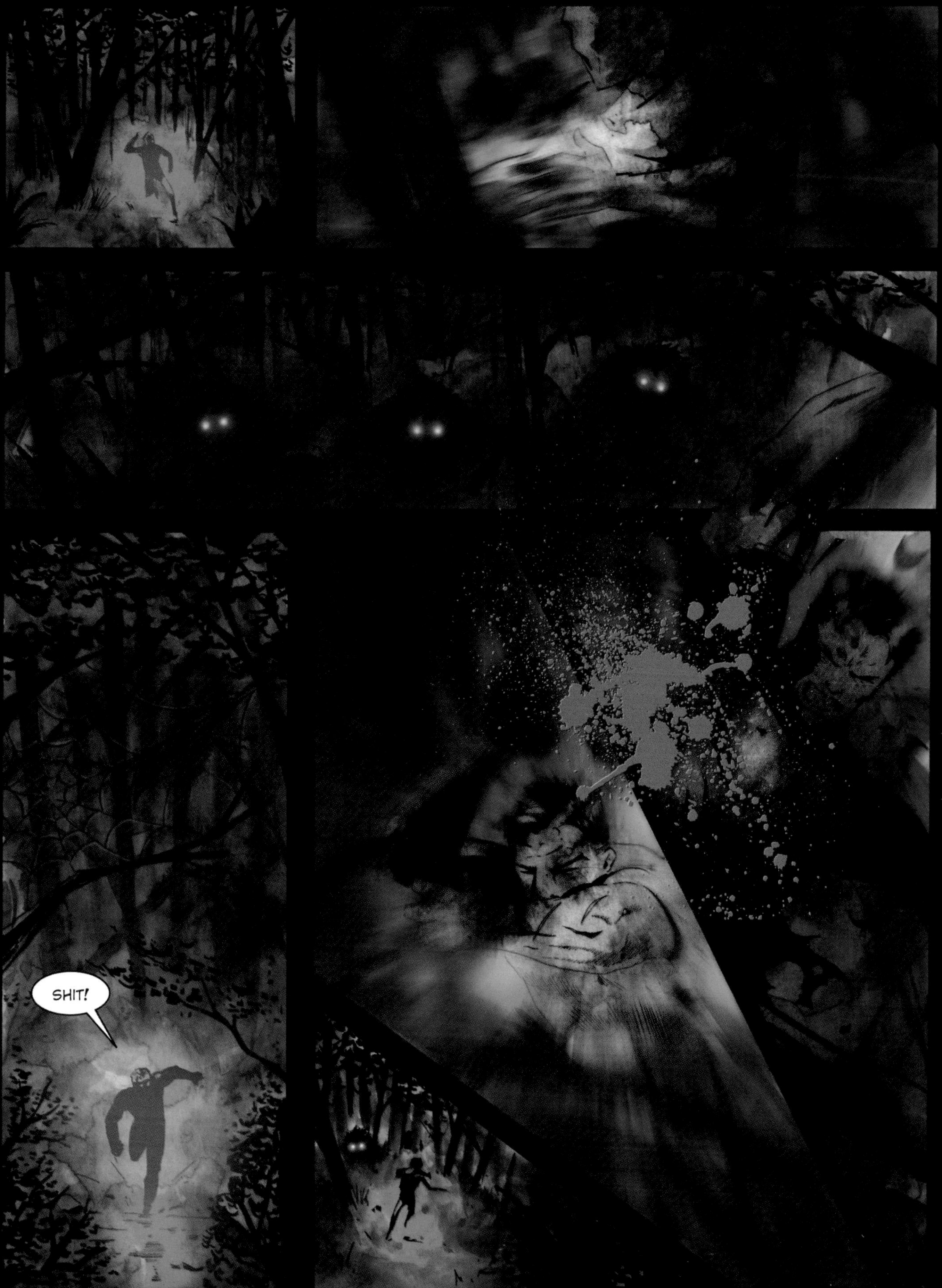
SHIT!

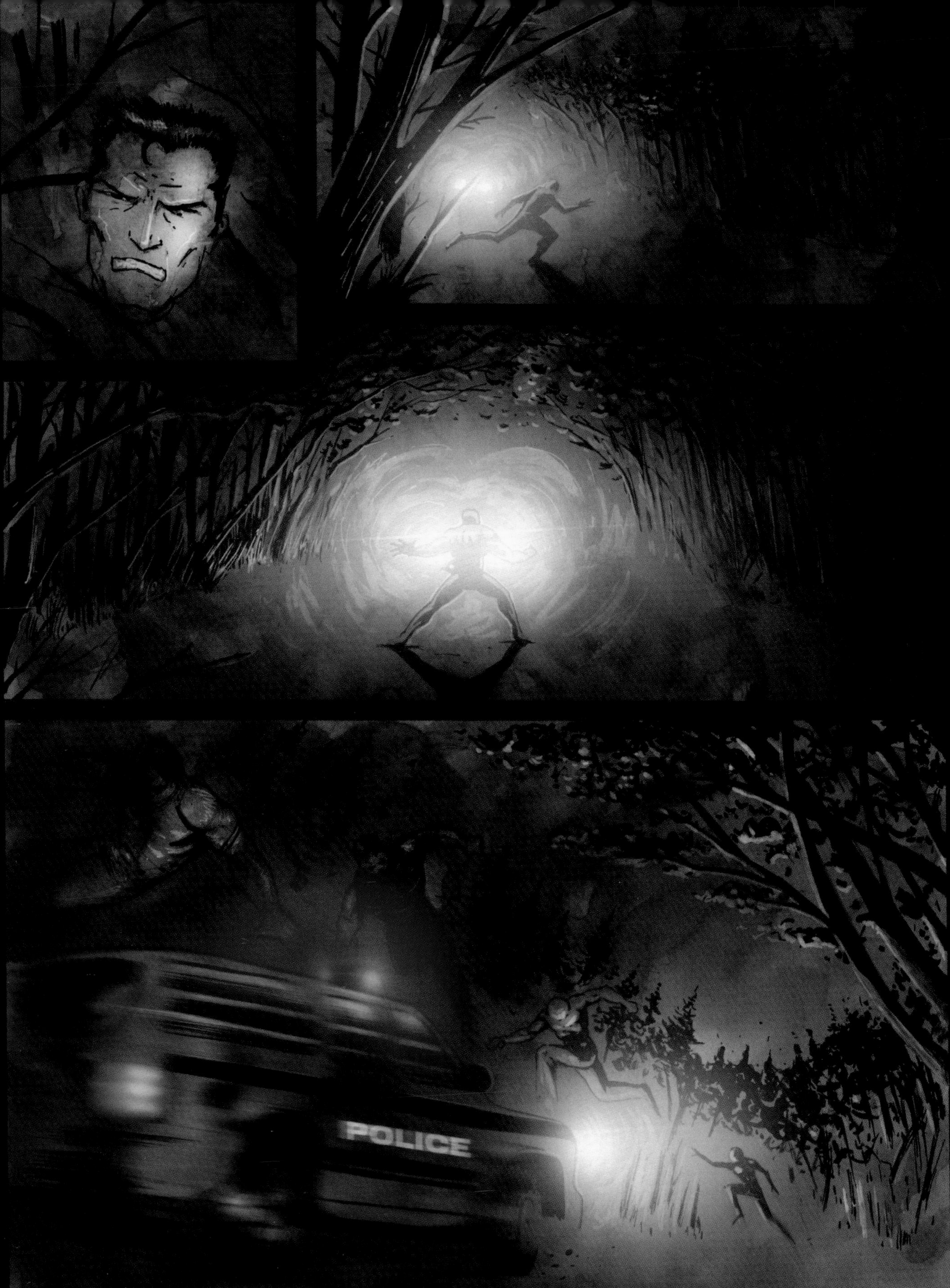
POLICE

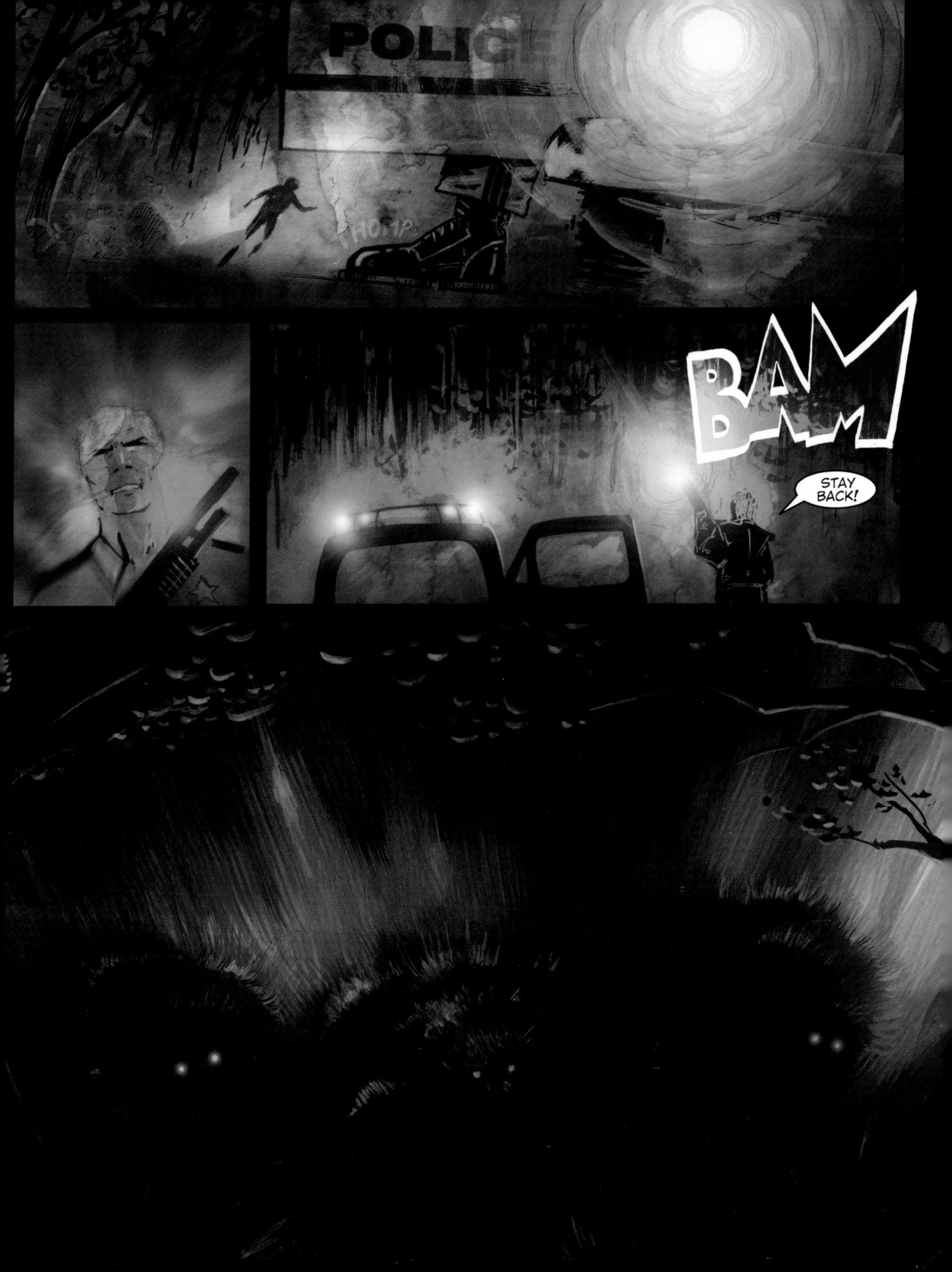
POLICE
THOMP.
BAM
STAY BACK!

THUD!

CALL THE STATE POLICE! TELL 'EM IT'S URGENT.

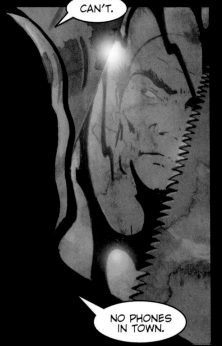

CAN'T.

NO PHONES IN TOWN.

WHAT?!

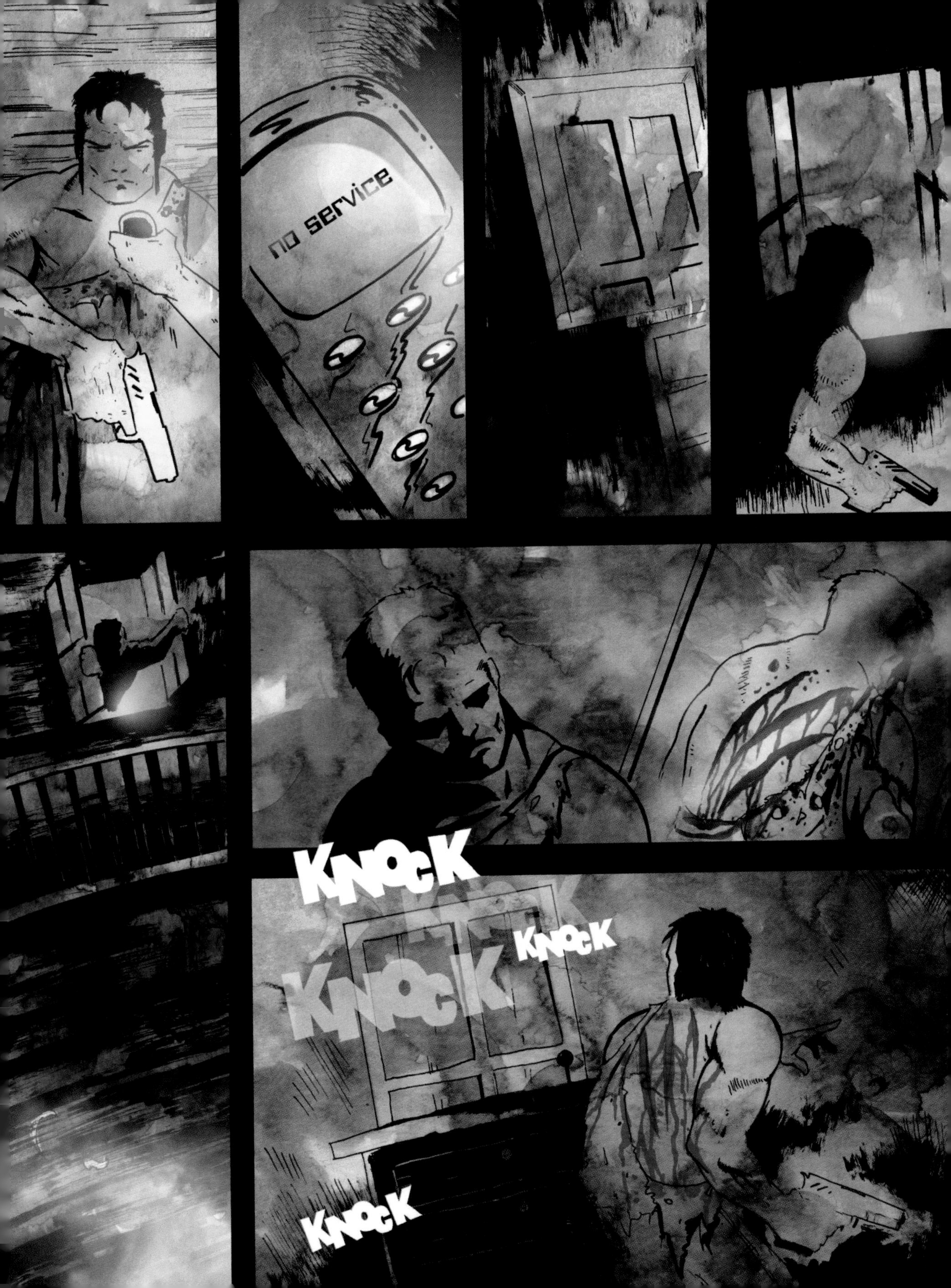
no service
KNOCK
KNOCK
KNOCK
KNOCK

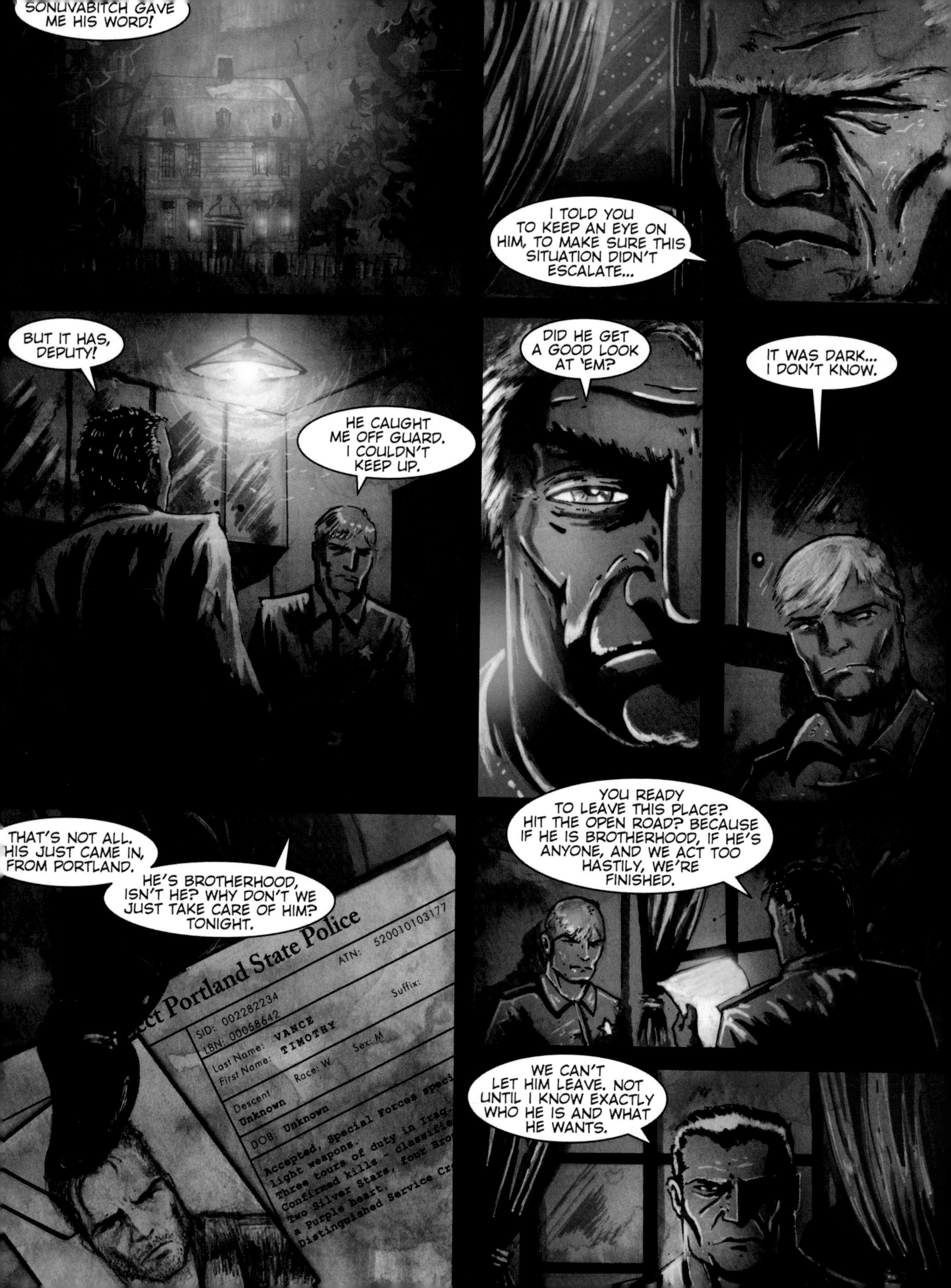
SONUVABITCH GAVE ME HIS WORD!
I TOLD YOU TO KEEP AN EYE ON HIM, TO MAKE SURE THIS SITUATION DIDN'T ESCALATE...
BUT IT HAS, DEPUTY!
HE CAUGHT ME OFF GUARD. I COULDN'T KEEP UP.
DID HE GET A GOOD LOOK AT 'EM?
IT WAS DARK... I DON'T KNOW.
THAT'S NOT ALL. HIS JUST CAME IN, FROM PORTLAND.
HE'S BROTHERHOOD, ISN'T HE? WHY DON'T WE JUST TAKE CARE OF HIM? TONIGHT.
Portland State Police
ATN: 520010103177
SID: 002282234
LBN: 00058642
Suffix:
Last Name: VANCE
First Name: TIMOTHY
Sex: M
Race: W
Descent Unknown
DOB: Unknown
light weapons.
Two Silver Stars,
a Purple heart,
YOU READY TO LEAVE THIS PLACE? HIT THE OPEN ROAD? BECAUSE IF HE IS BROTHERHOOD, IF HE'S ANYONE, AND WE ACT TOO HASTILY, WE'RE FINISHED.
WE CAN'T LET HIM LEAVE. NOT UNTIL I KNOW EXACTLY WHO HE IS AND WHAT HE WANTS.

KNOCK KNOCK

KNOCK

KNOCK

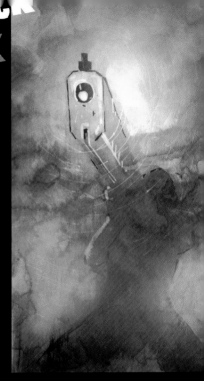

MR. VANCE!
IT'S SHERIFF
SULLIVAN.

PLEASE.
OPEN THE DOOR.
I KNOW YOU'RE IN
THERE. WE NEED
TO TALK.

THERE WAS
A BREAK-IN. ON THE
EDGE OF TOWN...

HAVEN'T
HAD A ROBBERY AS LONG
AS I'VE BEEN IN CHARGE.
HARBOR MOON'S A SAFE
PLACE.

I HEAR YOU GOT
THREE CORPSES IN AS MANY
WEEKS, SHERIFF. THAT SOUNDS
MORE LIKE BAGHDAD THAN
SAFE.

THAT'S JUST
THE THING, ISN'T IT? BODY
SHOWS UP JUST AS YOU STROLL
INTO TOWN. NOW I GOT A BREAK-IN
AND YOU WERE SPOTTED RUNNING
FROM THE SCENE OF
THE CRIME.

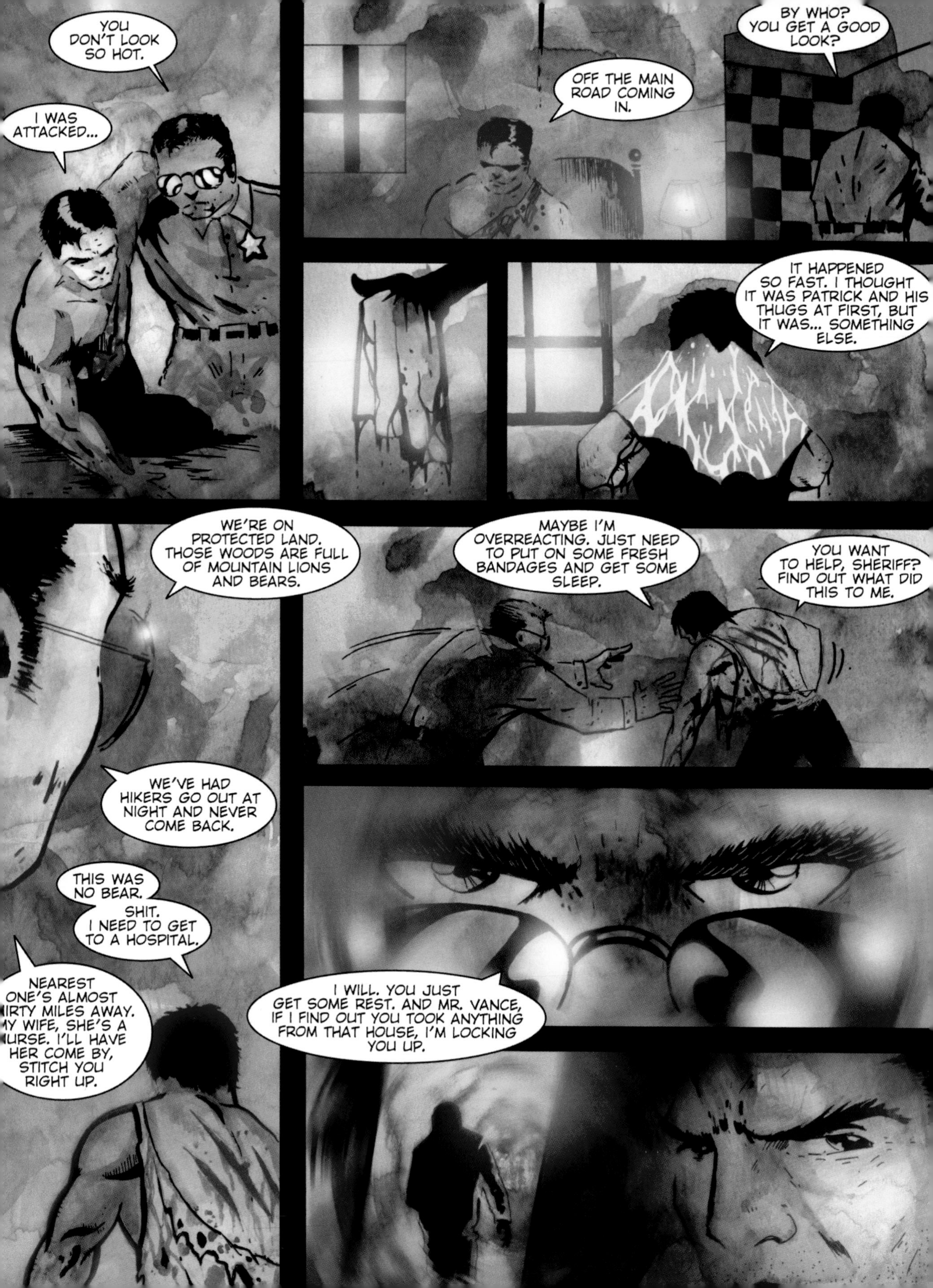

YOU DON'T LOOK SO HOT.
I WAS ATTACKED...
OFF THE MAIN ROAD COMING IN.
BY WHO? YOU GET A GOOD LOOK?
IT HAPPENED SO FAST. I THOUGHT IT WAS PATRICK AND HIS THUGS AT FIRST, BUT IT WAS... SOMETHING ELSE.
WE'RE ON PROTECTED LAND. THOSE WOODS ARE FULL OF MOUNTAIN LIONS AND BEARS.
WE'VE HAD HIKERS GO OUT AT NIGHT AND NEVER COME BACK.
THIS WAS NO BEAR.
SHIT. I NEED TO GET TO A HOSPITAL.
NEAREST ONE'S ALMOST IRTY MILES AWAY. Y WIFE, SHE'S A URSE. I'LL HAVE HER COME BY, STITCH YOU RIGHT UP.
MAYBE I'M OVERREACTING. JUST NEED TO PUT ON SOME FRESH BANDAGES AND GET SOME SLEEP.
YOU WANT TO HELP, SHERIFF? FIND OUT WHAT DID THIS TO ME.
I WILL. YOU JUST GET SOME REST. AND MR. VANCE, IF I FIND OUT YOU TOOK ANYTHING FROM THAT HOUSE, I'M LOCKING YOU UP.

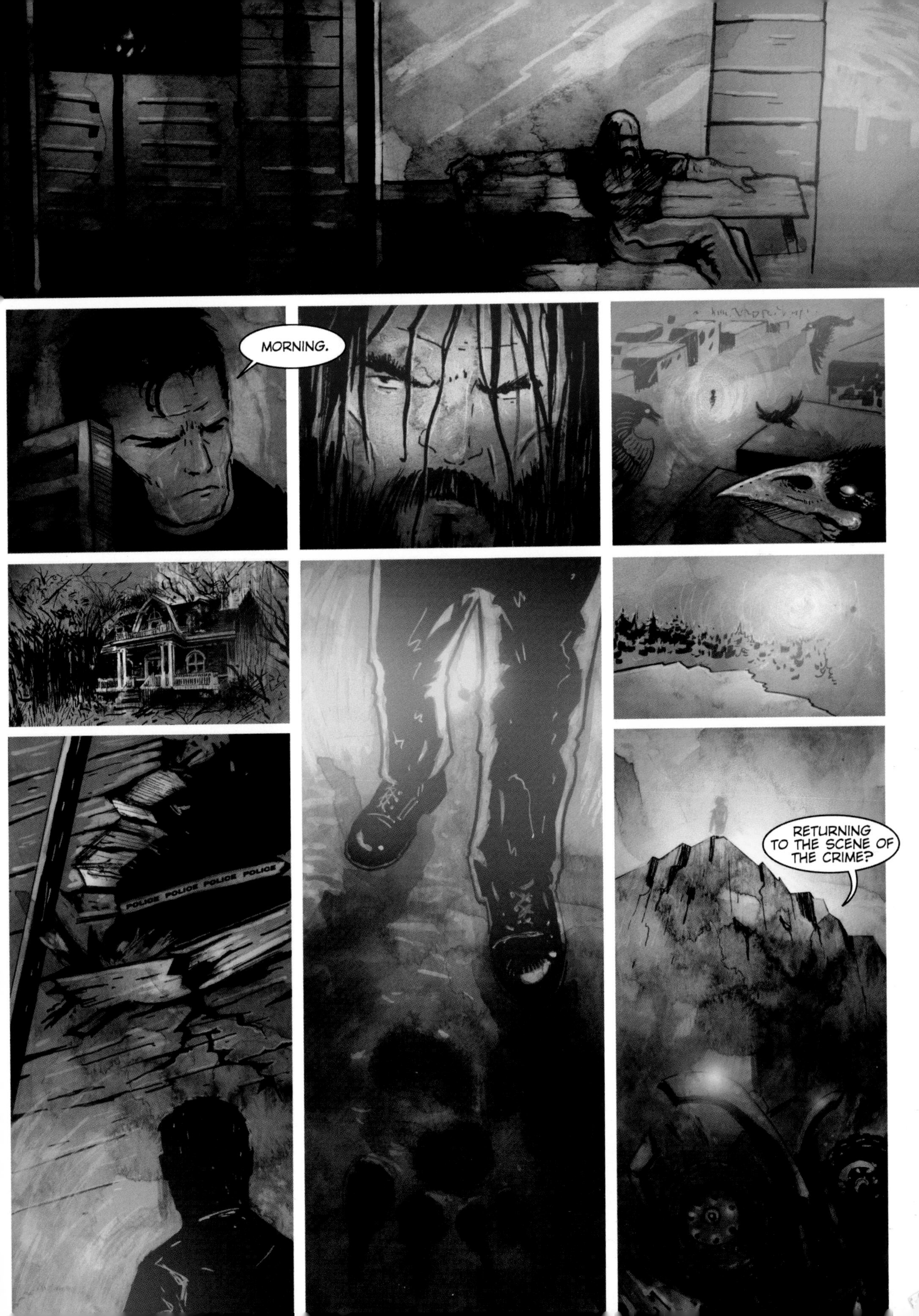
MORNING.
POLICE POLICE POLICE POLICE
RETURNING TO THE SCENE OF THE CRIME?

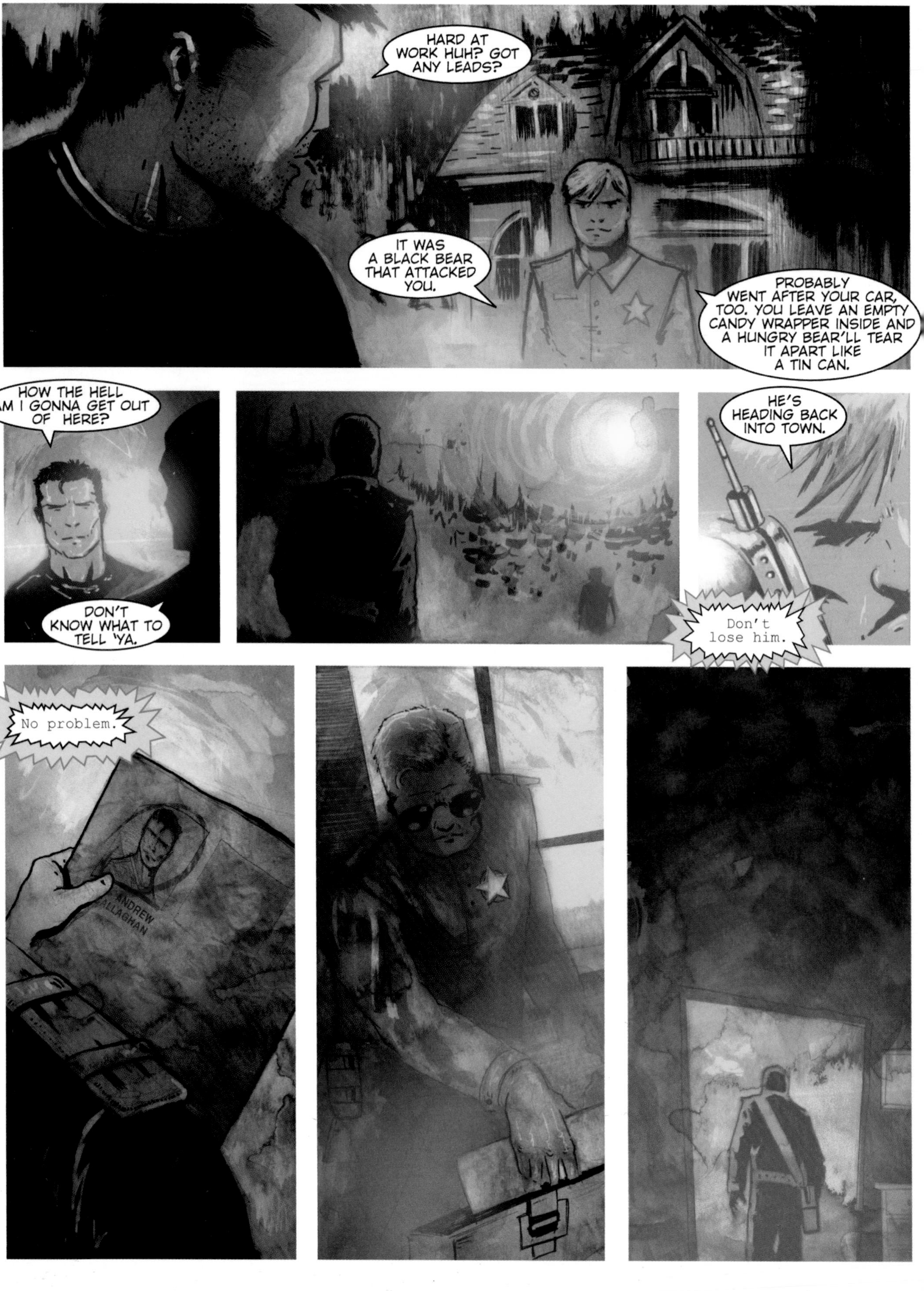
HARD AT WORK HUH? GOT ANY LEADS?
IT WAS A BLACK BEAR THAT ATTACKED YOU.
PROBABLY WENT AFTER YOUR CAR, TOO. YOU LEAVE AN EMPTY CANDY WRAPPER INSIDE AND A HUNGRY BEAR'LL TEAR IT APART LIKE A TIN CAN.
HOW THE HELL AM I GONNA GET OUT OF HERE?
DON'T KNOW WHAT TO TELL 'YA.
HE'S HEADING BACK INTO TOWN.
Don't lose him.
No problem.
ANDREW GALLAGHAN

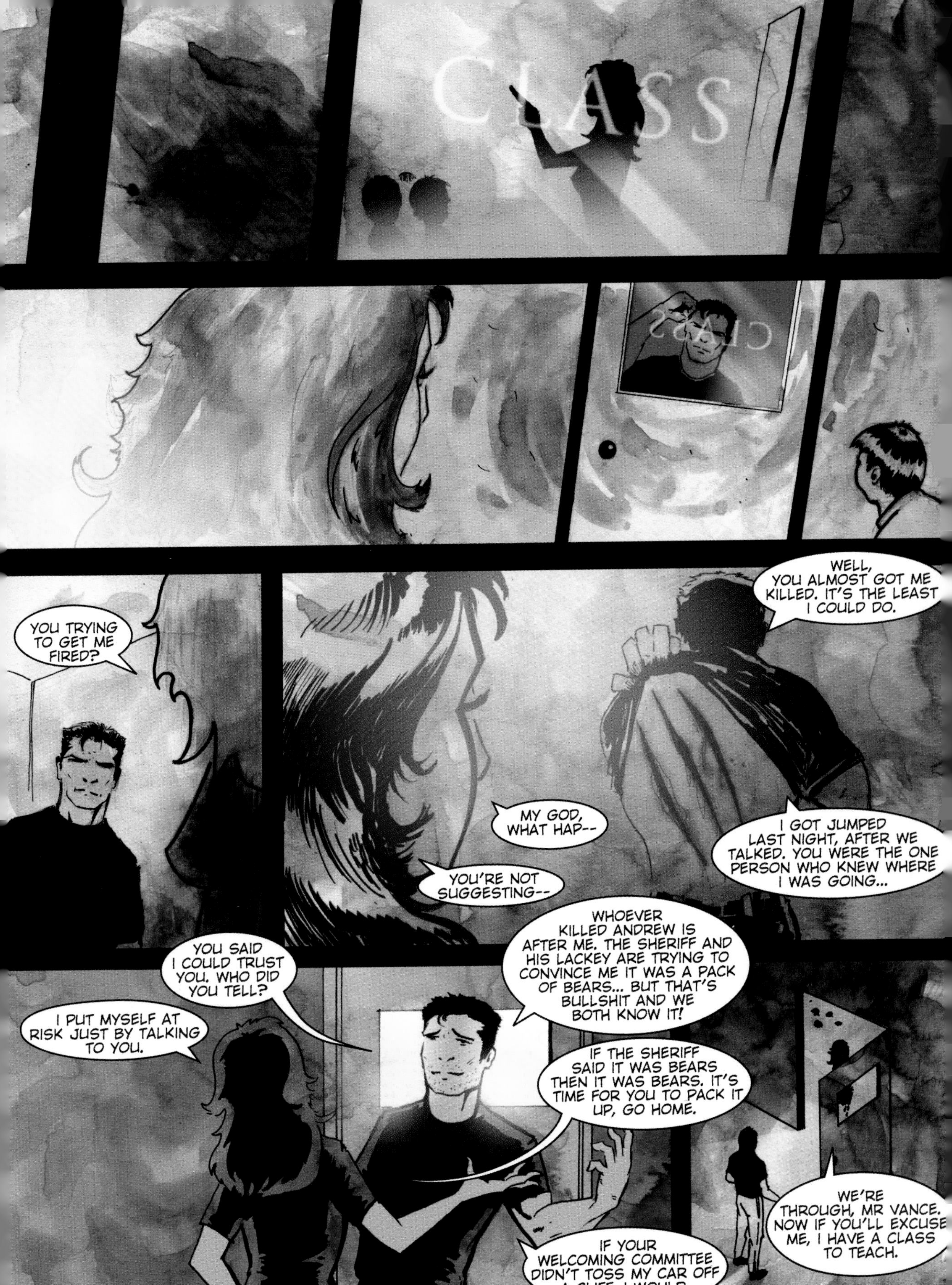
CLASS
YOU TRYING TO GET ME FIRED?
WELL, YOU ALMOST GOT ME KILLED. IT'S THE LEAST I COULD DO.
MY GOD, WHAT HAP--
I GOT JUMPED LAST NIGHT, AFTER WE TALKED. YOU WERE THE ONE PERSON WHO KNEW WHERE I WAS GOING...
YOU'RE NOT SUGGESTING--
YOU SAID I COULD TRUST YOU. WHO DID YOU TELL?
WHOEVER KILLED ANDREW IS AFTER ME. THE SHERIFF AND HIS LACKEY ARE TRYING TO CONVINCE ME IT WAS A PACK OF BEARS... BUT THAT'S BULLSHIT AND WE BOTH KNOW IT!
I PUT MYSELF AT RISK JUST BY TALKING TO YOU.
IF THE SHERIFF SAID IT WAS BEARS THEN IT WAS BEARS. IT'S TIME FOR YOU TO PACK IT UP, GO HOME.
IF YOUR WELCOMING COMMITTEE DIDN'T TOSS MY CAR OFF A CLIFF, I WOULD.
WE'RE THROUGH, MR VANCE. NOW IF YOU'LL EXCUSE ME, I HAVE A CLASS TO TEACH.

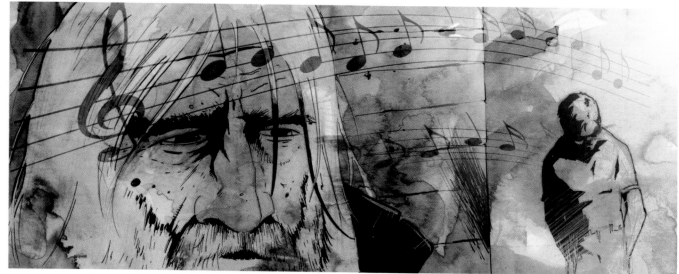

YOU WOULDN'T HAPPEN TO KNOW THE O'CALLAGHAN'S?

YOU. YOU'VE COME FOR US, HAVEN'T YOU? YOU'RE ONE OF THEM. STAY AWAY FROM ME!

STAY AWAY!

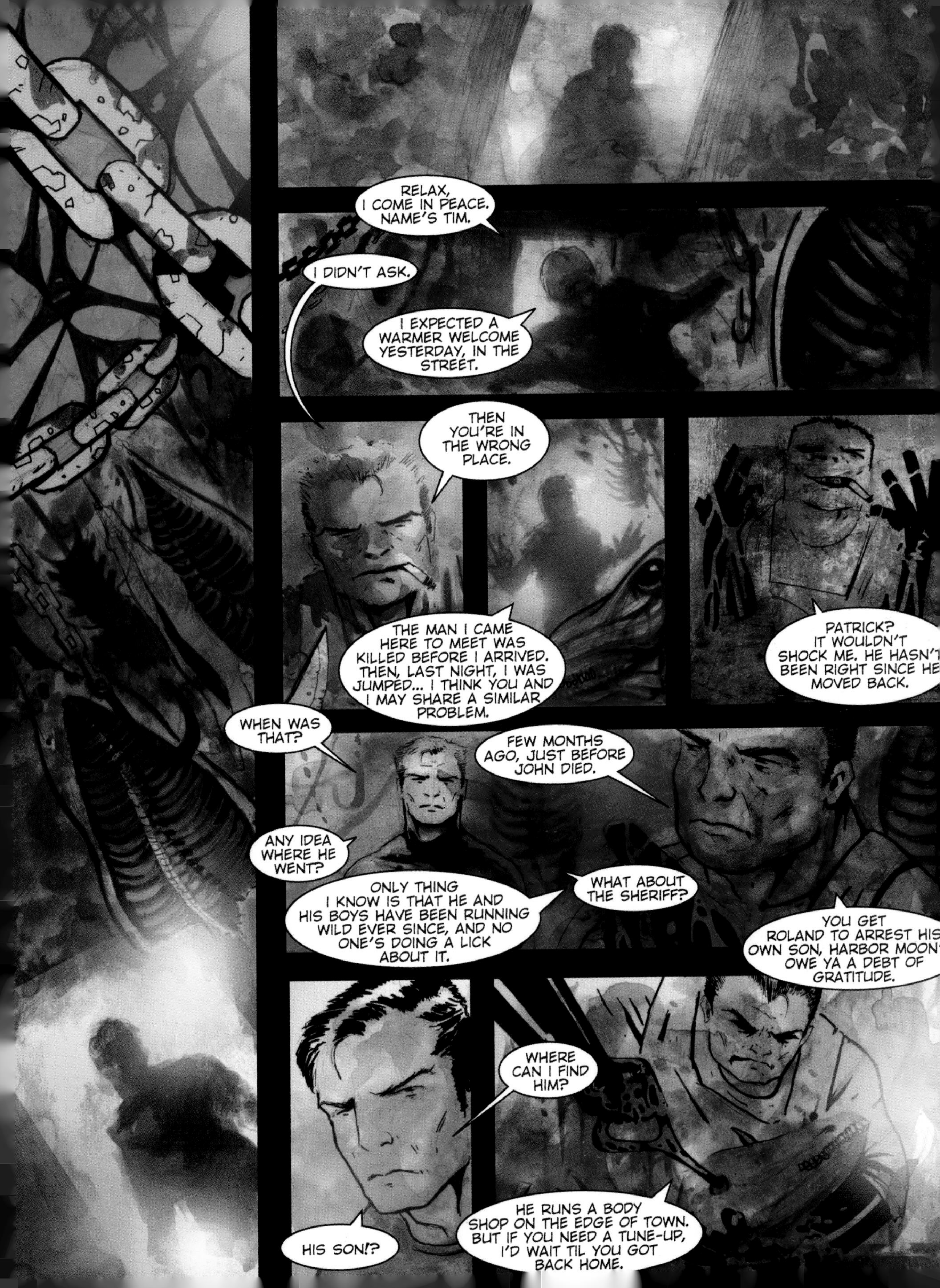

RELAX, I COME IN PEACE. NAME'S TIM.
I DIDN'T ASK.
I EXPECTED A WARMER WELCOME YESTERDAY, IN THE STREET.
THEN YOU'RE IN THE WRONG PLACE.
THE MAN I CAME HERE TO MEET WAS KILLED BEFORE I ARRIVED. THEN, LAST NIGHT, I WAS JUMPED... I THINK YOU AND I MAY SHARE A SIMILAR PROBLEM.
PATRICK? IT WOULDN'T SHOCK ME. HE HASN'T BEEN RIGHT SINCE HE MOVED BACK.
WHEN WAS THAT?
FEW MONTHS AGO, JUST BEFORE JOHN DIED.
ANY IDEA WHERE HE WENT?
ONLY THING I KNOW IS THAT HE AND HIS BOYS HAVE BEEN RUNNING WILD EVER SINCE, AND NO ONE'S DOING A LICK ABOUT IT.
WHAT ABOUT THE SHERIFF?
YOU GET ROLAND TO ARREST HIS OWN SON, HARBOR MOON'LL OWE YA A DEBT OF GRATITUDE.
HIS SON!?
WHERE CAN I FIND HIM?
HE RUNS A BODY SHOP ON THE EDGE OF TOWN. BUT IF YOU NEED A TUNE-UP, I'D WAIT TIL YOU GOT BACK HOME.

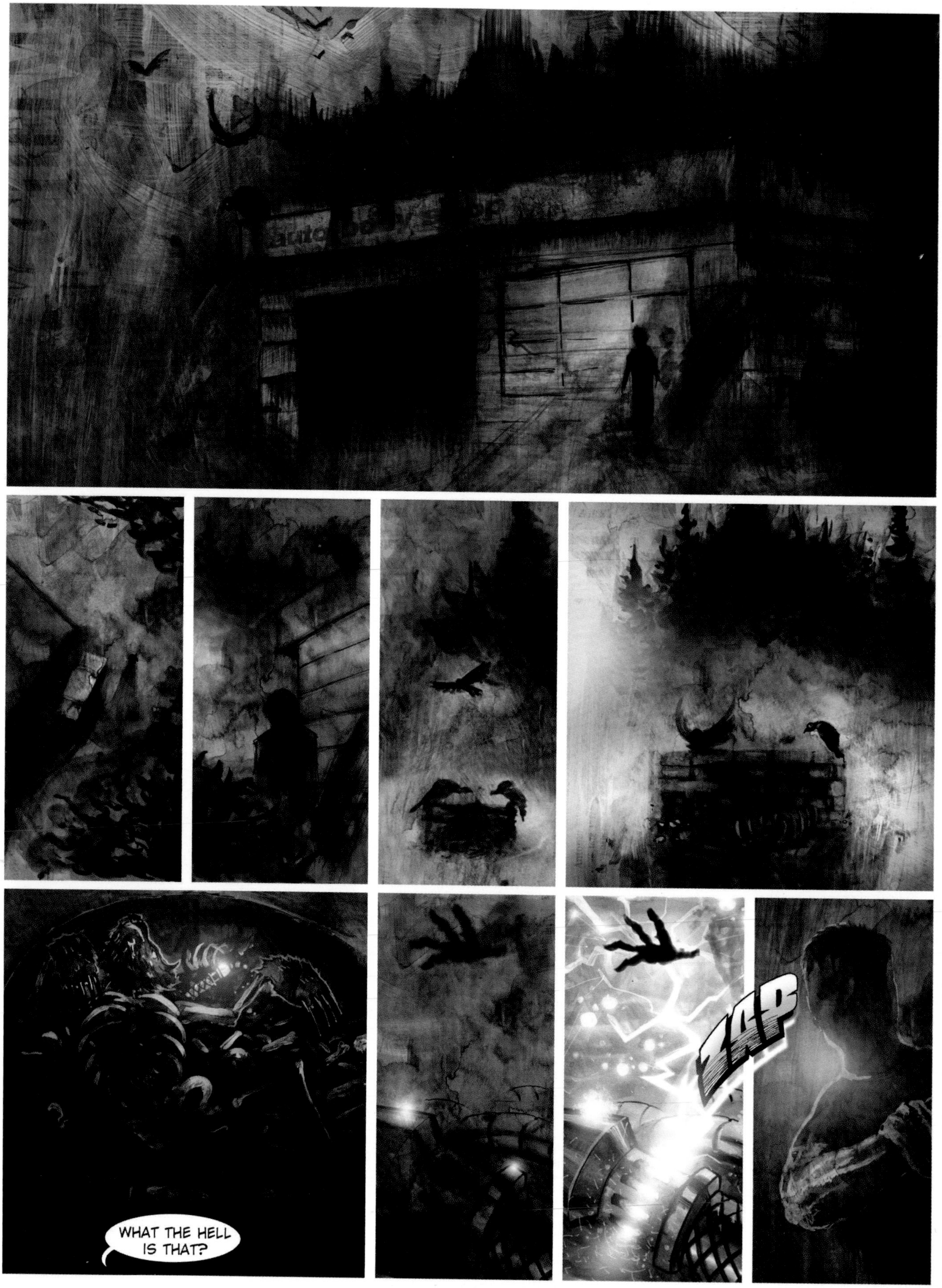
WHAT THE HELL IS THAT?
ZAP

County Morgue.
87 miles north of Portland, Maine.
IT WAS THE TARGET.
The target's dead...? What about Danforth?
HE MADE THE KILL.
Jesus. What now?
THERE ARE MORE OF THESE DOGS OUT THERE, I CAN FEEL IT. GET THE TEAM READY.
What are you gonna do?
I'M GOING TO FIND HIM.

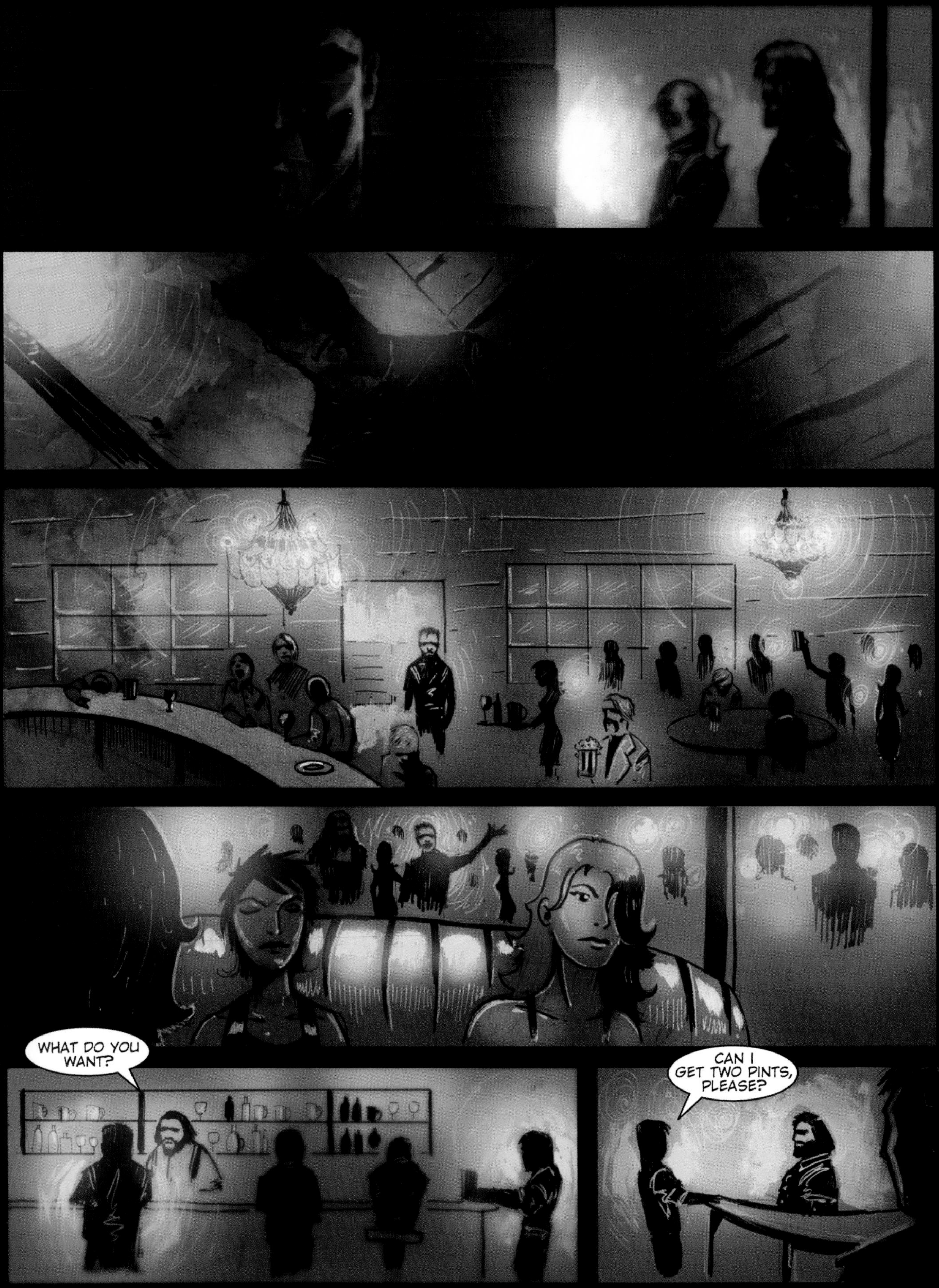
WHAT DO YOU WANT?
CAN I GET TWO PINTS, PLEASE?

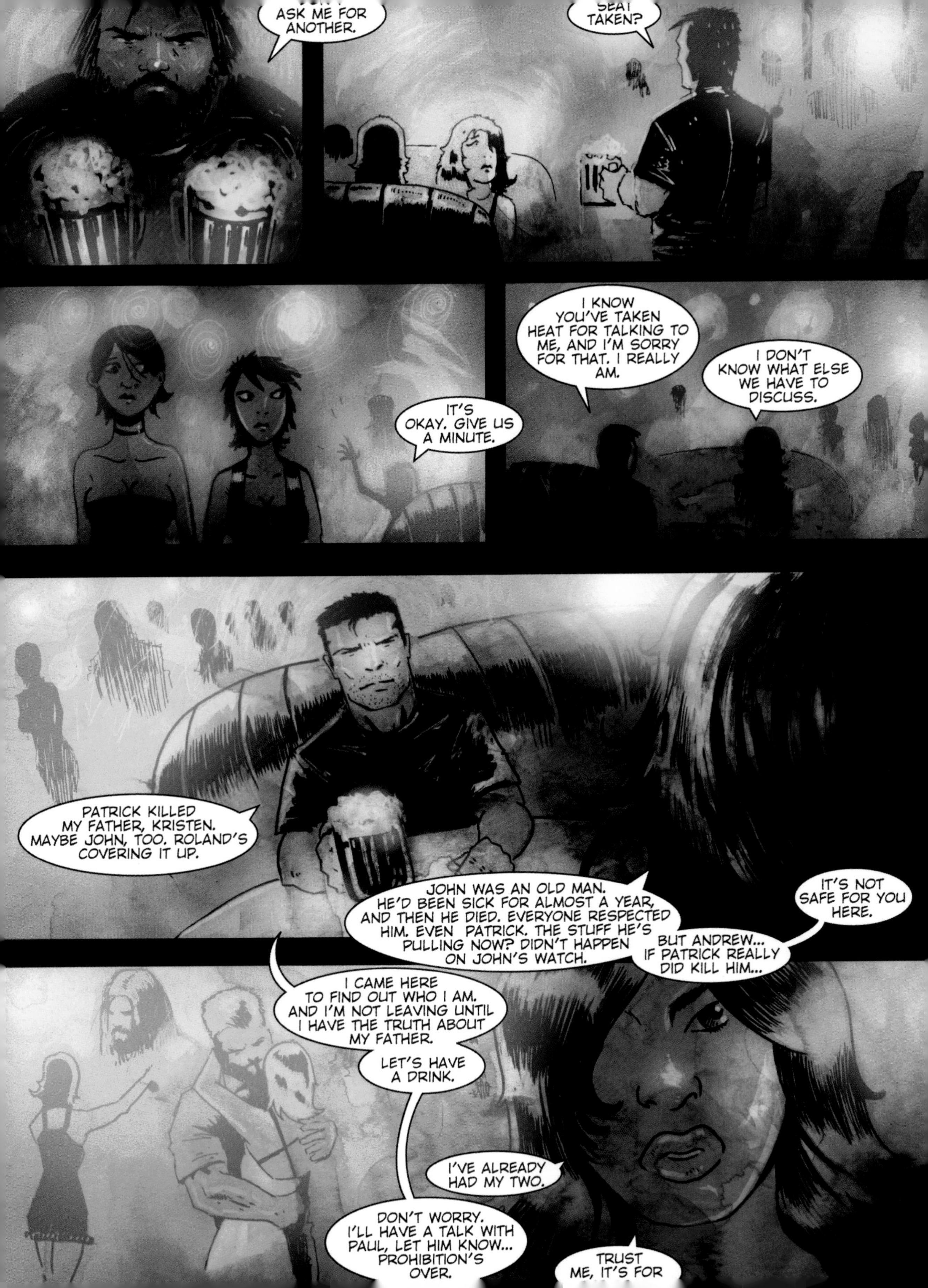
ASK ME FOR ANOTHER.
SEAT TAKEN?
IT'S OKAY. GIVE US A MINUTE.
I KNOW YOU'VE TAKEN HEAT FOR TALKING TO ME, AND I'M SORRY FOR THAT. I REALLY AM.
I DON'T KNOW WHAT ELSE WE HAVE TO DISCUSS.
PATRICK KILLED MY FATHER, KRISTEN. MAYBE JOHN, TOO. ROLAND'S COVERING IT UP.
JOHN WAS AN OLD MAN. HE'D BEEN SICK FOR ALMOST A YEAR, AND THEN HE DIED. EVERYONE RESPECTED HIM. EVEN PATRICK. THE STUFF HE'S PULLING NOW? DIDN'T HAPPEN ON JOHN'S WATCH.
BUT ANDREW... IF PATRICK REALLY DID KILL HIM...
IT'S NOT SAFE FOR YOU HERE.
I CAME HERE TO FIND OUT WHO I AM. AND I'M NOT LEAVING UNTIL I HAVE THE TRUTH ABOUT MY FATHER.
LET'S HAVE A DRINK.
I'VE ALREADY HAD MY TWO.
DON'T WORRY. I'LL HAVE A TALK WITH PAUL, LET HIM KNOW... PROHIBITION'S OVER.
TRUST ME, IT'S FOR

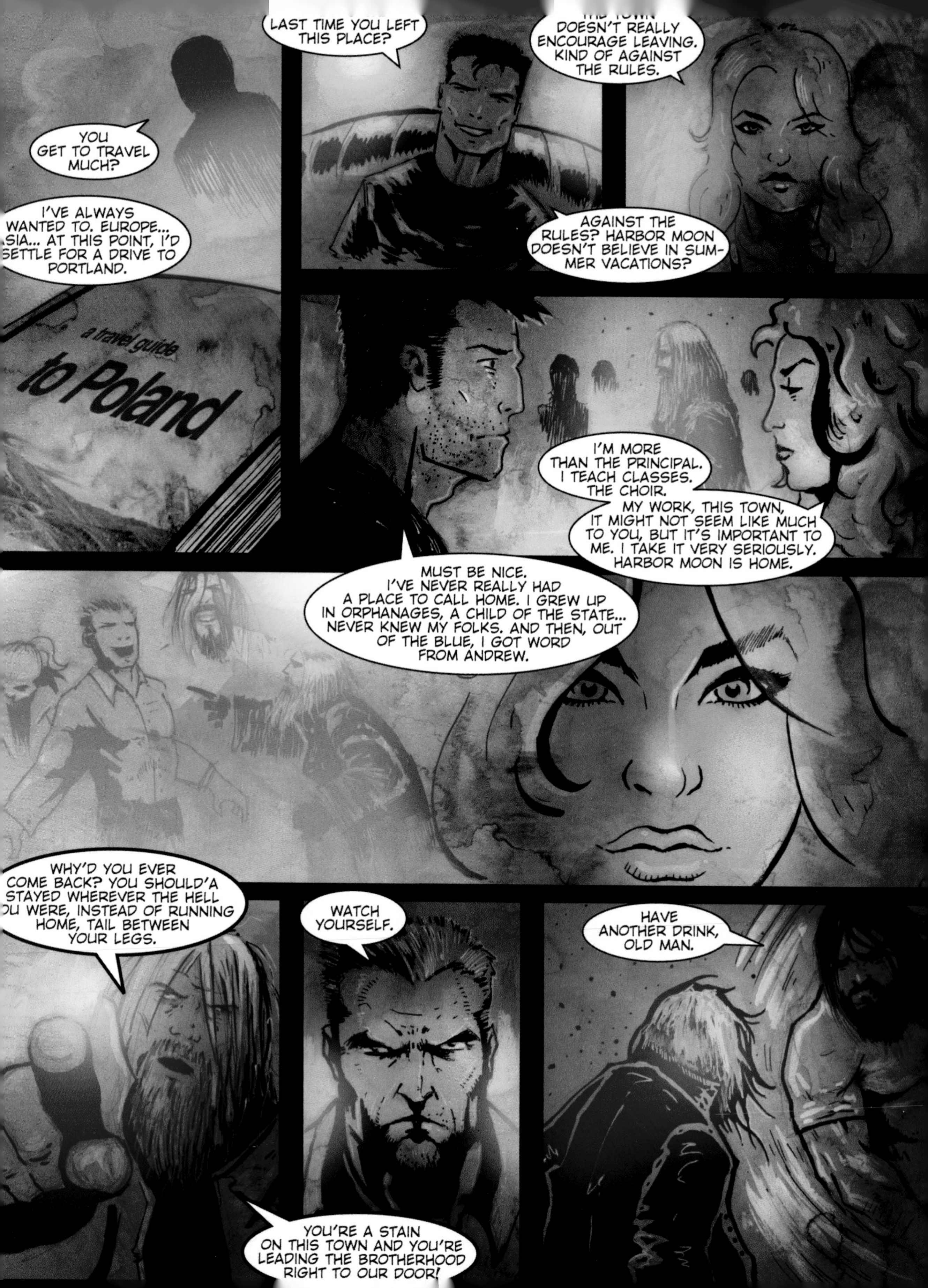
YOU GET TO TRAVEL MUCH?
I'VE ALWAYS WANTED TO. EUROPE... SIA... AT THIS POINT, I'D ETTLE FOR A DRIVE TO PORTLAND.
a travel guide to Poland
LAST TIME YOU LEFT THIS PLACE?
DOESN'T REALLY ENCOURAGE LEAVING. KIND OF AGAINST THE RULES.
AGAINST THE RULES? HARBOR MOON DOESN'T BELIEVE IN SUMMER VACATIONS?
I'M MORE THAN THE PRINCIPAL. I TEACH CLASSES. THE CHOIR.
MY WORK, THIS TOWN, IT MIGHT NOT SEEM LIKE MUCH TO YOU, BUT IT'S IMPORTANT TO ME. I TAKE IT VERY SERIOUSLY. HARBOR MOON IS HOME.
MUST BE NICE. I'VE NEVER REALLY HAD A PLACE TO CALL HOME. I GREW UP IN ORPHANAGES, A CHILD OF THE STATE... NEVER KNEW MY FOLKS. AND THEN, OUT OF THE BLUE, I GOT WORD FROM ANDREW.
WHY'D YOU EVER COME BACK? YOU SHOULD'A STAYED WHEREVER THE HELL OU WERE, INSTEAD OF RUNNING HOME, TAIL BETWEEN YOUR LEGS.
YOU'RE A STAIN ON THIS TOWN AND YOU'RE LEADING THE BROTHERHOOD RIGHT TO OUR DOOR!
WATCH YOURSELF.
HAVE ANOTHER DRINK, OLD MAN.

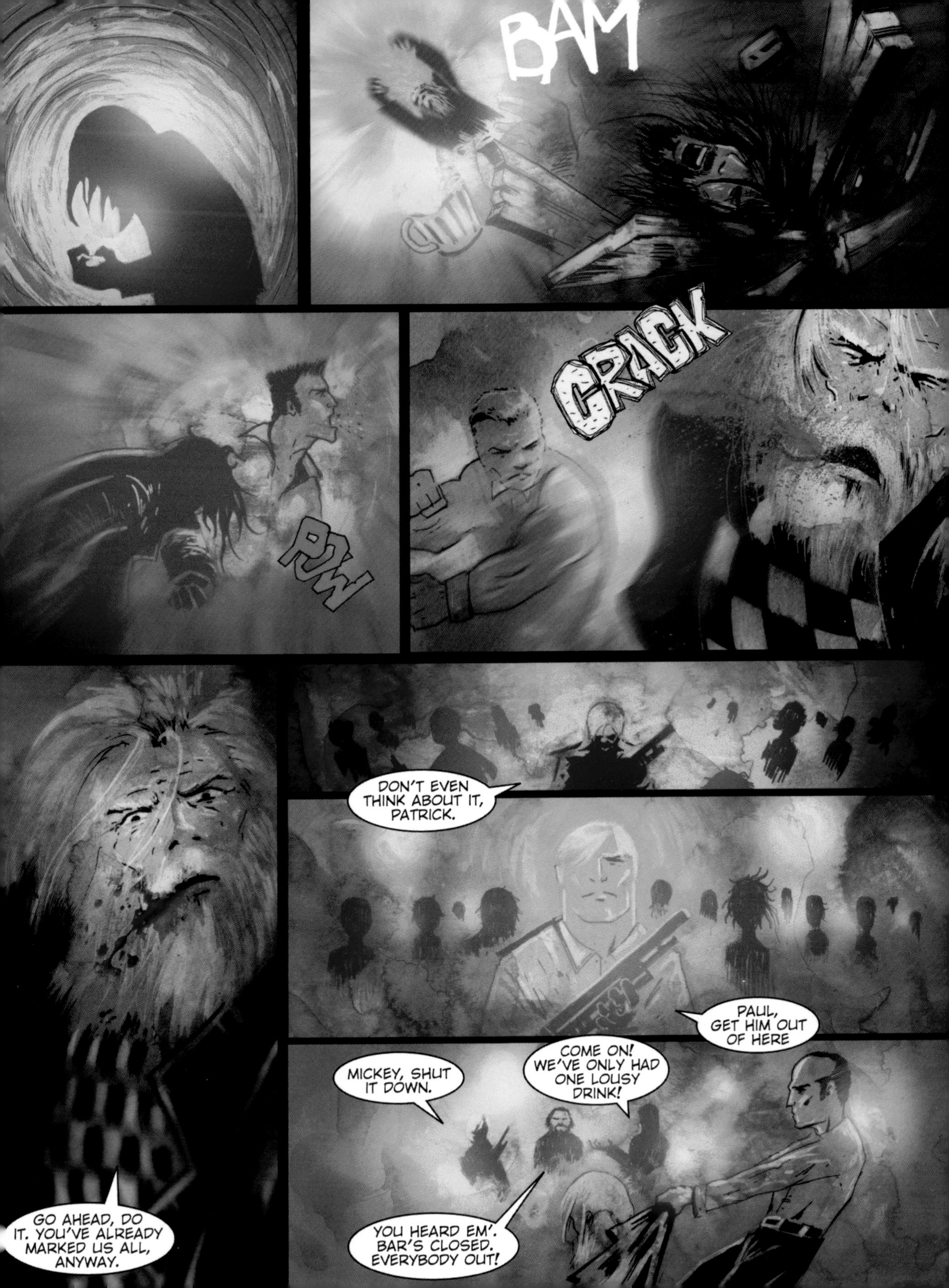
BAM
POW
CRACK
DON'T EVEN THINK ABOUT IT, PATRICK.
PAUL, GET HIM OUT OF HERE
MICKEY, SHUT IT DOWN.
COME ON! WE'VE ONLY HAD ONE LOUSY DRINK!
GO AHEAD, DO IT. YOU'VE ALREADY MARKED US ALL, ANYWAY.
YOU HEARD EM'. BAR'S CLOSED. EVERYBODY OUT!

TIM, DON'T!

WANT THAT LESSON NOW?

BREAK IT UP! RIGHT NOW!

I'M NOT GONNA ASK YOU AGAIN!

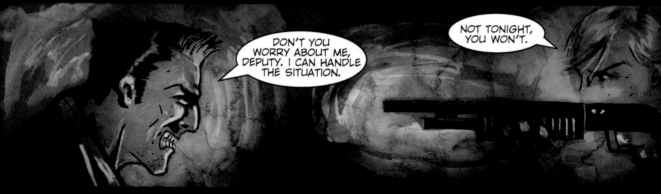

DON'T YOU WORRY ABOUT ME, DEPUTY. I CAN HANDLE THE SITUATION.

NOT TONIGHT, YOU WON'T.

SEEMS TO ME LIKE YOU GOT AN ANGEL WATCHING OVER YOUR SHOULDER.

WHERE'D HE GO?

NOT AGAIN--!

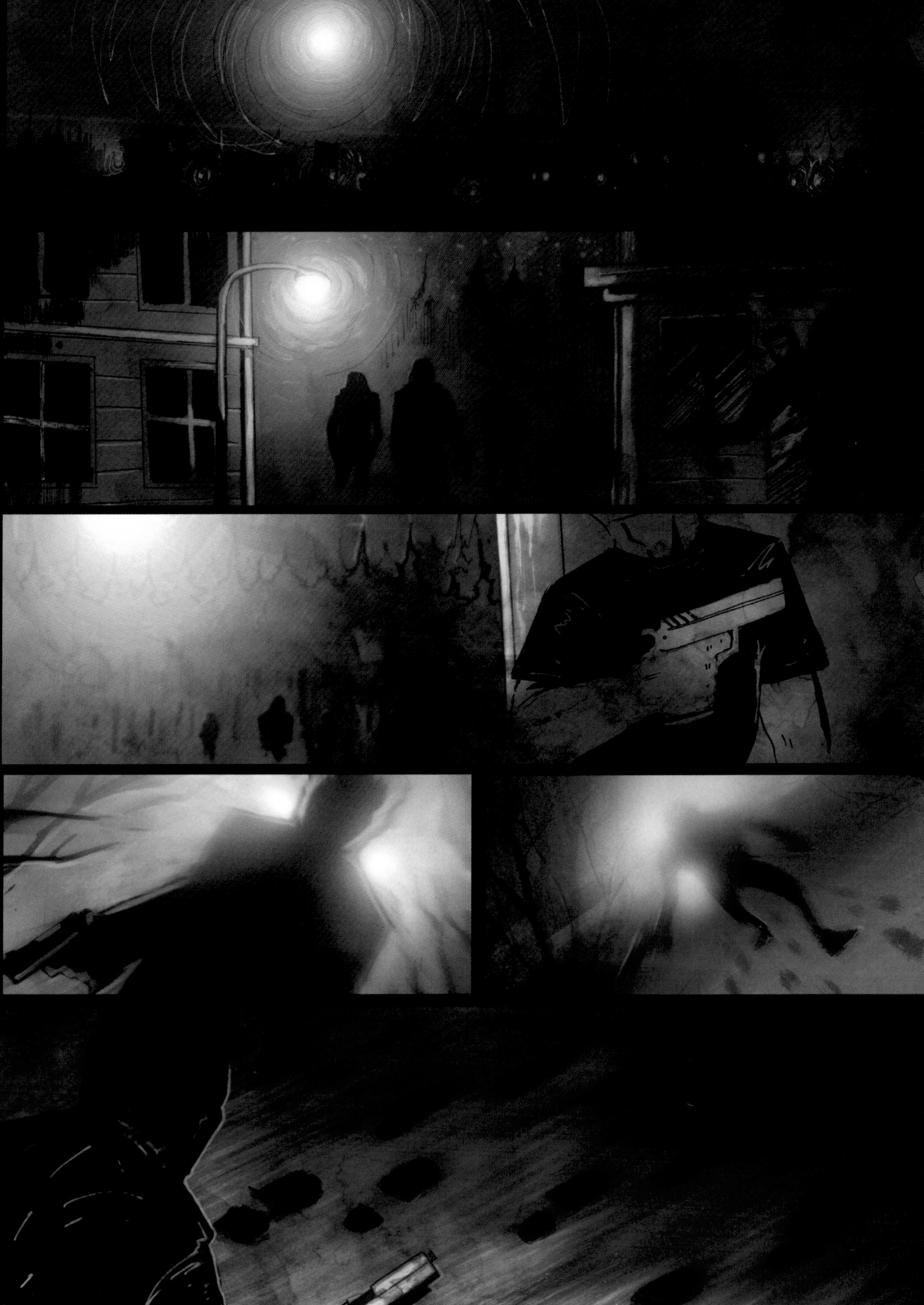

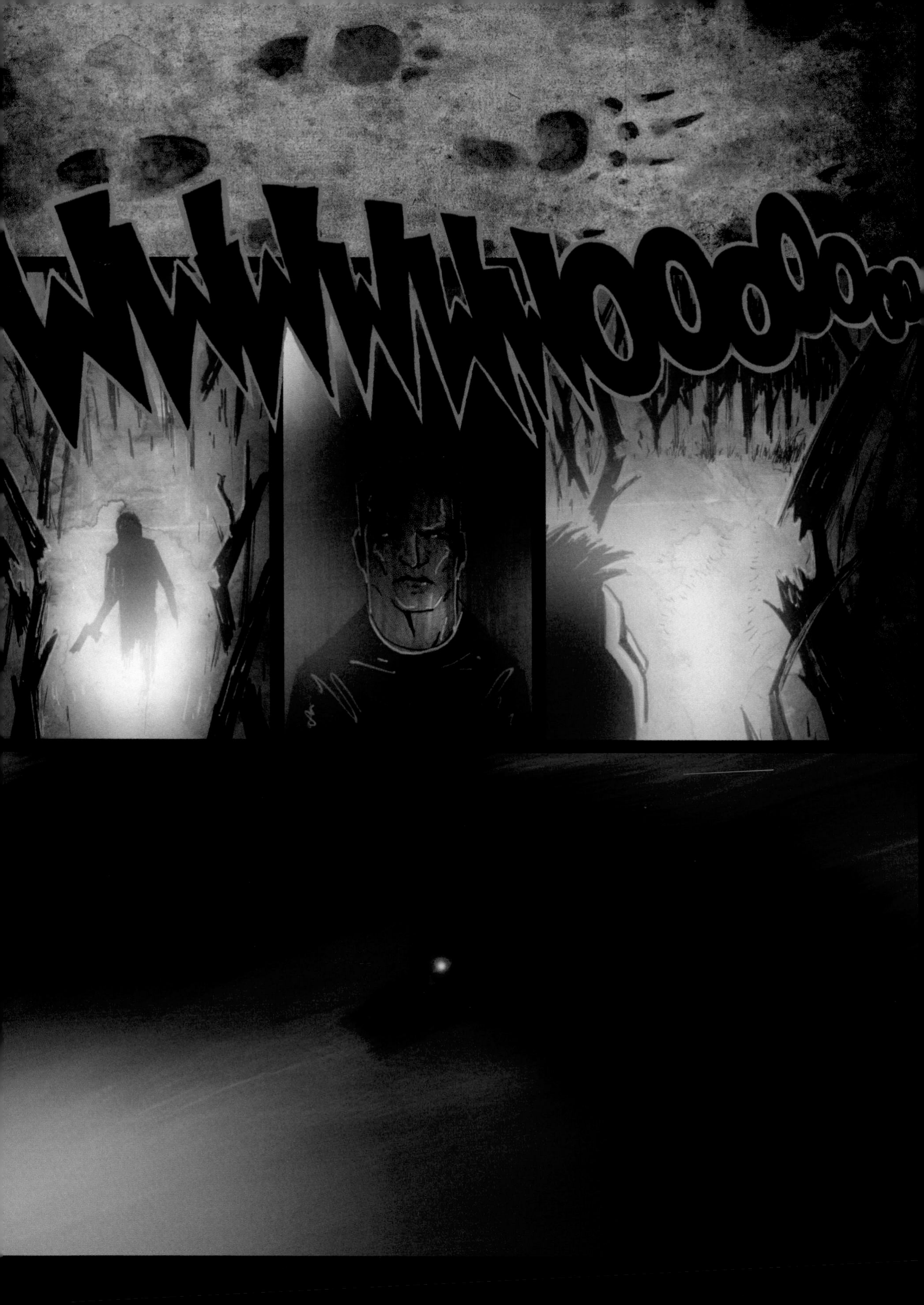

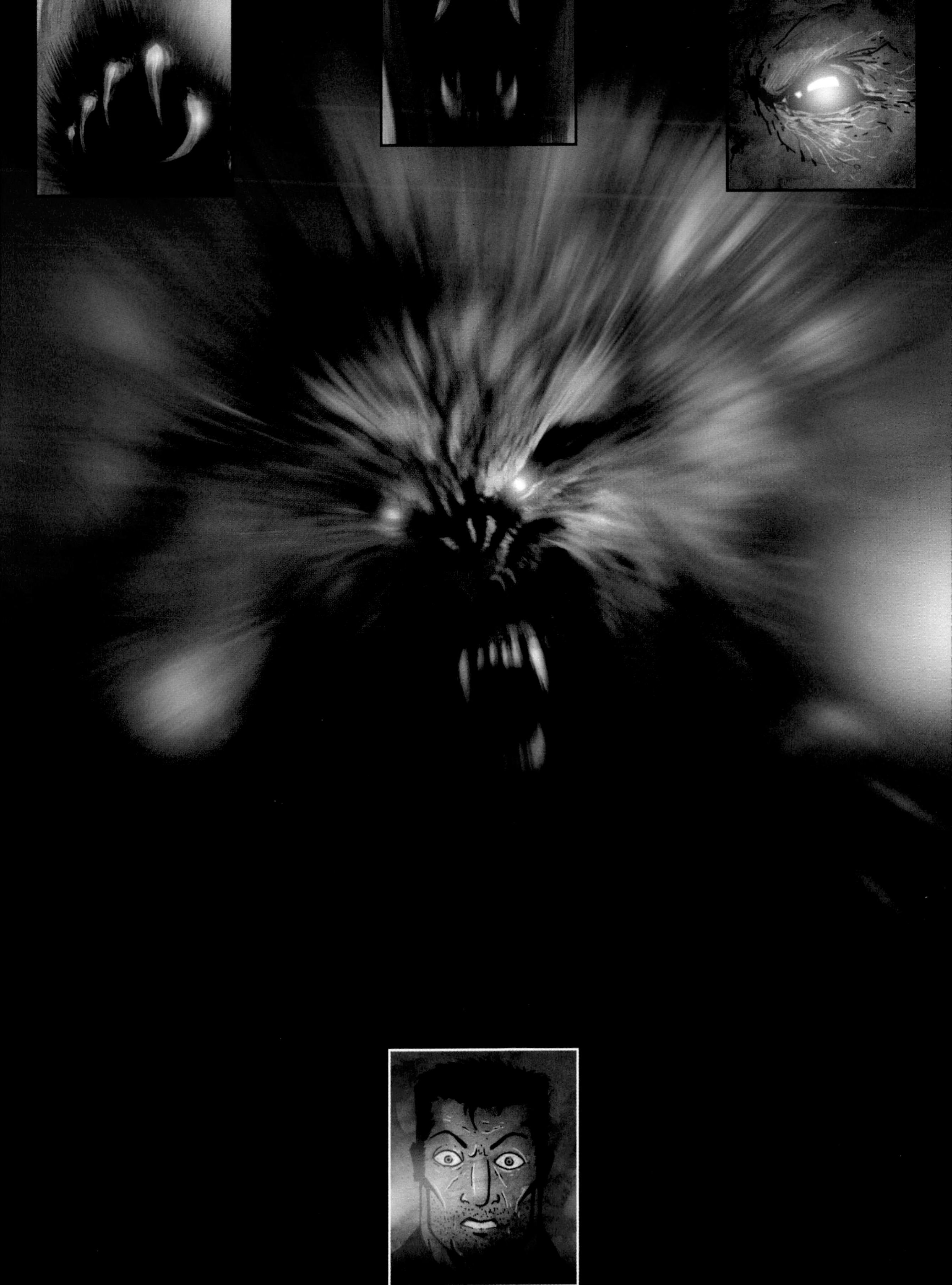

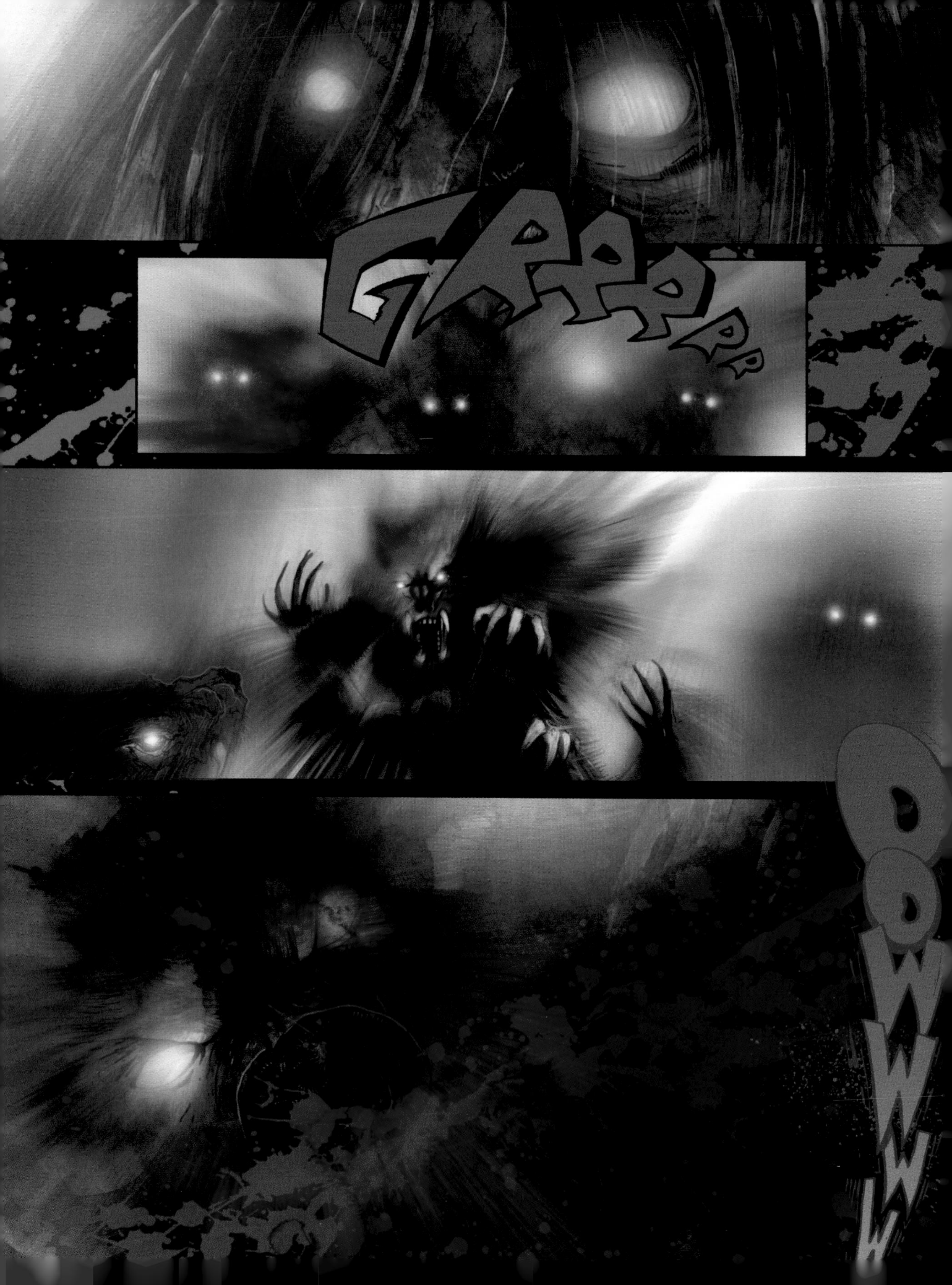
GRRRRR
OOWWWWW

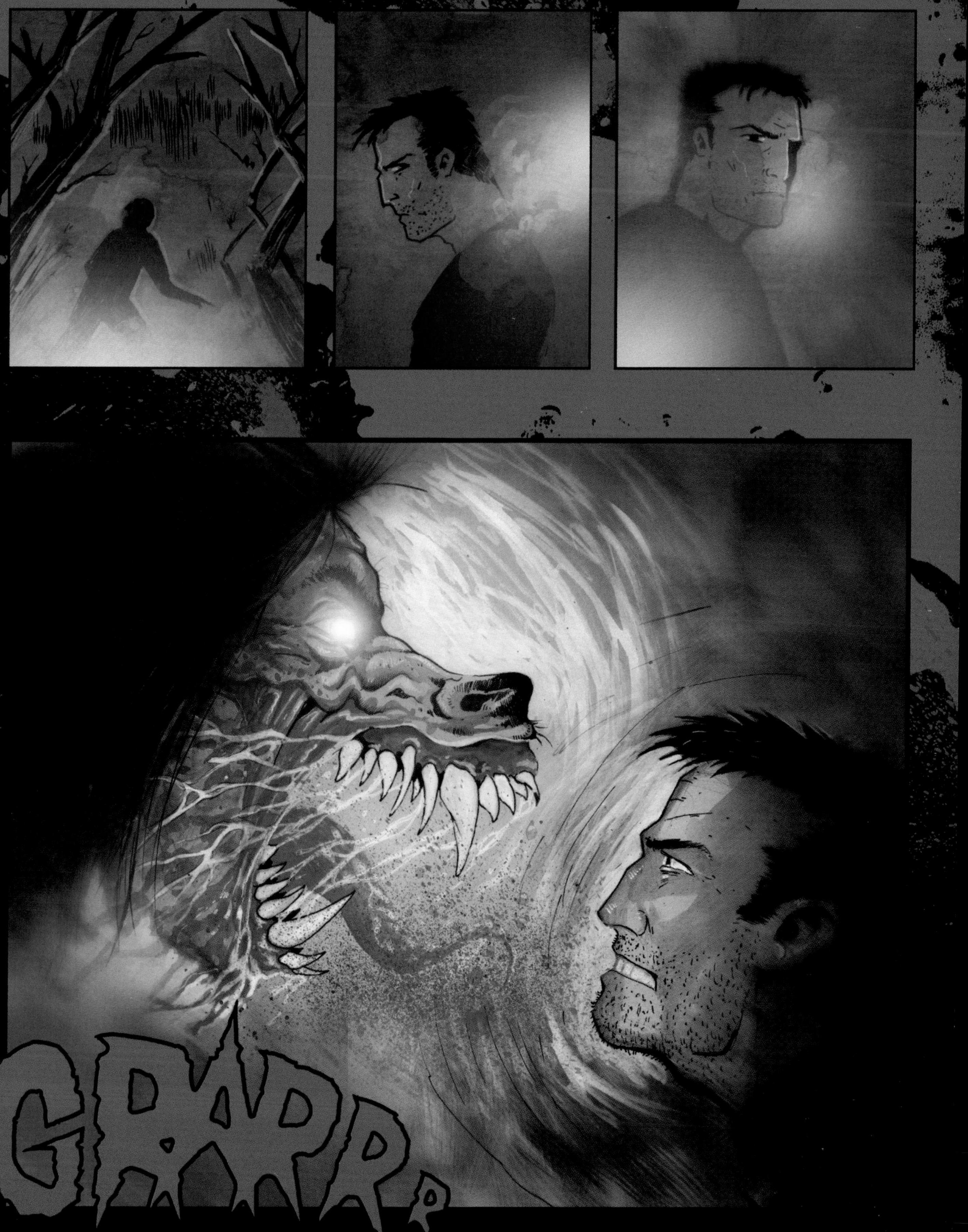
GRARRr

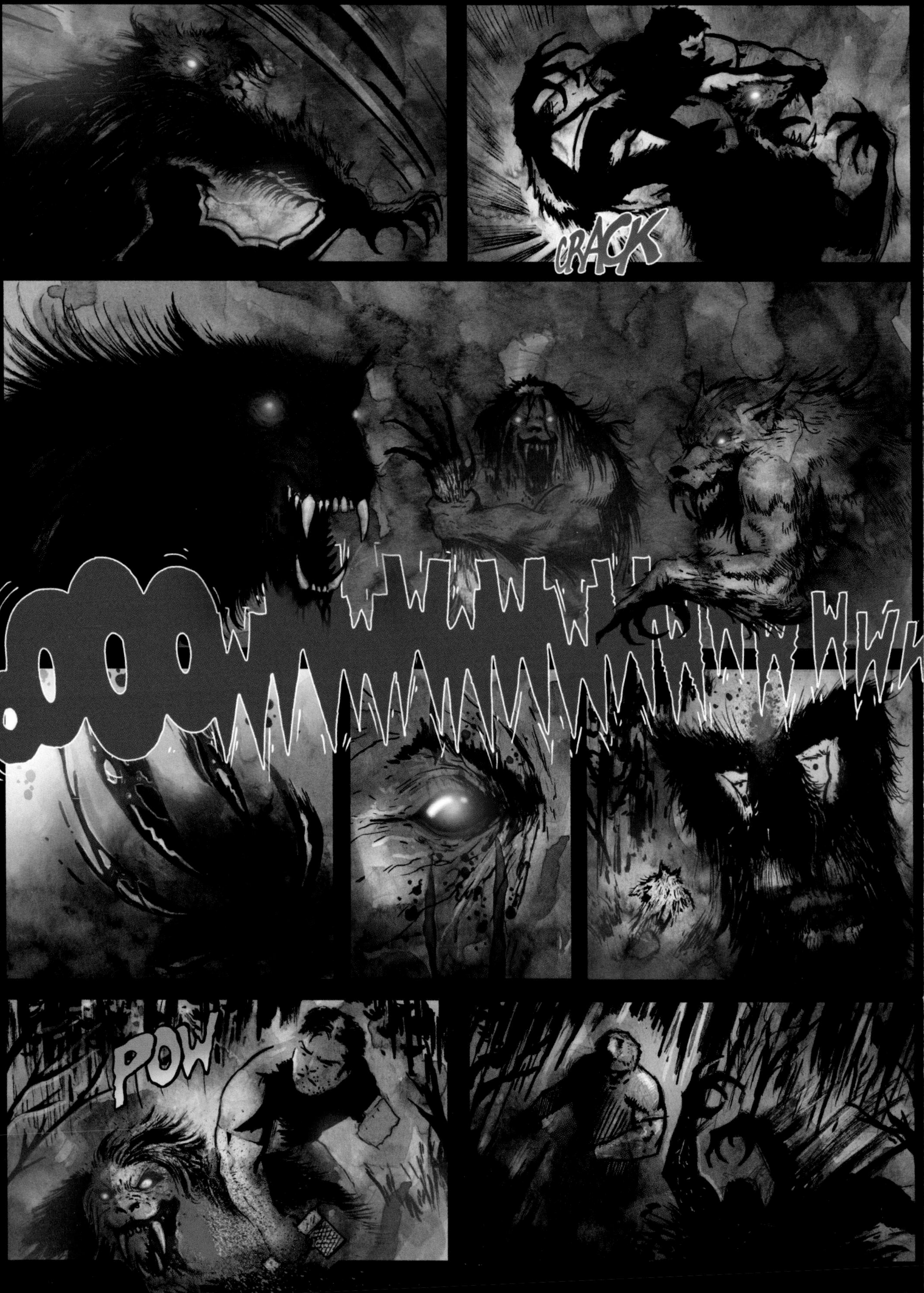
CRACK
POW

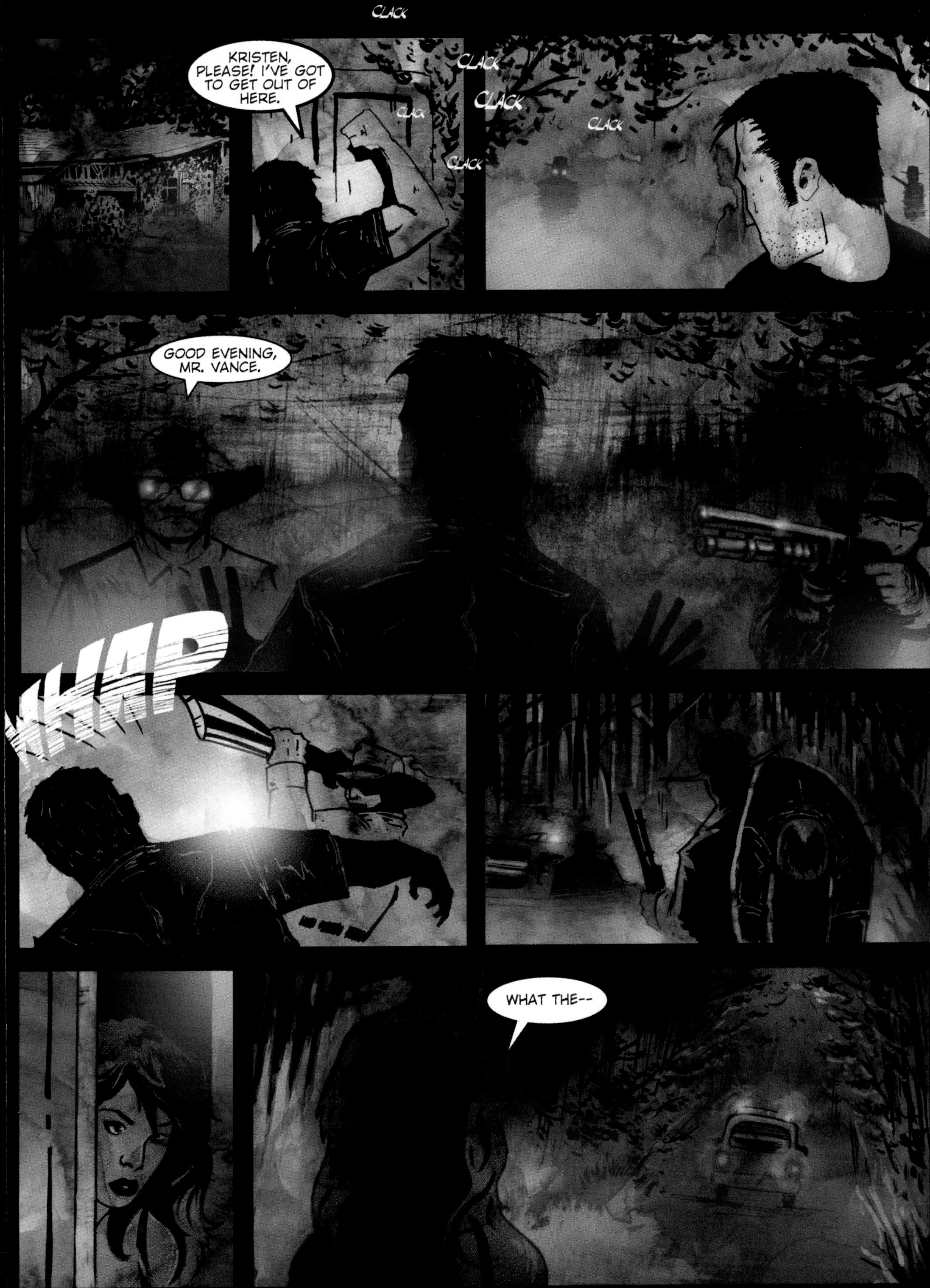
CLACK
KRISTEN, PLEASE! I'VE GOT TO GET OUT OF HERE.
CLACK
CLACK
CLACK
CLACK
CLACK
GOOD EVENING, MR. VANCE.
WHAP
WHAT THE--

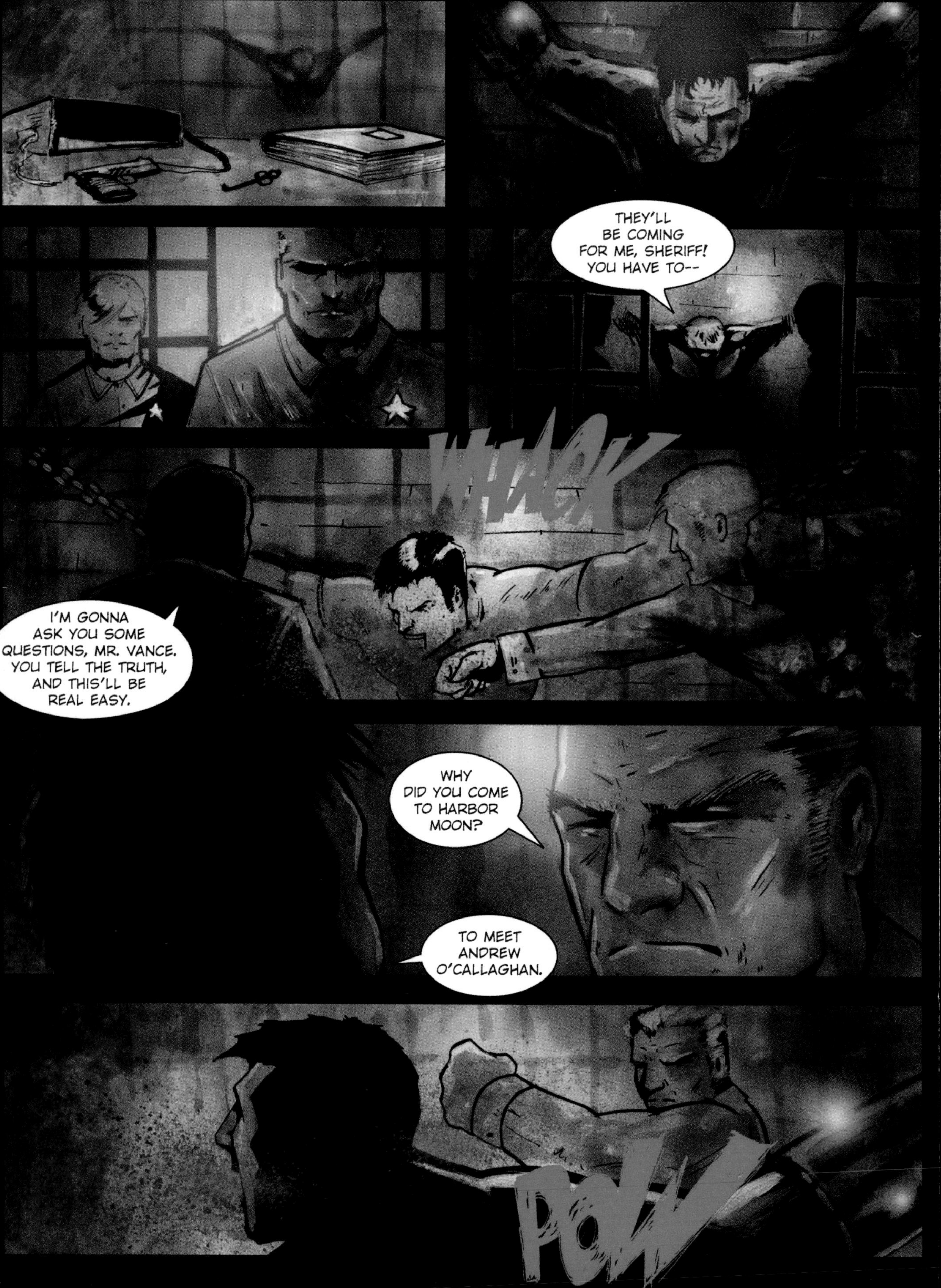
THEY'LL BE COMING FOR ME, SHERIFF! YOU HAVE TO--
WHACK
I'M GONNA ASK YOU SOME QUESTIONS, MR. VANCE. YOU TELL THE TRUTH, AND THIS'LL BE REAL EASY.
WHY DID YOU COME TO HARBOR MOON?
TO MEET ANDREW O'CALLAGHAN.
POW

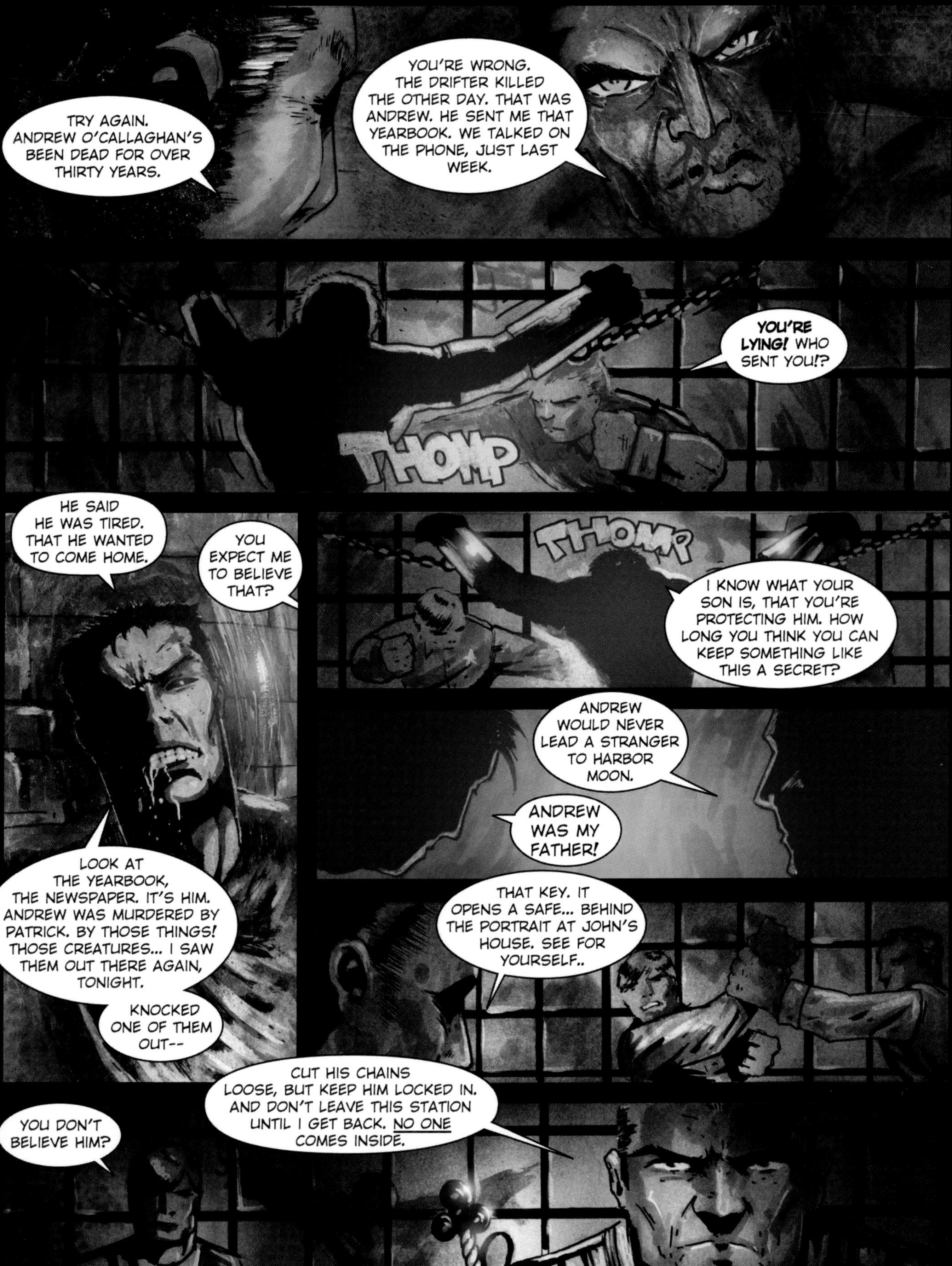
TRY AGAIN. ANDREW O'CALLAGHAN'S BEEN DEAD FOR OVER THIRTY YEARS.
YOU'RE WRONG. THE DRIFTER KILLED THE OTHER DAY. THAT WAS ANDREW. HE SENT ME THAT YEARBOOK. WE TALKED ON THE PHONE, JUST LAST WEEK.
YOU'RE LYING! WHO SENT YOU!?
THOMP
HE SAID HE WAS TIRED. THAT HE WANTED TO COME HOME.
YOU EXPECT ME TO BELIEVE THAT?
THOMP
I KNOW WHAT YOUR SON IS, THAT YOU'RE PROTECTING HIM. HOW LONG YOU THINK YOU CAN KEEP SOMETHING LIKE THIS A SECRET?
ANDREW WOULD NEVER LEAD A STRANGER TO HARBOR MOON.
ANDREW WAS MY FATHER!
LOOK AT THE YEARBOOK, THE NEWSPAPER. IT'S HIM. ANDREW WAS MURDERED BY PATRICK. BY THOSE THINGS! THOSE CREATURES... I SAW THEM OUT THERE AGAIN, TONIGHT.
KNOCKED ONE OF THEM OUT--
THAT KEY. IT OPENS A SAFE... BEHIND THE PORTRAIT AT JOHN'S HOUSE. SEE FOR YOURSELF..
YOU DON'T BELIEVE HIM?
CUT HIS CHAINS LOOSE, BUT KEEP HIM LOCKED IN. AND DON'T LEAVE THIS STATION UNTIL I GET BACK. NO ONE COMES INSIDE.

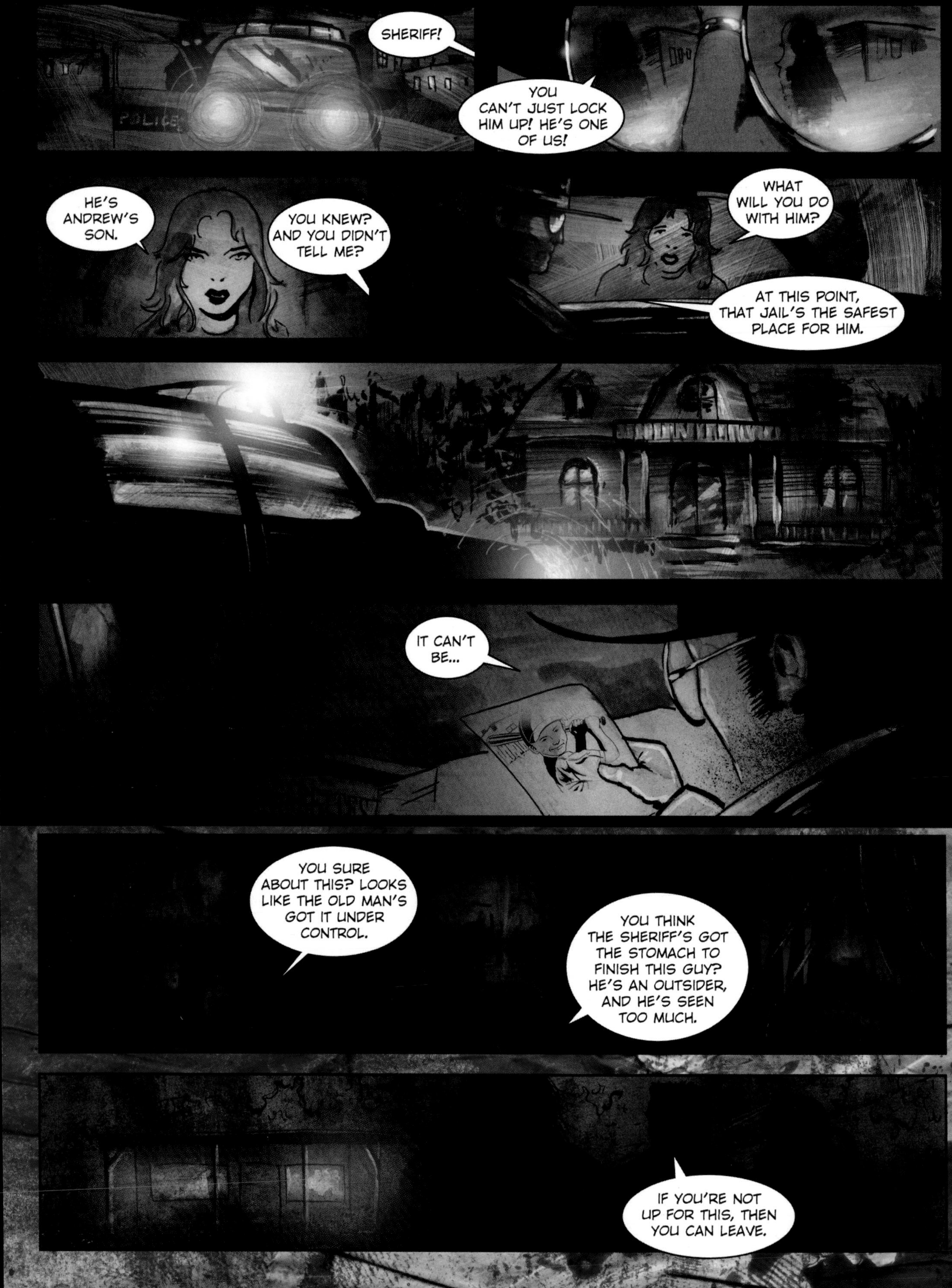
SHERIFF!
YOU CAN'T JUST LOCK HIM UP! HE'S ONE OF US!
HE'S ANDREW'S SON.
YOU KNEW? AND YOU DIDN'T TELL ME?
WHAT WILL YOU DO WITH HIM?
AT THIS POINT, THAT JAIL'S THE SAFEST PLACE FOR HIM.
IT CAN'T BE...
YOU SURE ABOUT THIS? LOOKS LIKE THE OLD MAN'S GOT IT UNDER CONTROL.
YOU THINK THE SHERIFF'S GOT THE STOMACH TO FINISH THIS GUY? HE'S AN OUTSIDER, AND HE'S SEEN TOO MUCH.
IF YOU'RE NOT UP FOR THIS, THEN YOU CAN LEAVE.

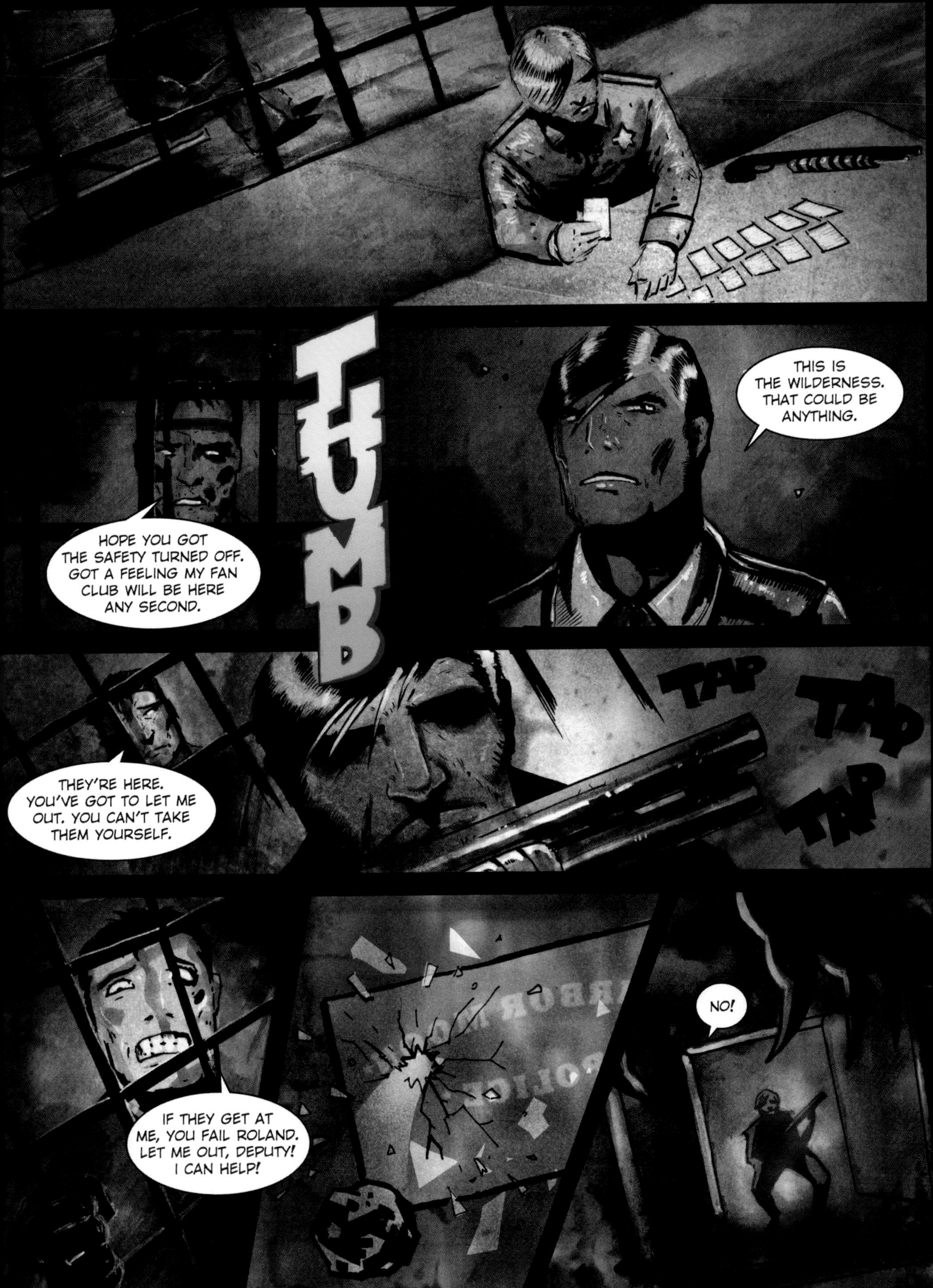
TUMB
THIS IS THE WILDERNESS. THAT COULD BE ANYTHING.
HOPE YOU GOT THE SAFETY TURNED OFF. GOT A FEELING MY FAN CLUB WILL BE HERE ANY SECOND.
TAP TAP TAP
THEY'RE HERE. YOU'VE GOT TO LET ME OUT. YOU CAN'T TAKE THEM YOURSELF.
IF THEY GET AT ME, YOU FAIL ROLAND. LET ME OUT, DEPUTY! I CAN HELP!
NO!

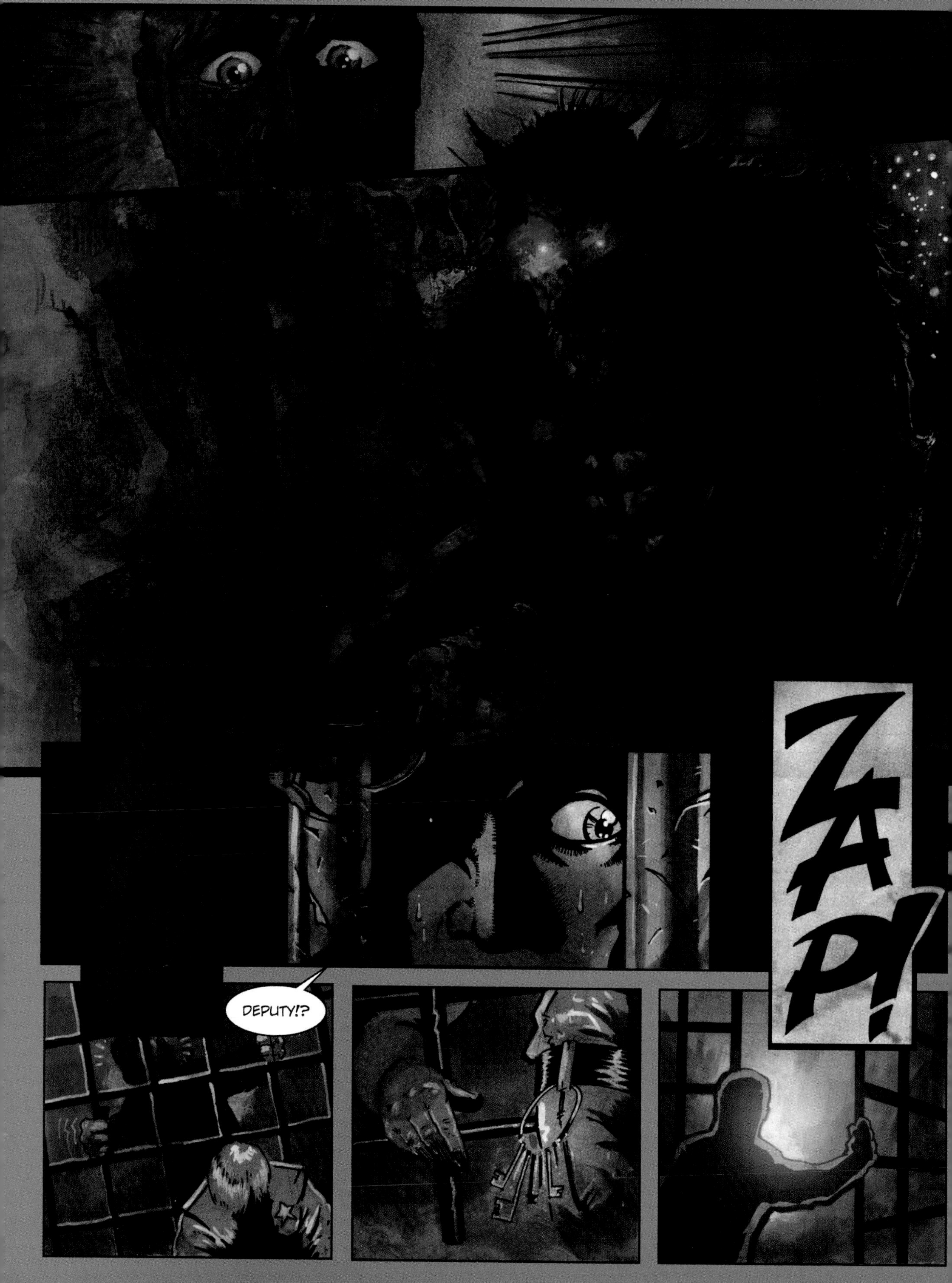
ZAP!
DEPUTY!?

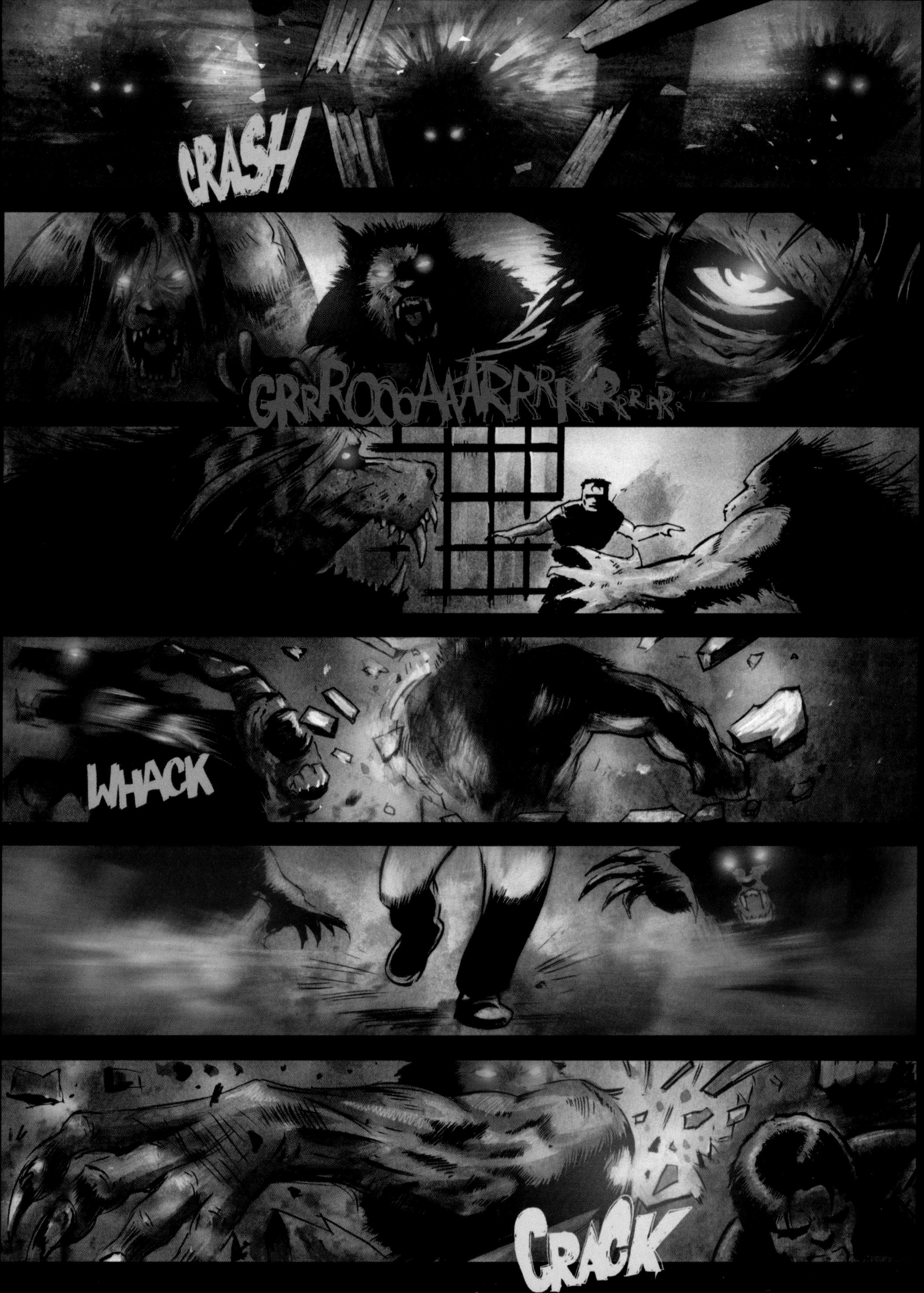
CRASH
GRRROOOAAARRRRRRRRR
WHACK
CRACK

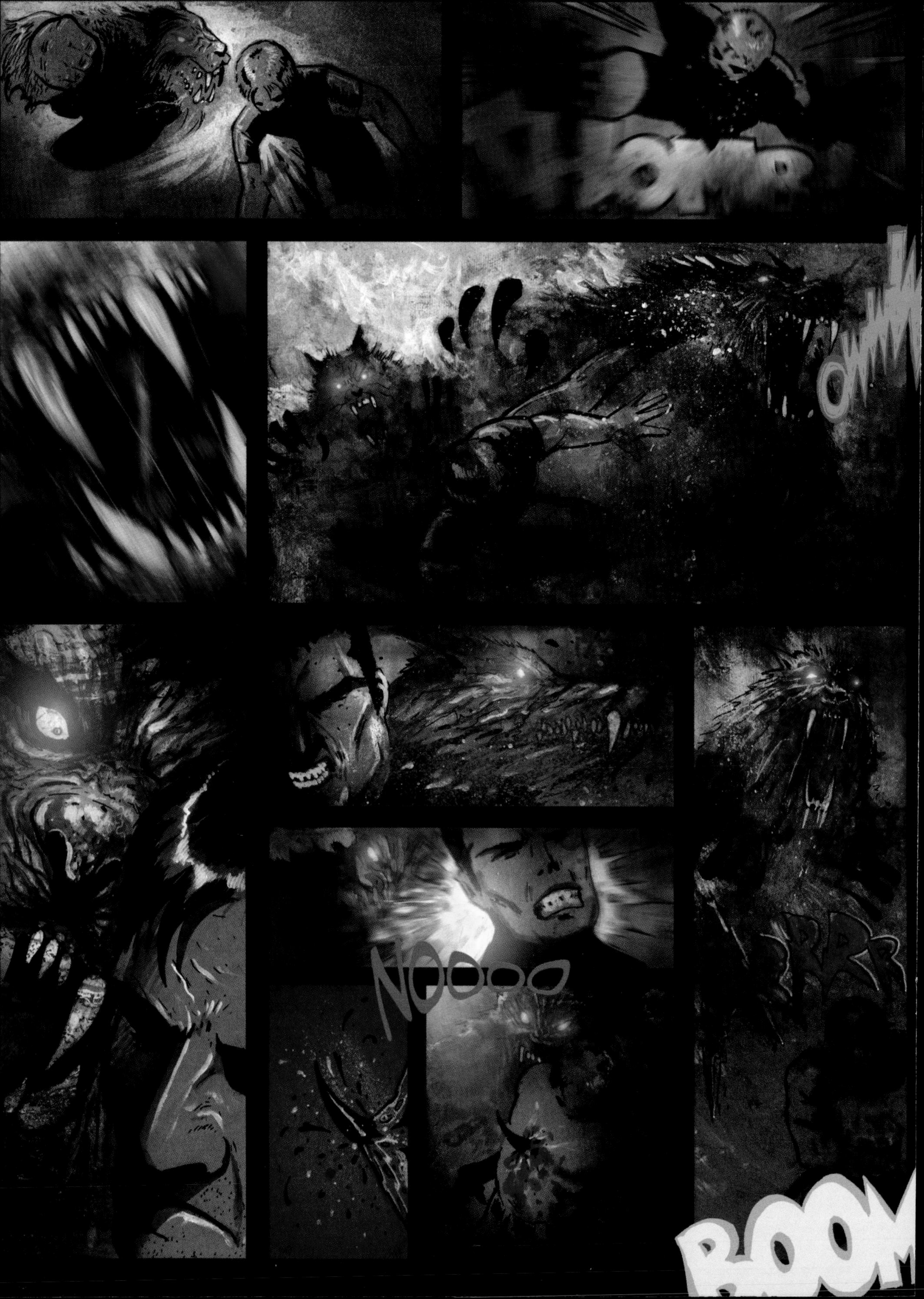
NOOOO
BOOM

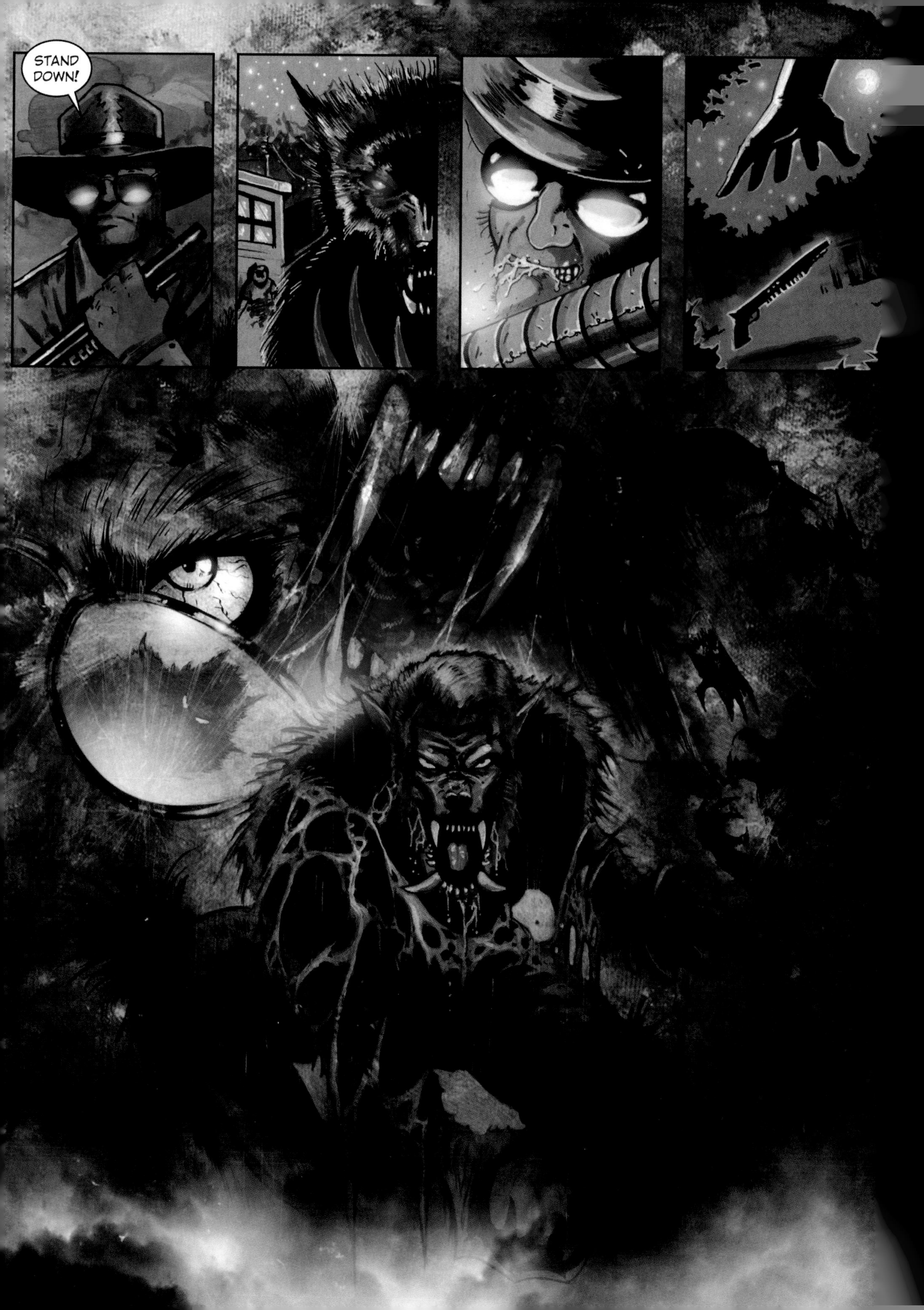
STAND DOWN!

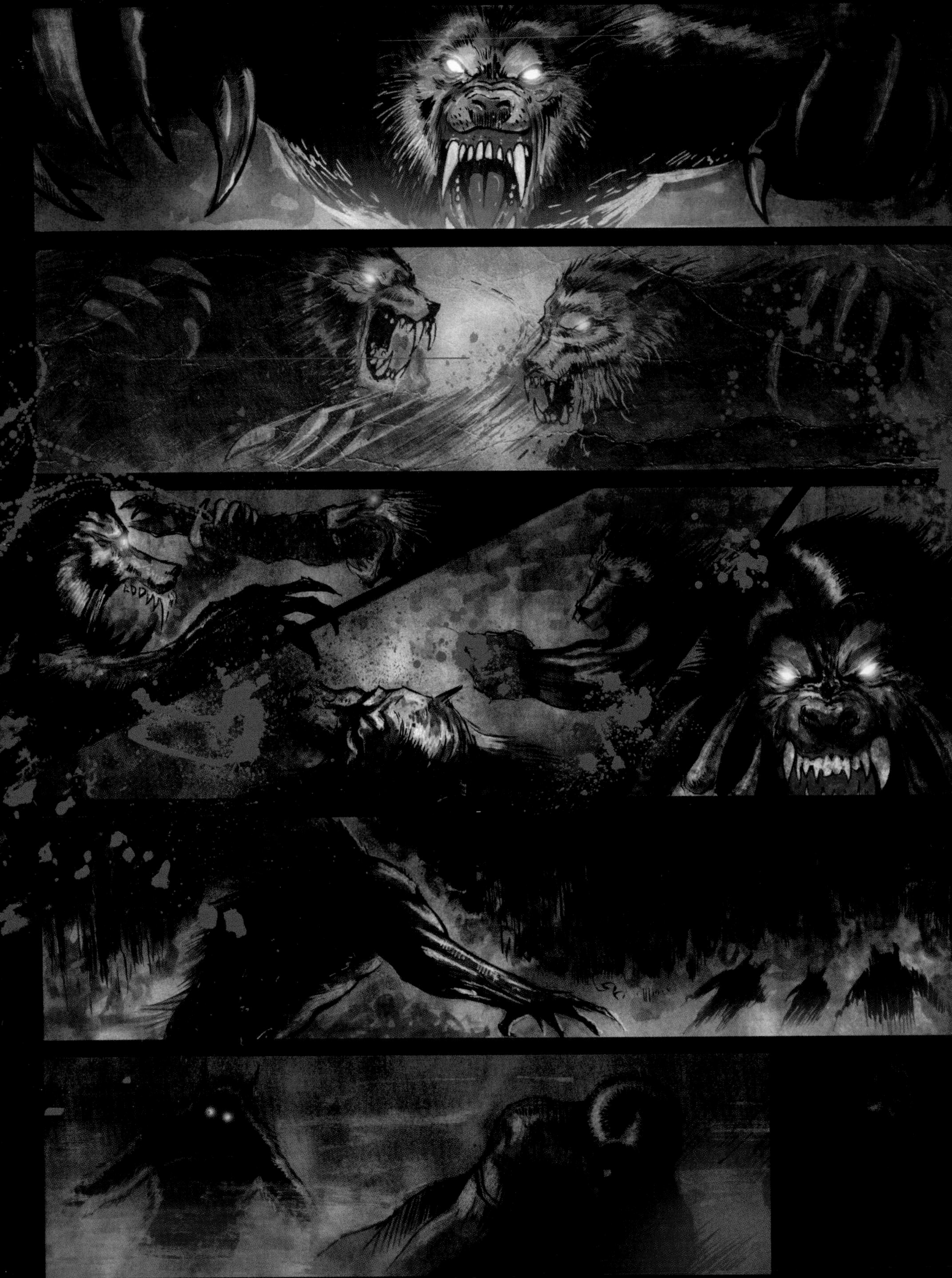

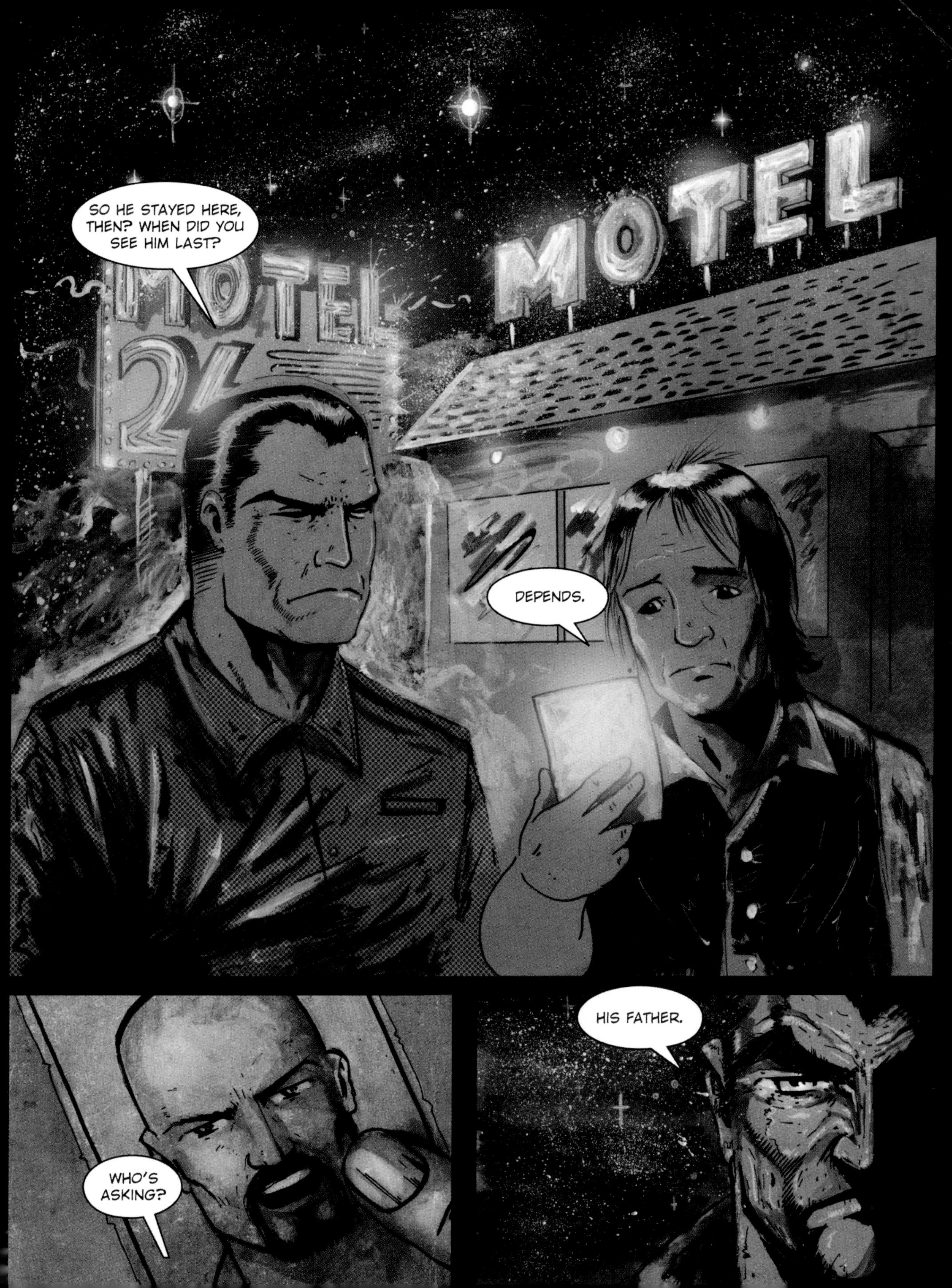
SO HE STAYED HERE, THEN? WHEN DID YOU SEE HIM LAST?
MOTEL
MOTEL
24
DEPENDS.
WHO'S ASKING?
HIS FATHER.

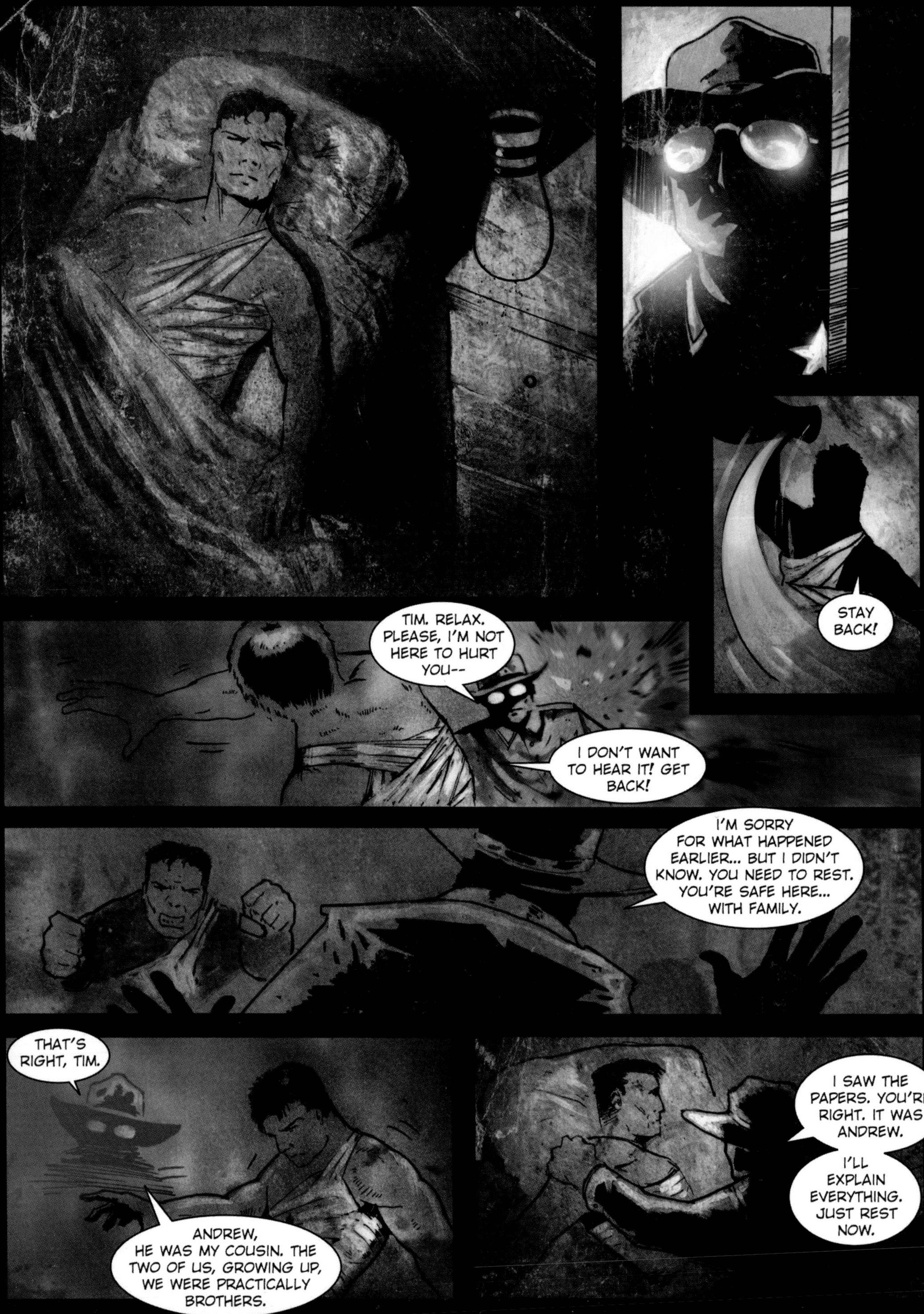
STAY BACK!
TIM. RELAX. PLEASE, I'M NOT HERE TO HURT YOU--
I DON'T WANT TO HEAR IT! GET BACK!
I'M SORRY FOR WHAT HAPPENED EARLIER... BUT I DIDN'T KNOW. YOU NEED TO REST. YOU'RE SAFE HERE... WITH FAMILY.
THAT'S RIGHT, TIM.
ANDREW, HE WAS MY COUSIN. THE TWO OF US, GROWING UP, WE WERE PRACTICALLY BROTHERS.
I SAW THE PAPERS. YOU'RE RIGHT. IT WAS ANDREW.
I'LL EXPLAIN EVERYTHING. JUST REST NOW.

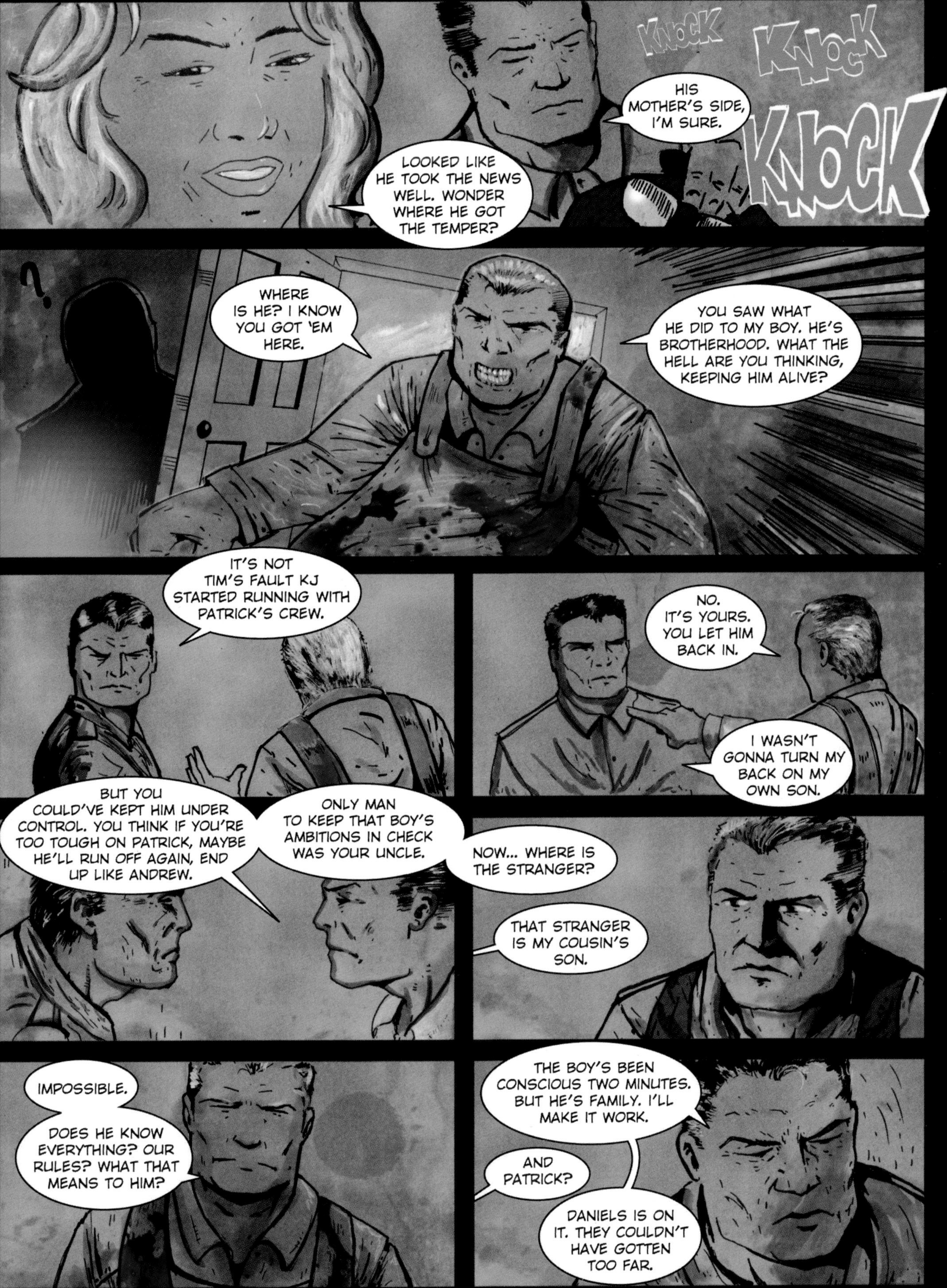
LOOKED LIKE HE TOOK THE NEWS WELL. WONDER WHERE HE GOT THE TEMPER?
HIS MOTHER'S SIDE, I'M SURE.
KNOCK KNOCK KNOCK
?
WHERE IS HE? I KNOW YOU GOT 'EM HERE.
YOU SAW WHAT HE DID TO MY BOY. HE'S BROTHERHOOD. WHAT THE HELL ARE YOU THINKING, KEEPING HIM ALIVE?
IT'S NOT TIM'S FAULT KJ STARTED RUNNING WITH PATRICK'S CREW.
NO. IT'S YOURS. YOU LET HIM BACK IN.
I WASN'T GONNA TURN MY BACK ON MY OWN SON.
BUT YOU COULD'VE KEPT HIM UNDER CONTROL. YOU THINK IF YOU'RE TOO TOUGH ON PATRICK, MAYBE HE'LL RUN OFF AGAIN, END UP LIKE ANDREW.
ONLY MAN TO KEEP THAT BOY'S AMBITIONS IN CHECK WAS YOUR UNCLE.
NOW... WHERE IS THE STRANGER?
THAT STRANGER IS MY COUSIN'S SON.
IMPOSSIBLE.
DOES HE KNOW EVERYTHING? OUR RULES? WHAT THAT MEANS TO HIM?
THE BOY'S BEEN CONSCIOUS TWO MINUTES. BUT HE'S FAMILY. I'LL MAKE IT WORK.
AND PATRICK?
DANIELS IS ON IT. THEY COULDN'T HAVE GOTTEN TOO FAR.

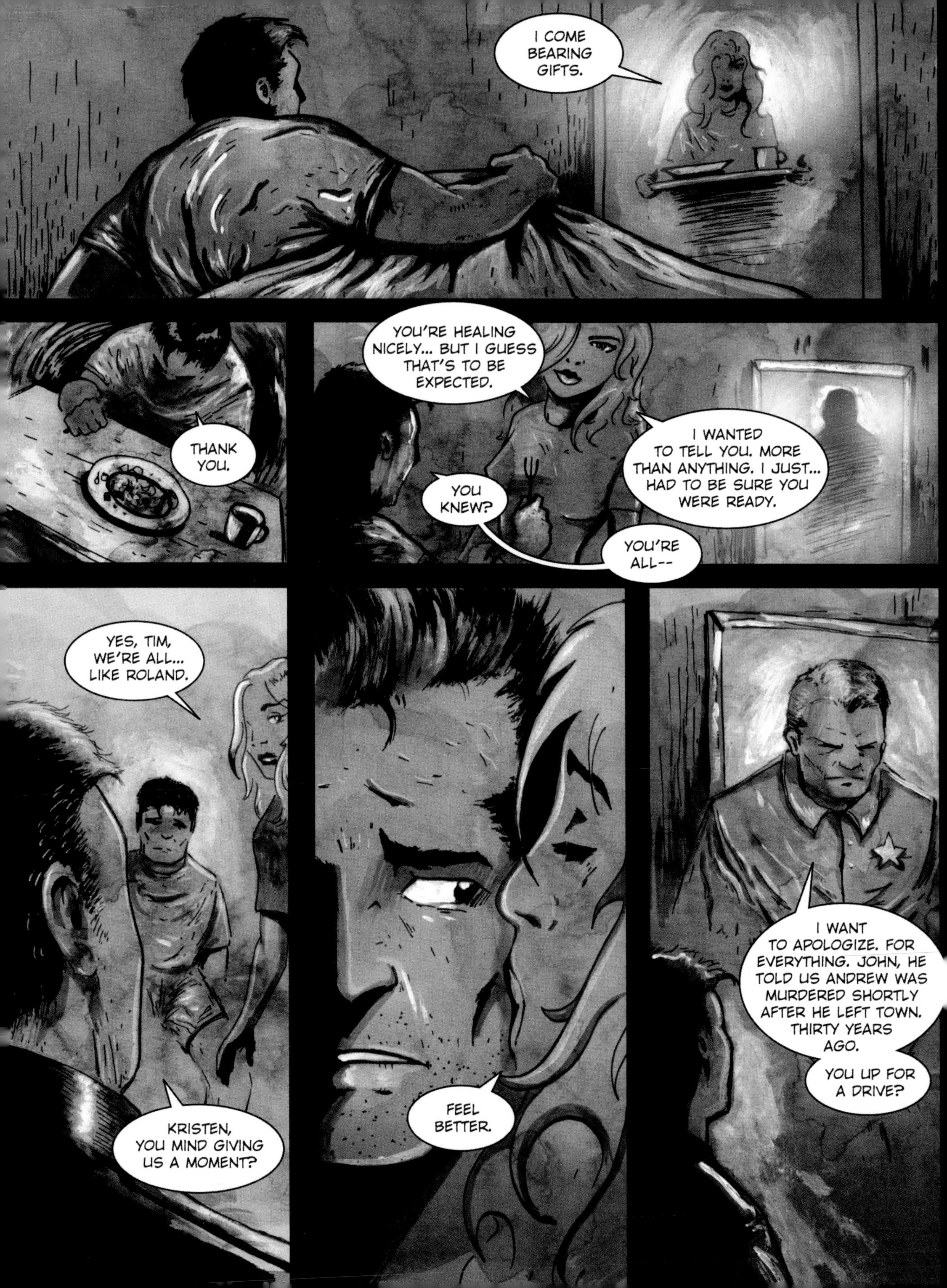
I COME BEARING GIFTS.
THANK YOU.
YOU'RE HEALING NICELY... BUT I GUESS THAT'S TO BE EXPECTED.
YOU KNEW?
I WANTED TO TELL YOU. MORE THAN ANYTHING. I JUST... HAD TO BE SURE YOU WERE READY.
YOU'RE ALL--
YES, TIM, WE'RE ALL... LIKE ROLAND.
KRISTEN, YOU MIND GIVING US A MOMENT?
FEEL BETTER.
I WANT TO APOLOGIZE. FOR EVERYTHING. JOHN, HE TOLD US ANDREW WAS MURDERED SHORTLY AFTER HE LEFT TOWN. THIRTY YEARS AGO.
YOU UP FOR A DRIVE?

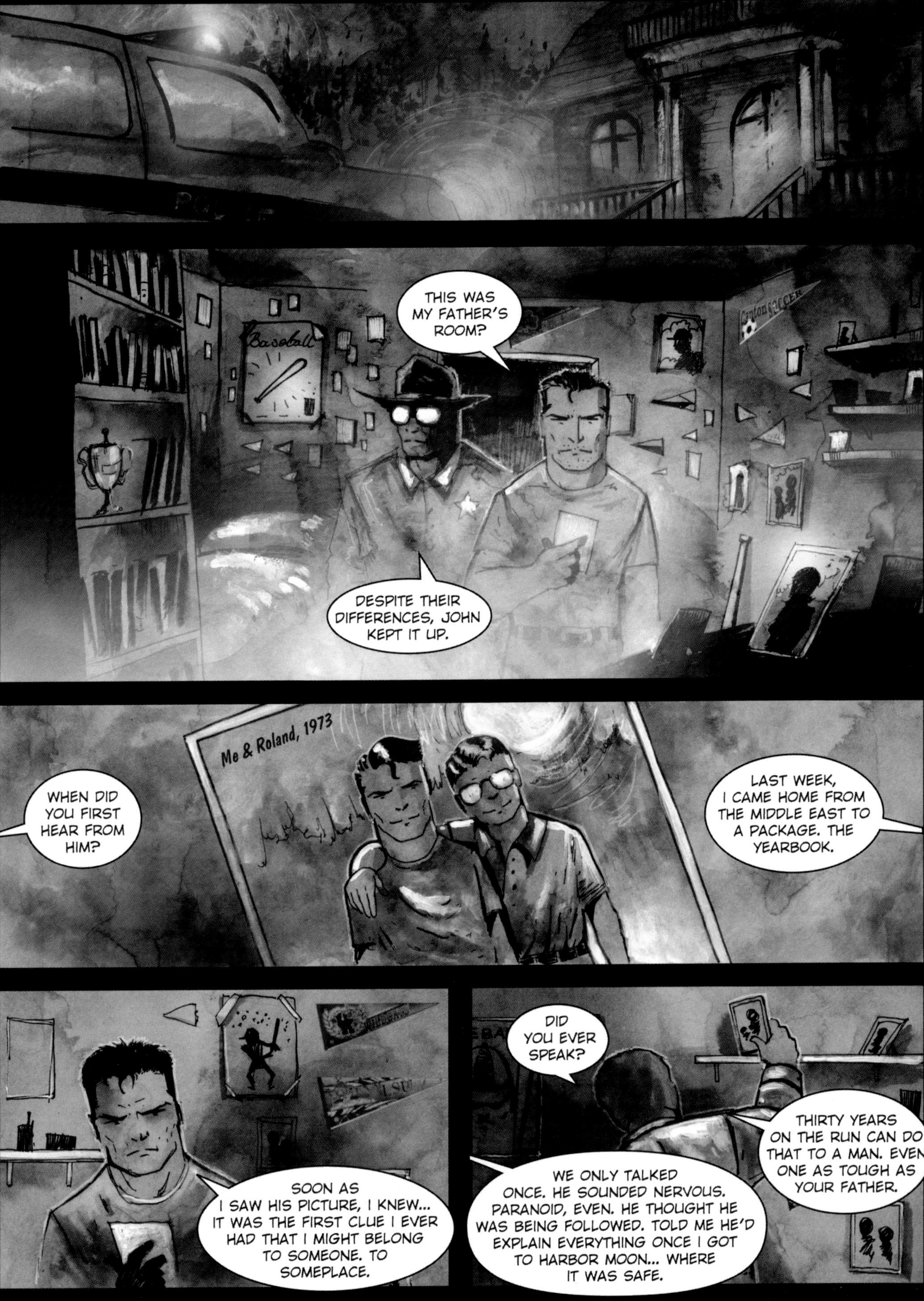
THIS WAS MY FATHER'S ROOM?
DESPITE THEIR DIFFERENCES, JOHN KEPT IT UP.
Me & Roland, 1973
WHEN DID YOU FIRST HEAR FROM HIM?
LAST WEEK, I CAME HOME FROM THE MIDDLE EAST TO A PACKAGE. THE YEARBOOK.
SOON AS I SAW HIS PICTURE, I KNEW... IT WAS THE FIRST CLUE I EVER HAD THAT I MIGHT BELONG TO SOMEONE. TO SOMEPLACE.
DID YOU EVER SPEAK?
WE ONLY TALKED ONCE. HE SOUNDED NERVOUS. PARANOID, EVEN. HE THOUGHT HE WAS BEING FOLLOWED. TOLD ME HE'D EXPLAIN EVERYTHING ONCE I GOT TO HARBOR MOON... WHERE IT WAS SAFE.
THIRTY YEARS ON THE RUN CAN DO THAT TO A MAN. EVEN ONE AS TOUGH AS YOUR FATHER.

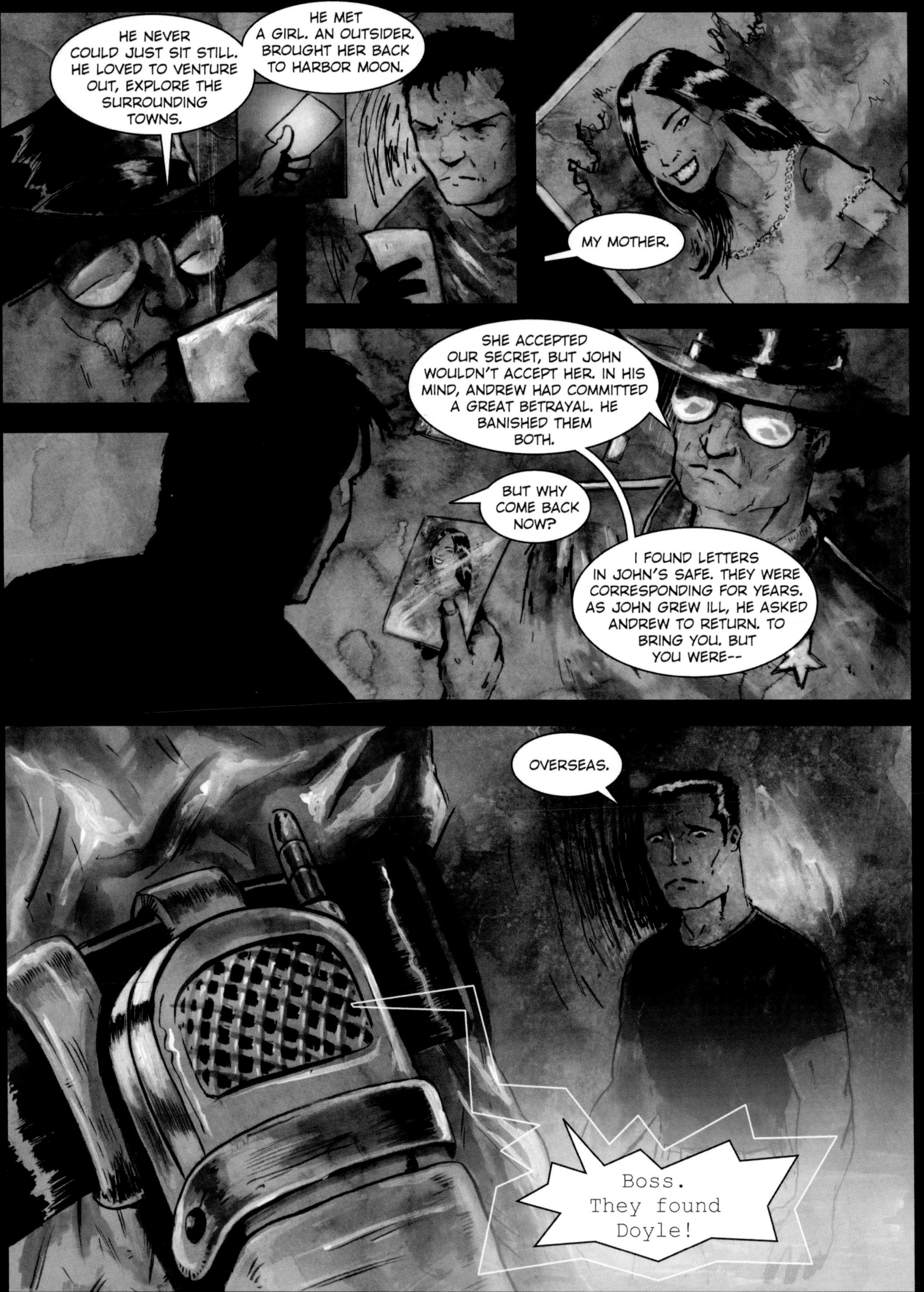
HE NEVER COULD JUST SIT STILL. HE LOVED TO VENTURE OUT, EXPLORE THE SURROUNDING TOWNS.
HE MET A GIRL. AN OUTSIDER. BROUGHT HER BACK TO HARBOR MOON.
MY MOTHER.
SHE ACCEPTED OUR SECRET, BUT JOHN WOULDN'T ACCEPT HER. IN HIS MIND, ANDREW HAD COMMITTED A GREAT BETRAYAL. HE BANISHED THEM BOTH.
BUT WHY COME BACK NOW?
I FOUND LETTERS IN JOHN'S SAFE. THEY WERE CORRESPONDING FOR YEARS. AS JOHN GREW ILL, HE ASKED ANDREW TO RETURN. TO BRING YOU. BUT YOU WERE--
OVERSEAS.
Boss. They found Doyle!

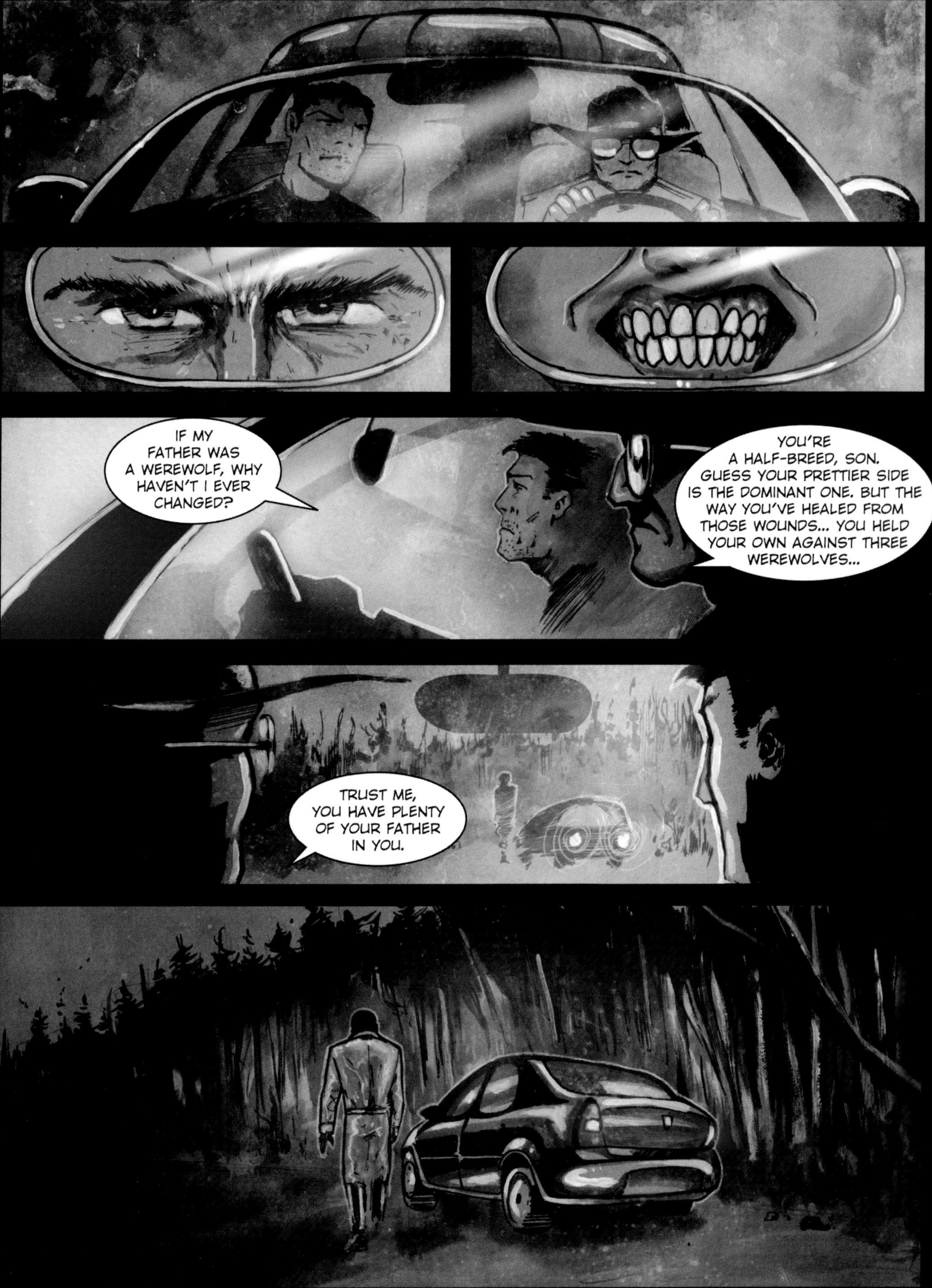
IF MY FATHER WAS A WEREWOLF, WHY HAVEN'T I EVER CHANGED?
YOU'RE A HALF-BREED, SON. GUESS YOUR PRETTIER SIDE IS THE DOMINANT ONE. BUT THE WAY YOU'VE HEALED FROM THOSE WOUNDS... YOU HELD YOUR OWN AGAINST THREE WEREWOLVES...
TRUST ME, YOU HAVE PLENTY OF YOUR FATHER IN YOU.

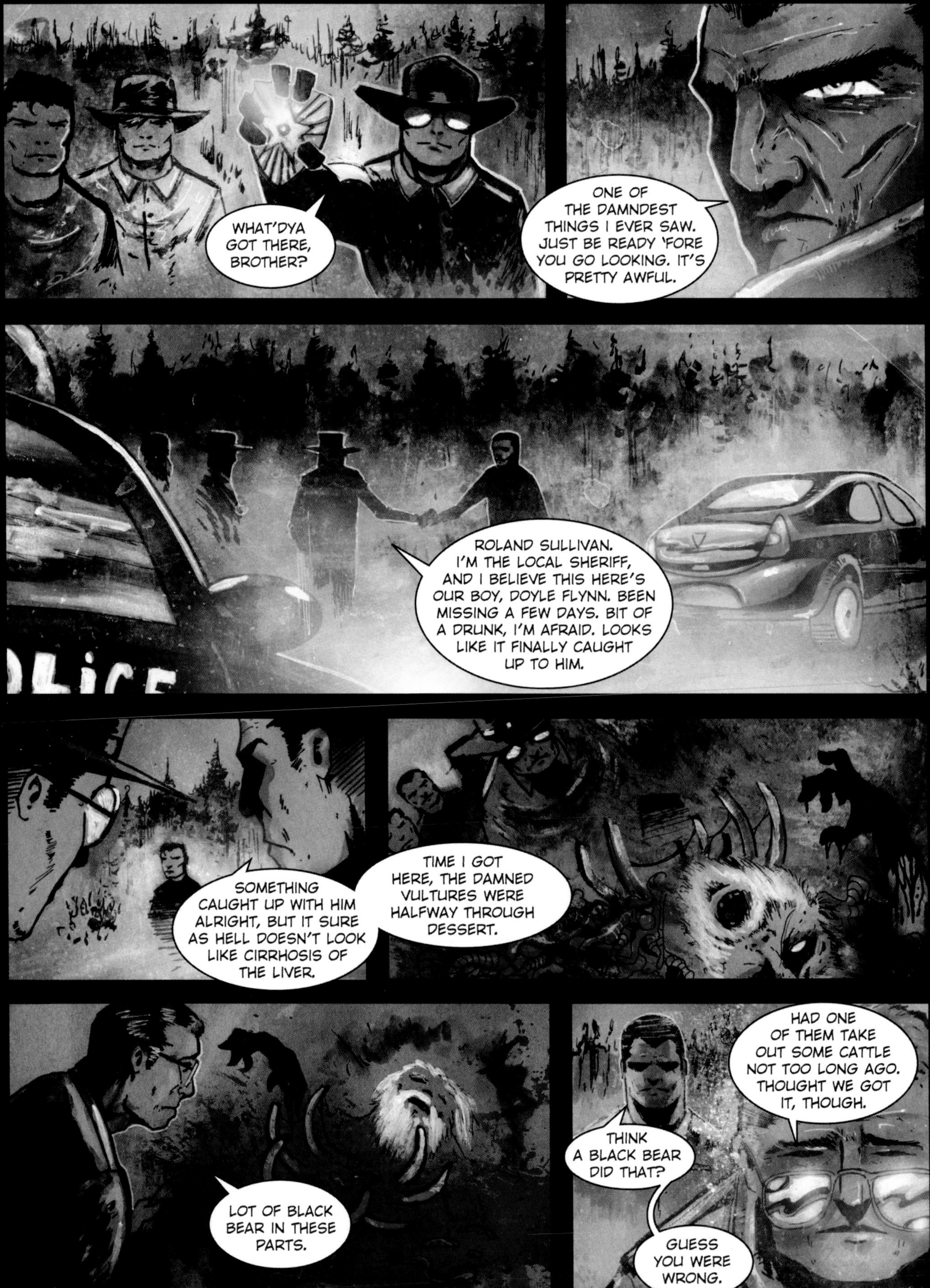
WHAT'DYA GOT THERE, BROTHER?
ONE OF THE DAMNDEST THINGS I EVER SAW. JUST BE READY 'FORE YOU GO LOOKING. IT'S PRETTY AWFUL.
ROLAND SULLIVAN. I'M THE LOCAL SHERIFF, AND I BELIEVE THIS HERE'S OUR BOY, DOYLE FLYNN. BEEN MISSING A FEW DAYS. BIT OF A DRUNK, I'M AFRAID. LOOKS LIKE IT FINALLY CAUGHT UP TO HIM.
POLICE
SOMETHING CAUGHT UP WITH HIM ALRIGHT, BUT IT SURE AS HELL DOESN'T LOOK LIKE CIRRHOSIS OF THE LIVER.
TIME I GOT HERE, THE DAMNED VULTURES WERE HALFWAY THROUGH DESSERT.
LOT OF BLACK BEAR IN THESE PARTS.
HAD ONE OF THEM TAKE OUT SOME CATTLE NOT TOO LONG AGO. THOUGHT WE GOT IT, THOUGH.
THINK A BLACK BEAR DID THAT?
GUESS YOU WERE WRONG.

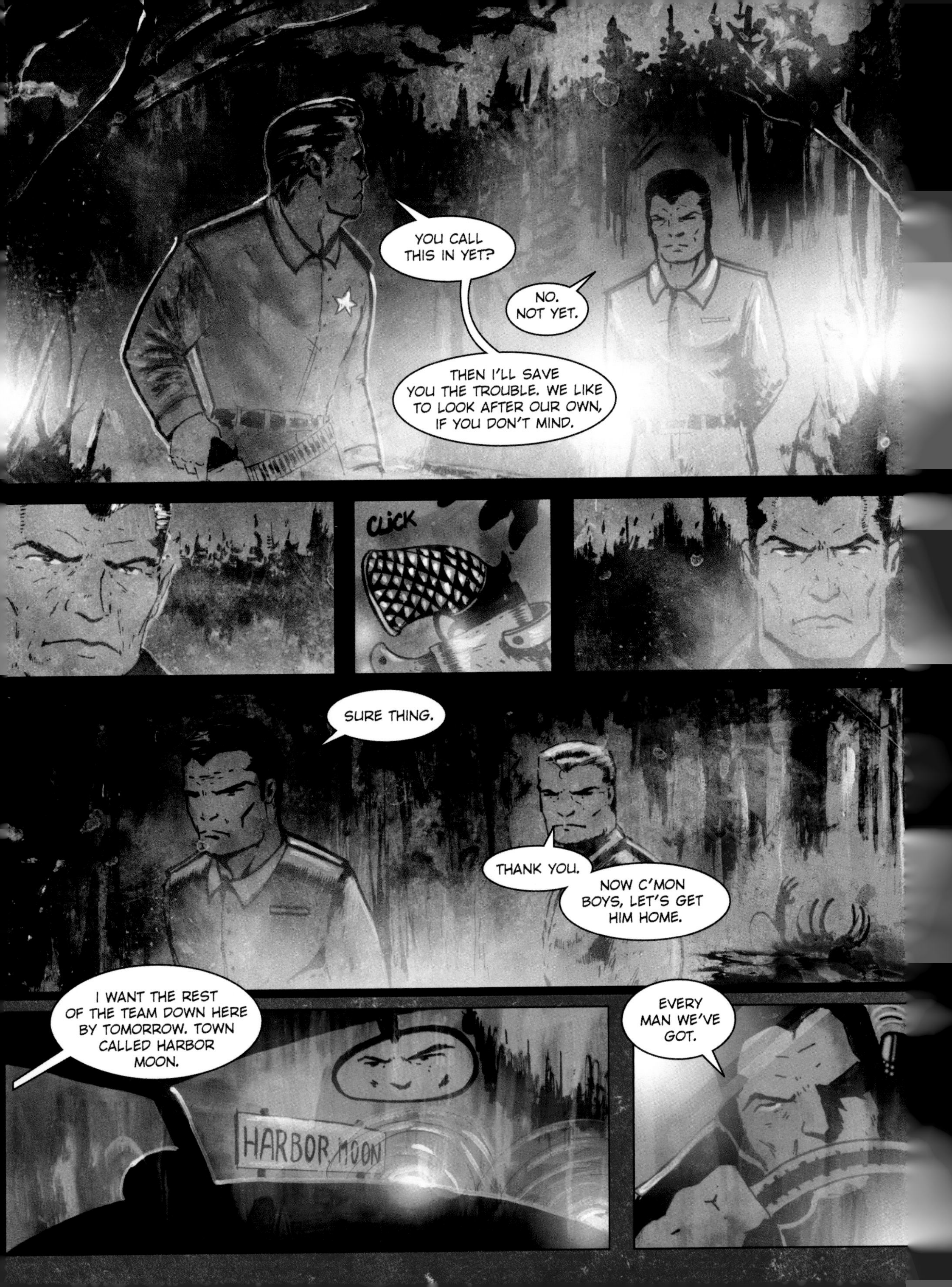
YOU CALL THIS IN YET?
NO. NOT YET.
THEN I'LL SAVE YOU THE TROUBLE. WE LIKE TO LOOK AFTER OUR OWN, IF YOU DON'T MIND.
CLICK
SURE THING.
THANK YOU.
NOW C'MON BOYS, LET'S GET HIM HOME.
I WANT THE REST OF THE TEAM DOWN HERE BY TOMORROW. TOWN CALLED HARBOR MOON.
HARBOR MOON
EVERY MAN WE'VE GOT.

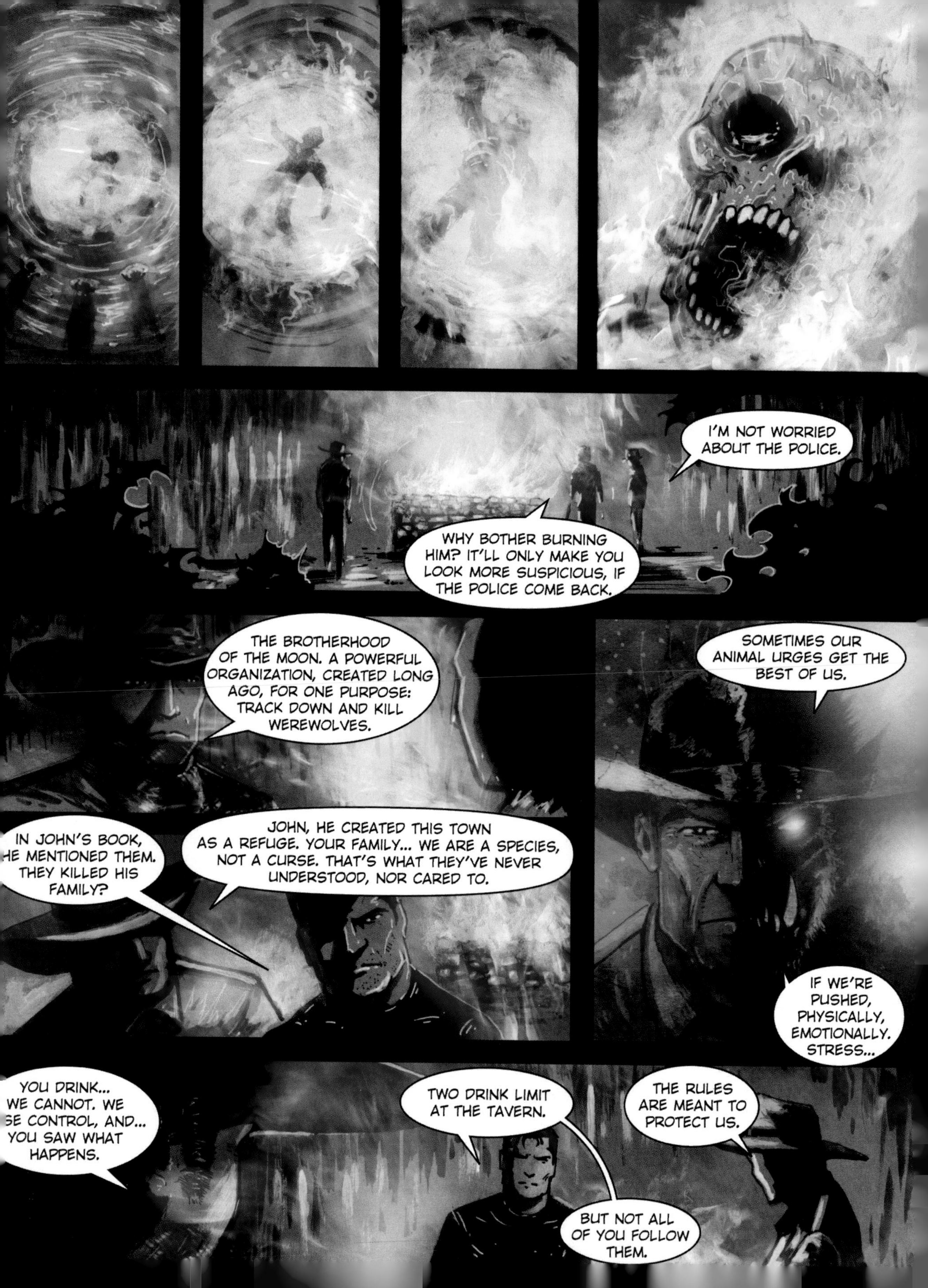
I'M NOT WORRIED ABOUT THE POLICE.
WHY BOTHER BURNING HIM? IT'LL ONLY MAKE YOU LOOK MORE SUSPICIOUS, IF THE POLICE COME BACK.
THE BROTHERHOOD OF THE MOON. A POWERFUL ORGANIZATION, CREATED LONG AGO, FOR ONE PURPOSE: TRACK DOWN AND KILL WEREWOLVES.
IN JOHN'S BOOK, HE MENTIONED THEM. THEY KILLED HIS FAMILY?
JOHN, HE CREATED THIS TOWN AS A REFUGE. YOUR FAMILY... WE ARE A SPECIES, NOT A CURSE. THAT'S WHAT THEY'VE NEVER UNDERSTOOD, NOR CARED TO.
SOMETIMES OUR ANIMAL URGES GET THE BEST OF US.
IF WE'RE PUSHED, PHYSICALLY, EMOTIONALLY. STRESS...
YOU DRINK... WE CANNOT. WE SE CONTROL, AND... YOU SAW WHAT HAPPENS.
TWO DRINK LIMIT AT THE TAVERN.
THE RULES ARE MEANT TO PROTECT US.
BUT NOT ALL OF YOU FOLLOW THEM.

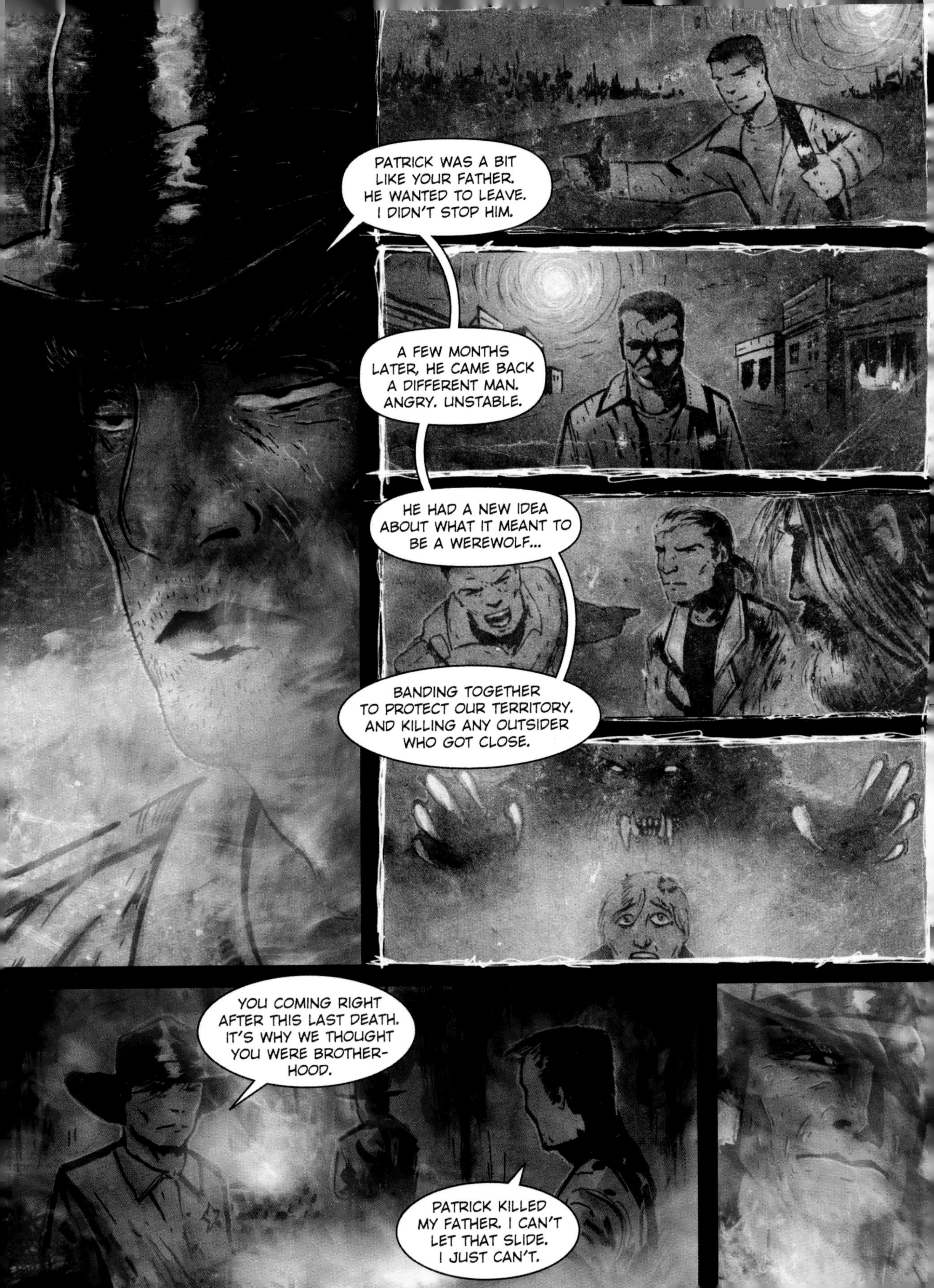
PATRICK WAS A BIT LIKE YOUR FATHER. HE WANTED TO LEAVE. I DIDN'T STOP HIM.
A FEW MONTHS LATER, HE CAME BACK A DIFFERENT MAN. ANGRY. UNSTABLE.
HE HAD A NEW IDEA ABOUT WHAT IT MEANT TO BE A WEREWOLF...
BANDING TOGETHER TO PROTECT OUR TERRITORY. AND KILLING ANY OUTSIDER WHO GOT CLOSE.
YOU COMING RIGHT AFTER THIS LAST DEATH. IT'S WHY WE THOUGHT YOU WERE BROTHER-HOOD.
PATRICK KILLED MY FATHER. I CAN'T LET THAT SLIDE. I JUST CAN'T.

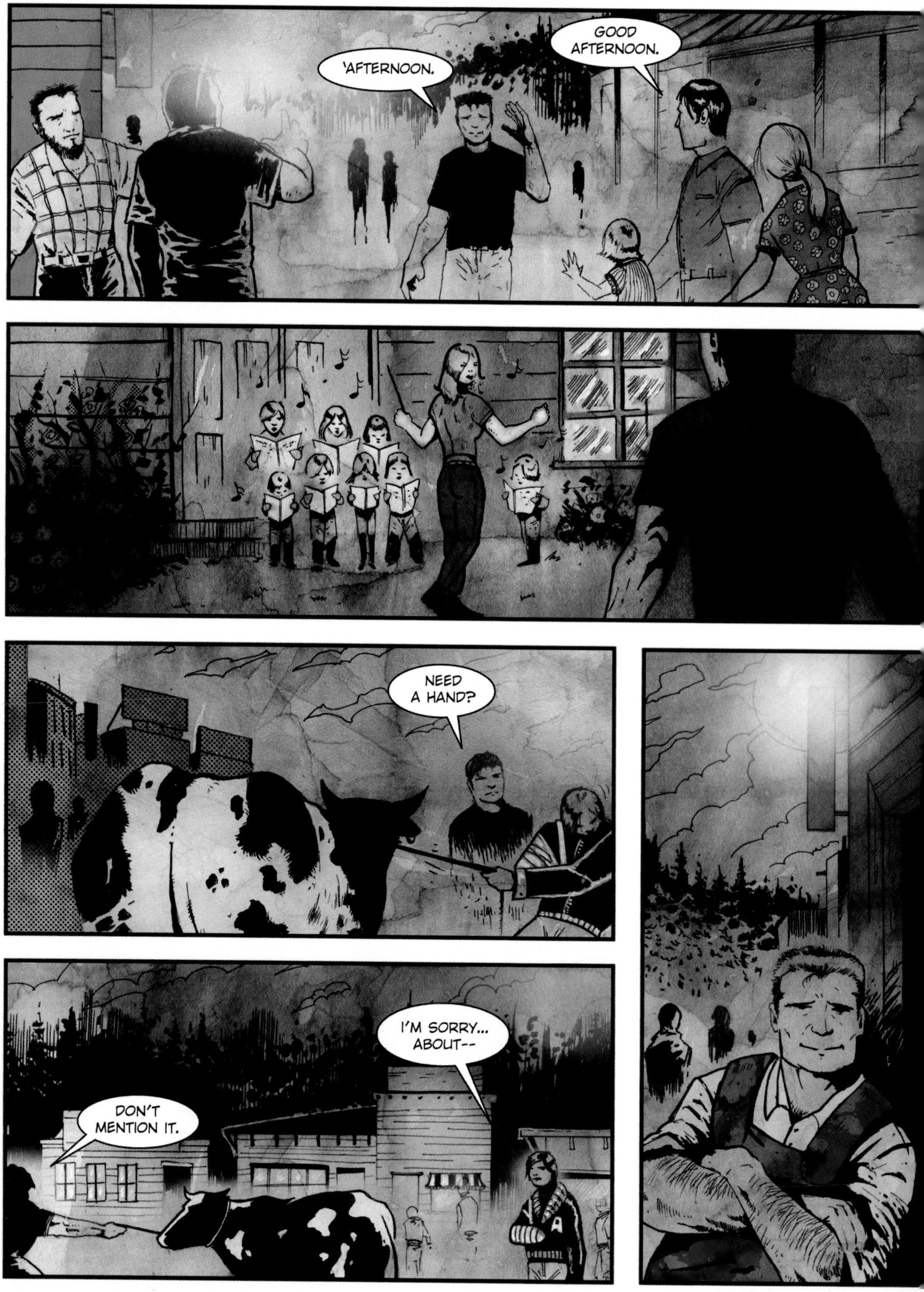
'AFTERNOON.
GOOD AFTERNOON.
NEED A HAND?
I'M SORRY... ABOUT--
DON'T MENTION IT.

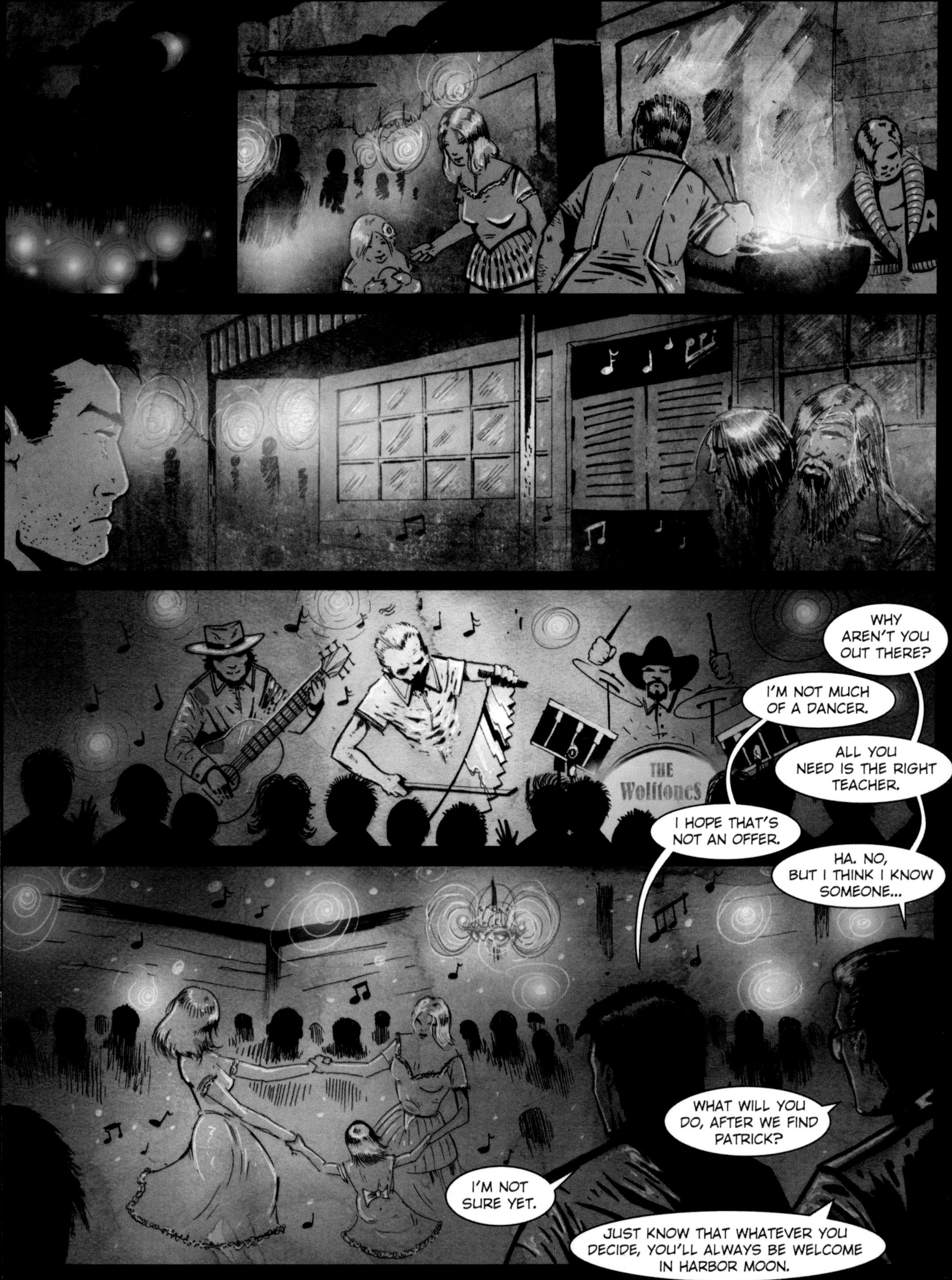

THE Wolftones
WHY AREN'T YOU OUT THERE?
I'M NOT MUCH OF A DANCER.
ALL YOU NEED IS THE RIGHT TEACHER.
I HOPE THAT'S NOT AN OFFER.
HA. NO, BUT I THINK I KNOW SOMEONE...
WHAT WILL YOU DO, AFTER WE FIND PATRICK?
I'M NOT SURE YET.
JUST KNOW THAT WHATEVER YOU DECIDE, YOU'LL ALWAYS BE WELCOME IN HARBOR MOON.

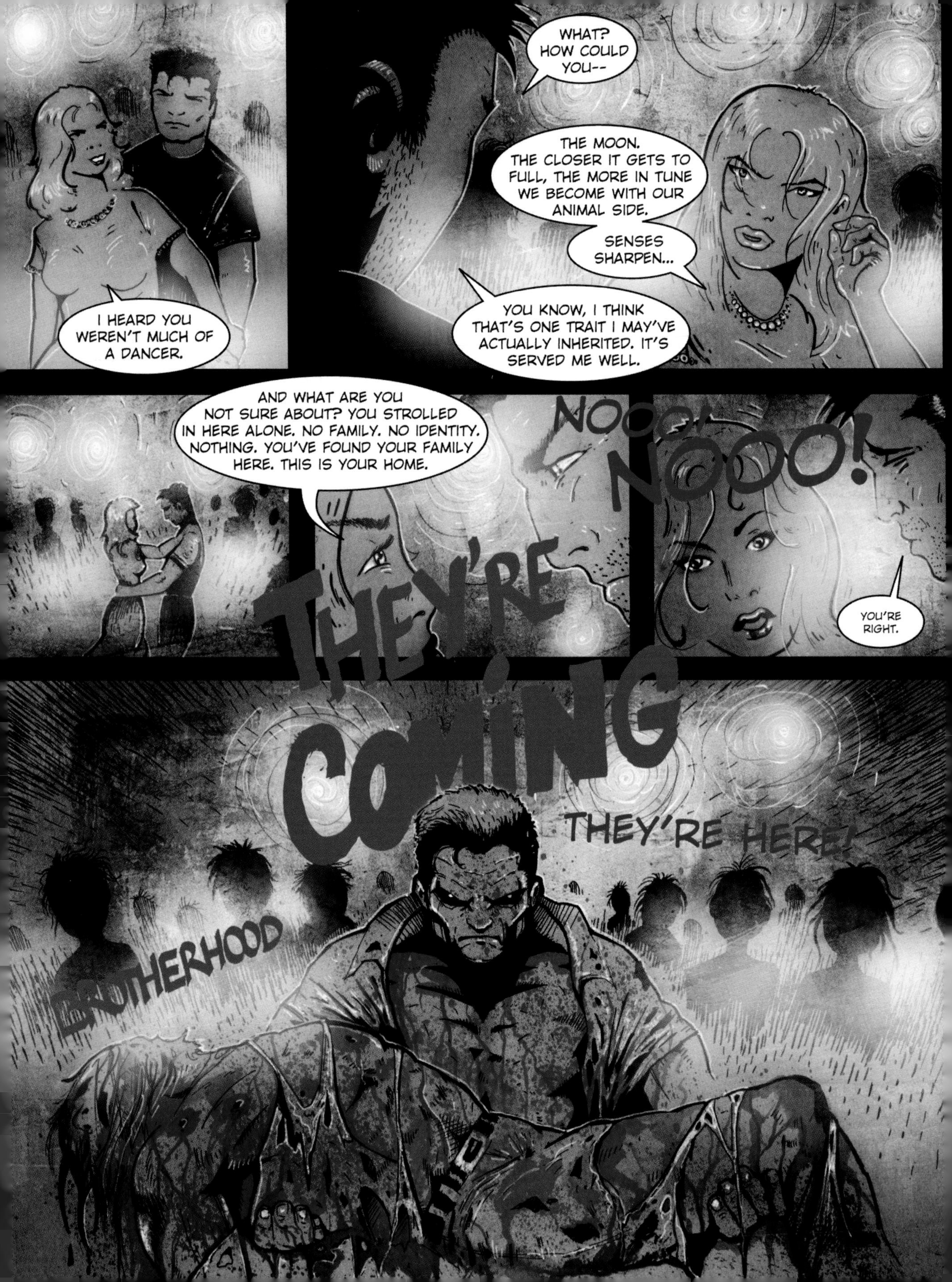
I HEARD YOU WEREN'T MUCH OF A DANCER.
WHAT? HOW COULD YOU--
THE MOON. THE CLOSER IT GETS TO FULL, THE MORE IN TUNE WE BECOME WITH OUR ANIMAL SIDE.
SENSES SHARPEN...
YOU KNOW, I THINK THAT'S ONE TRAIT I MAY'VE ACTUALLY INHERITED. IT'S SERVED ME WELL.
AND WHAT ARE YOU NOT SURE ABOUT? YOU STROLLED IN HERE ALONE. NO FAMILY. NO IDENTITY. NOTHING. YOU'VE FOUND YOUR FAMILY HERE. THIS IS YOUR HOME.
NOOO!
NOOO!
YOU'RE RIGHT.
THEY'RE COMING
THEY'RE HERE!
BROTHERHOOD

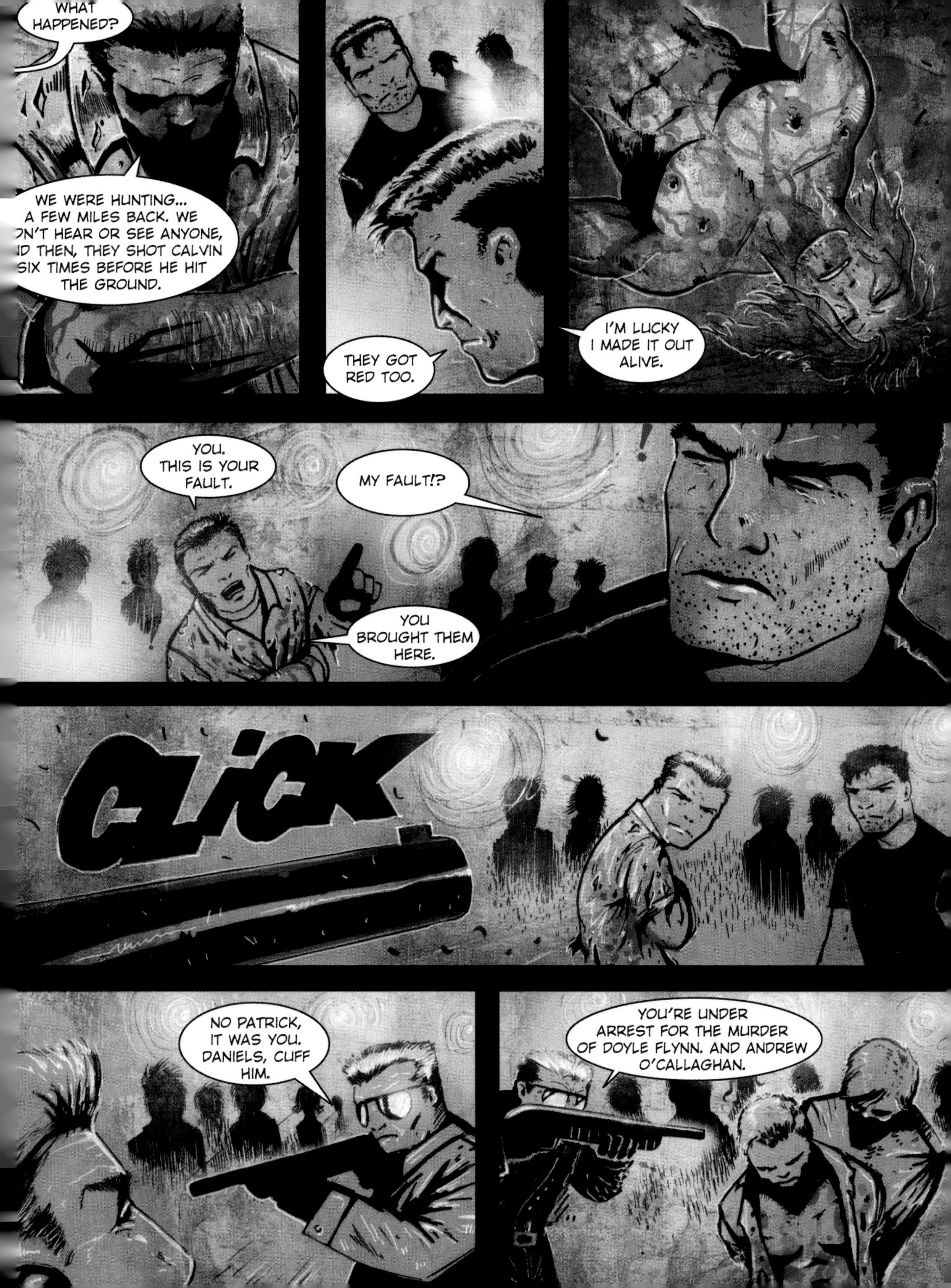
WHAT HAPPENED?
WE WERE HUNTING... A FEW MILES BACK. WE
N'T HEAR OR SEE ANYONE,
D THEN, THEY SHOT CALVIN
SIX TIMES BEFORE HE HIT THE GROUND.
THEY GOT RED TOO.
I'M LUCKY I MADE IT OUT ALIVE.
YOU. THIS IS YOUR FAULT.
MY FAULT!?
YOU BROUGHT THEM HERE.
CLICK
NO PATRICK, IT WAS YOU. DANIELS, CUFF HIM.
YOU'RE UNDER ARREST FOR THE MURDER OF DOYLE FLYNN. AND ANDREW O'CALLAGHAN.

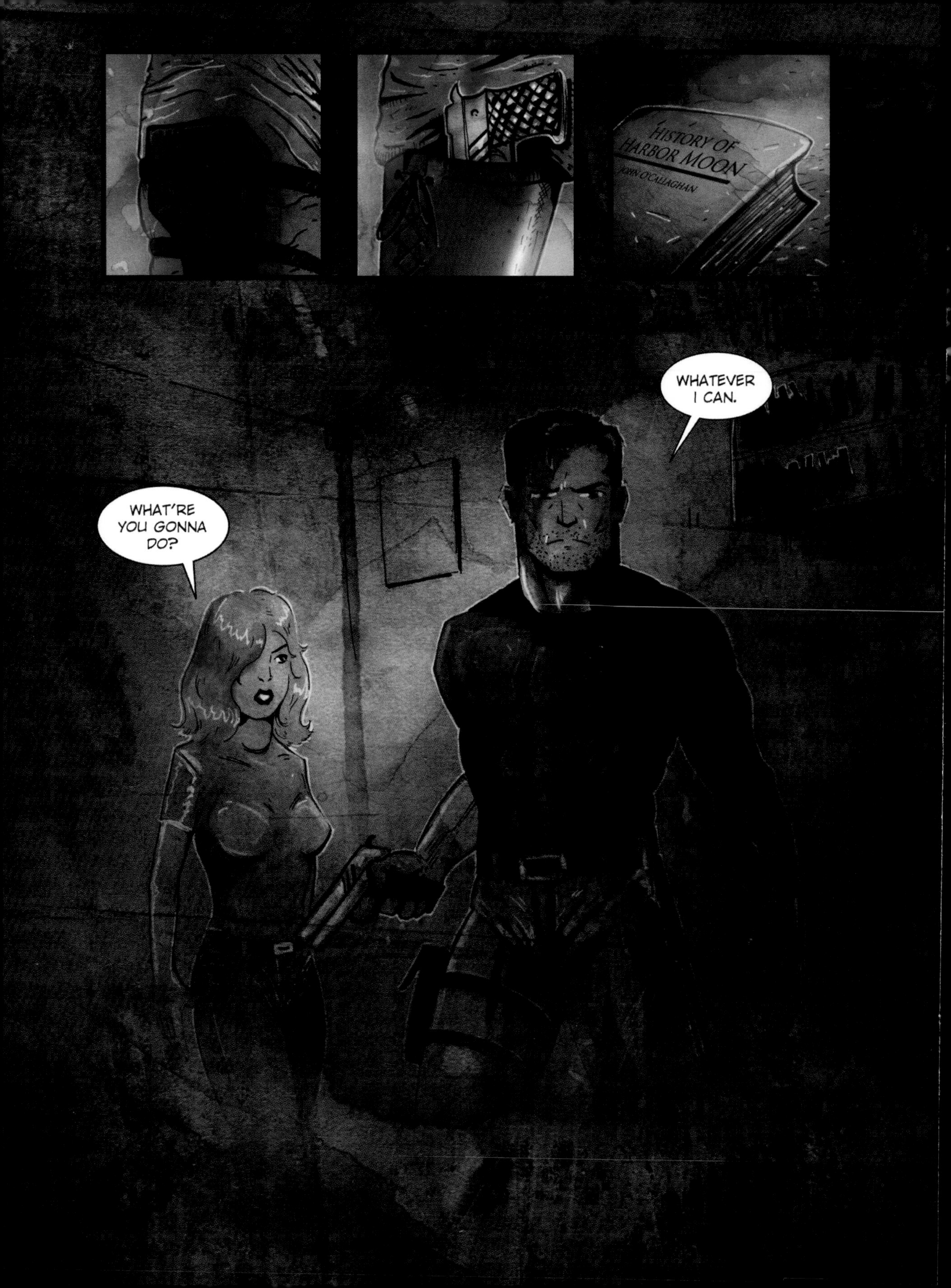
HISTORY OF HARBOR MOON
JOHN O'CALLAGHAN
WHAT'RE YOU GONNA DO?
WHATEVER I CAN.

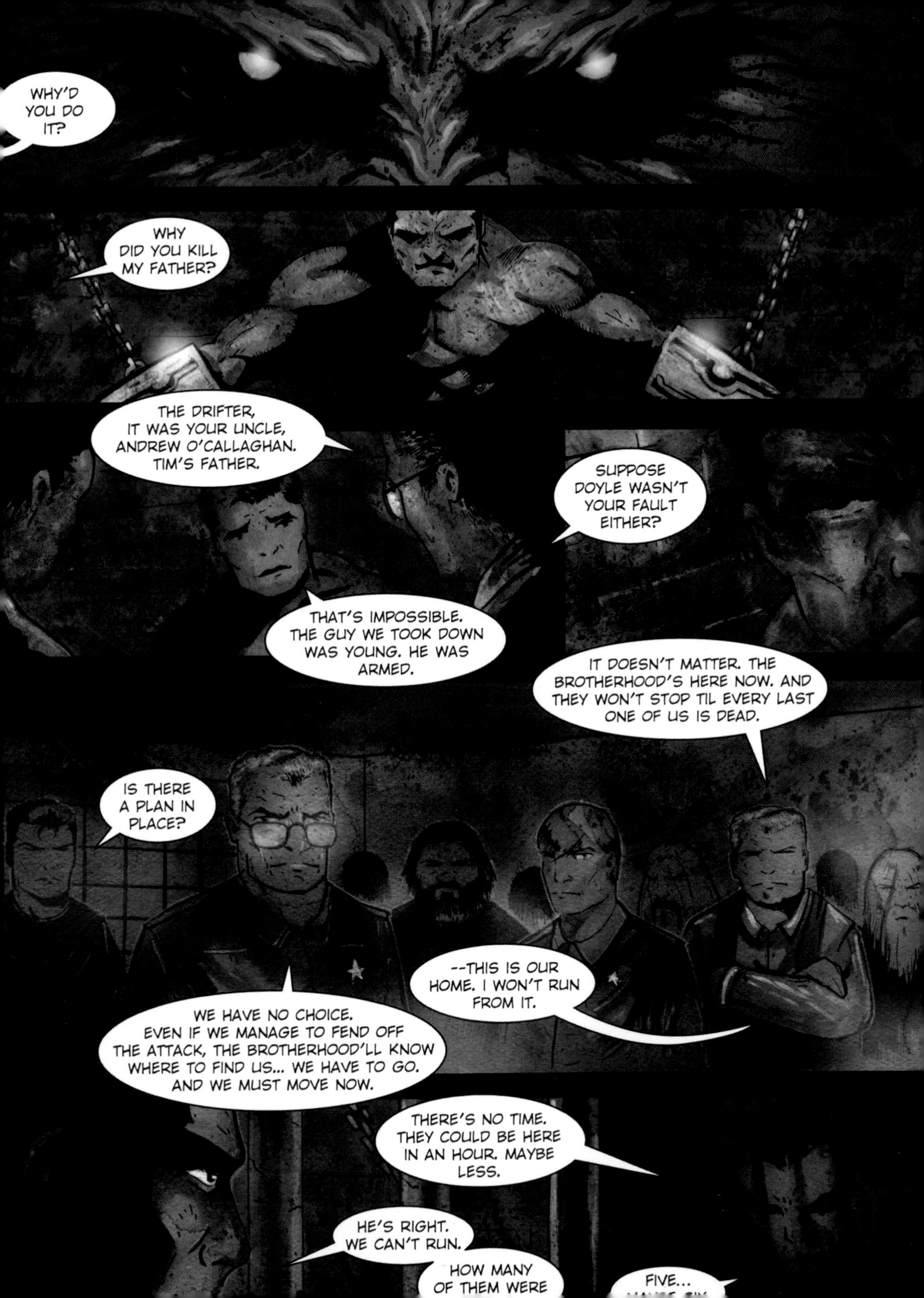
WHY'D YOU DO IT?
WHY DID YOU KILL MY FATHER?
THE DRIFTER, IT WAS YOUR UNCLE, ANDREW O'CALLAGHAN. TIM'S FATHER.
THAT'S IMPOSSIBLE. THE GUY WE TOOK DOWN WAS YOUNG. HE WAS ARMED.
SUPPOSE DOYLE WASN'T YOUR FAULT EITHER?
IT DOESN'T MATTER. THE BROTHERHOOD'S HERE NOW. AND THEY WON'T STOP TIL EVERY LAST ONE OF US IS DEAD.
IS THERE A PLAN IN PLACE?
WE HAVE NO CHOICE. EVEN IF WE MANAGE TO FEND OFF THE ATTACK, THE BROTHERHOOD'LL KNOW WHERE TO FIND US... WE HAVE TO GO. AND WE MUST MOVE NOW.
--THIS IS OUR HOME. I WON'T RUN FROM IT.
THERE'S NO TIME. THEY COULD BE HERE IN AN HOUR. MAYBE LESS.
HE'S RIGHT. WE CAN'T RUN.
HOW MANY OF THEM WERE
FIVE...

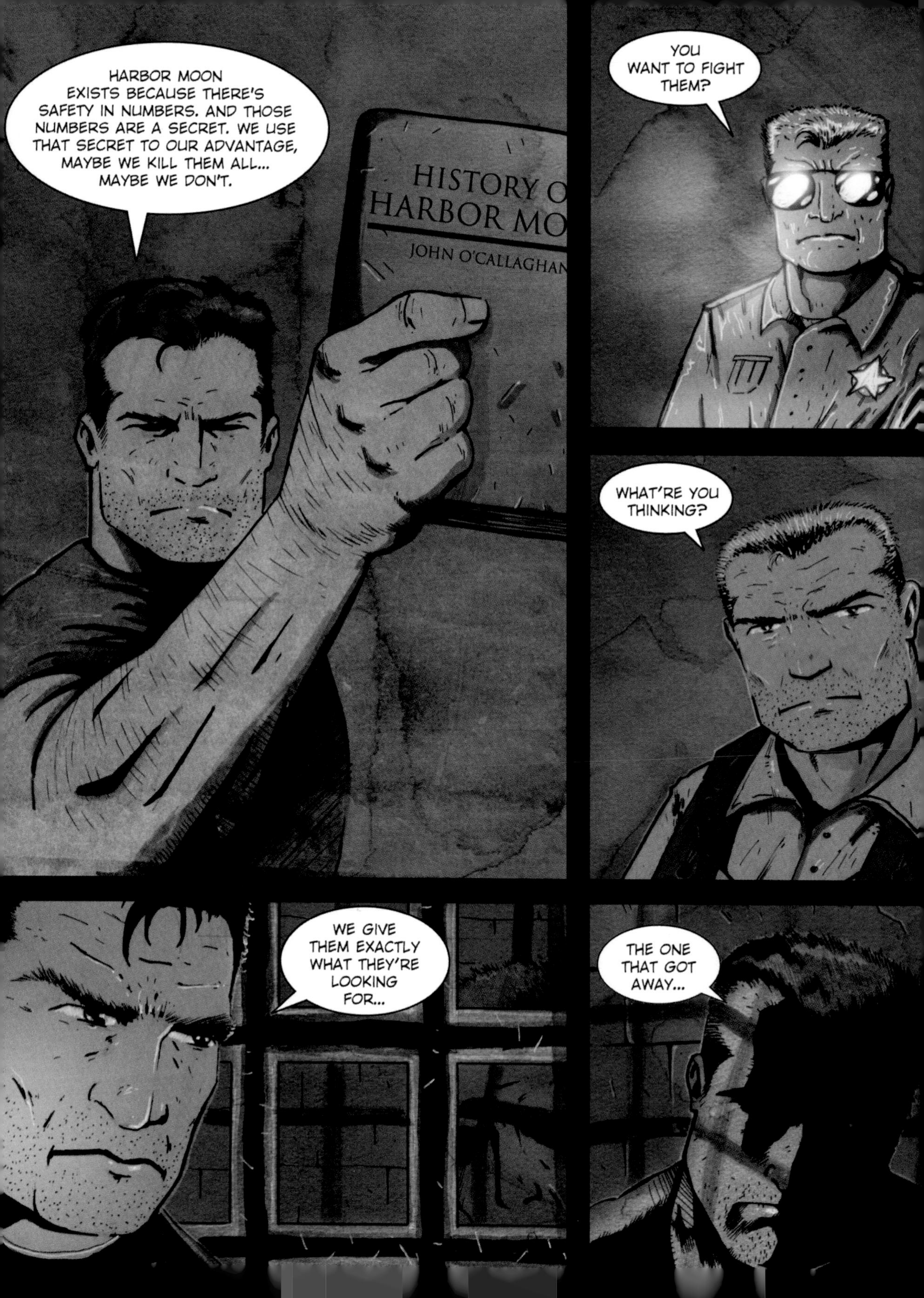
HARBOR MOON EXISTS BECAUSE THERE'S SAFETY IN NUMBERS. AND THOSE NUMBERS ARE A SECRET. WE USE THAT SECRET TO OUR ADVANTAGE, MAYBE WE KILL THEM ALL... MAYBE WE DON'T.
HISTORY O
HARBOR MO
JOHN O'CALLAGHAN
YOU WANT TO FIGHT THEM?
WHAT'RE YOU THINKING?
WE GIVE THEM EXACTLY WHAT THEY'RE LOOKING FOR...
THE ONE THAT GOT AWAY...

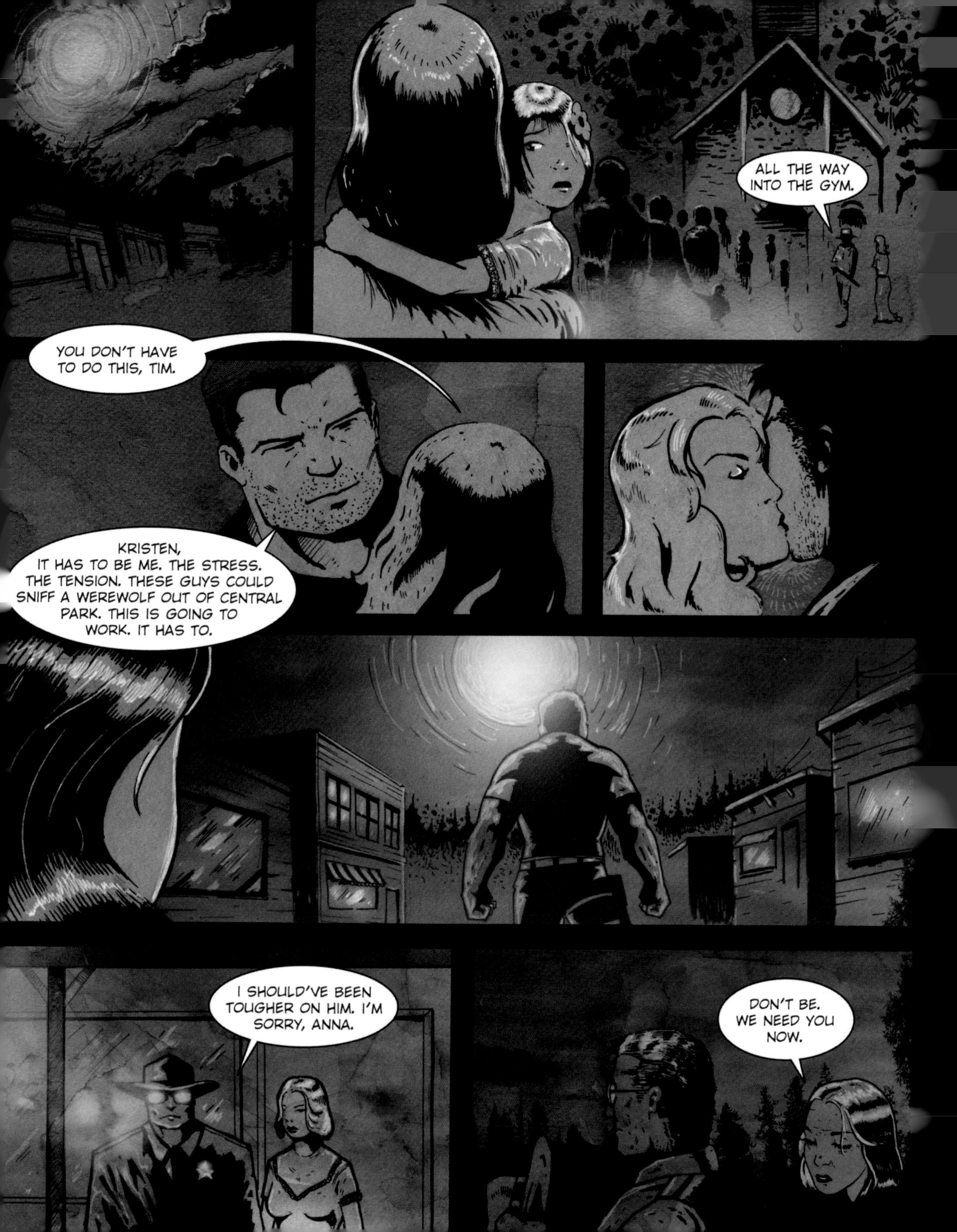
ALL THE WAY INTO THE GYM.
YOU DON'T HAVE TO DO THIS, TIM.
KRISTEN, IT HAS TO BE ME. THE STRESS. THE TENSION. THESE GUYS COULD SNIFF A WEREWOLF OUT OF CENTRAL PARK. THIS IS GOING TO WORK. IT HAS TO.
I SHOULD'VE BEEN TOUGHER ON HIM. I'M SORRY, ANNA.
DON'T BE. WE NEED YOU NOW.

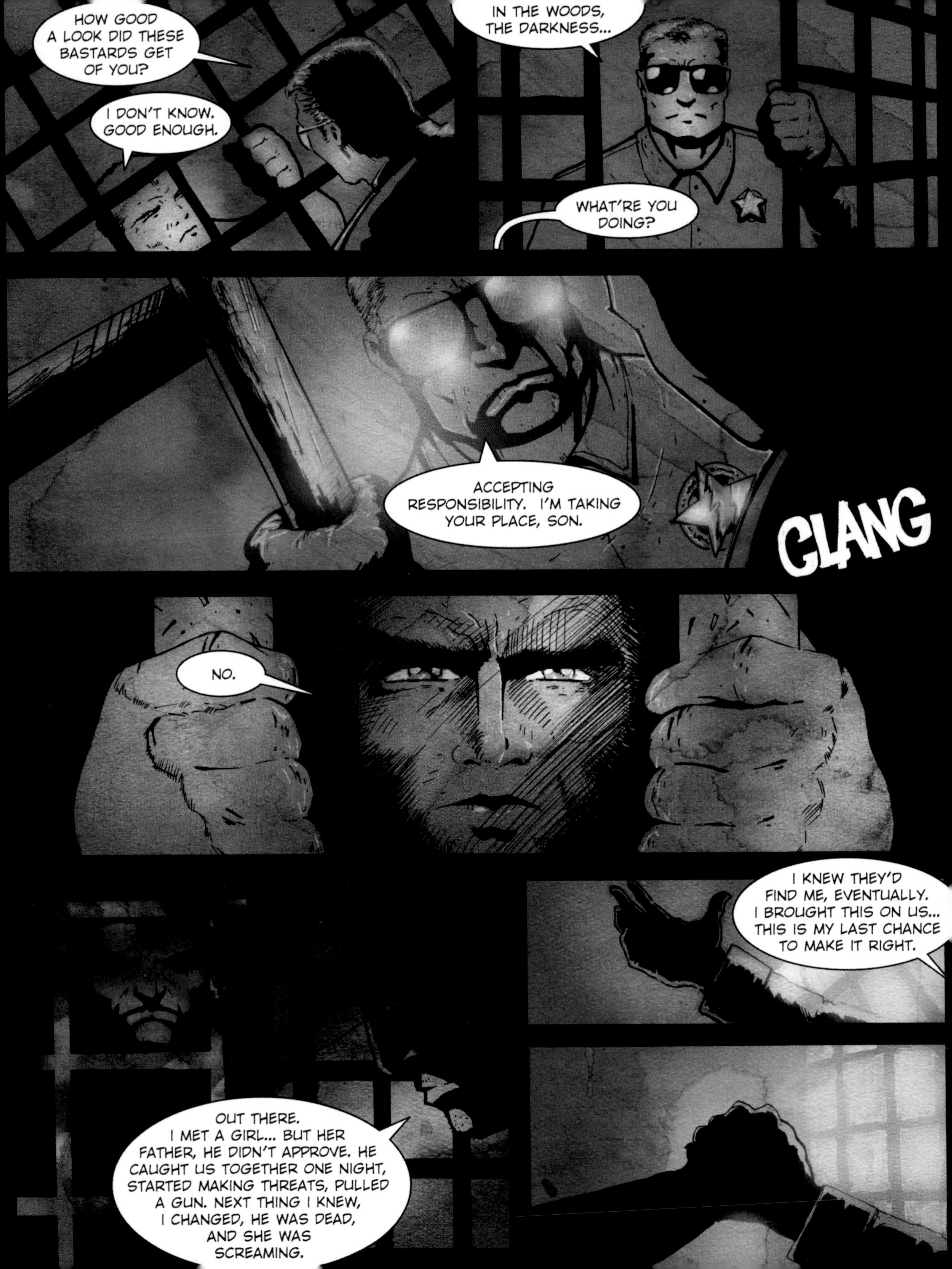
HOW GOOD A LOOK DID THESE BASTARDS GET OF YOU?
I DON'T KNOW. GOOD ENOUGH.
IN THE WOODS, THE DARKNESS...
WHAT'RE YOU DOING?
ACCEPTING RESPONSIBILITY. I'M TAKING YOUR PLACE, SON.
CLANG
NO.
OUT THERE. I MET A GIRL... BUT HER FATHER, HE DIDN'T APPROVE. HE CAUGHT US TOGETHER ONE NIGHT, STARTED MAKING THREATS, PULLED A GUN. NEXT THING I KNEW, I CHANGED, HE WAS DEAD, AND SHE WAS SCREAMING.
I KNEW THEY'D FIND ME, EVENTUALLY. I BROUGHT THIS ON US... THIS IS MY LAST CHANCE TO MAKE IT RIGHT.

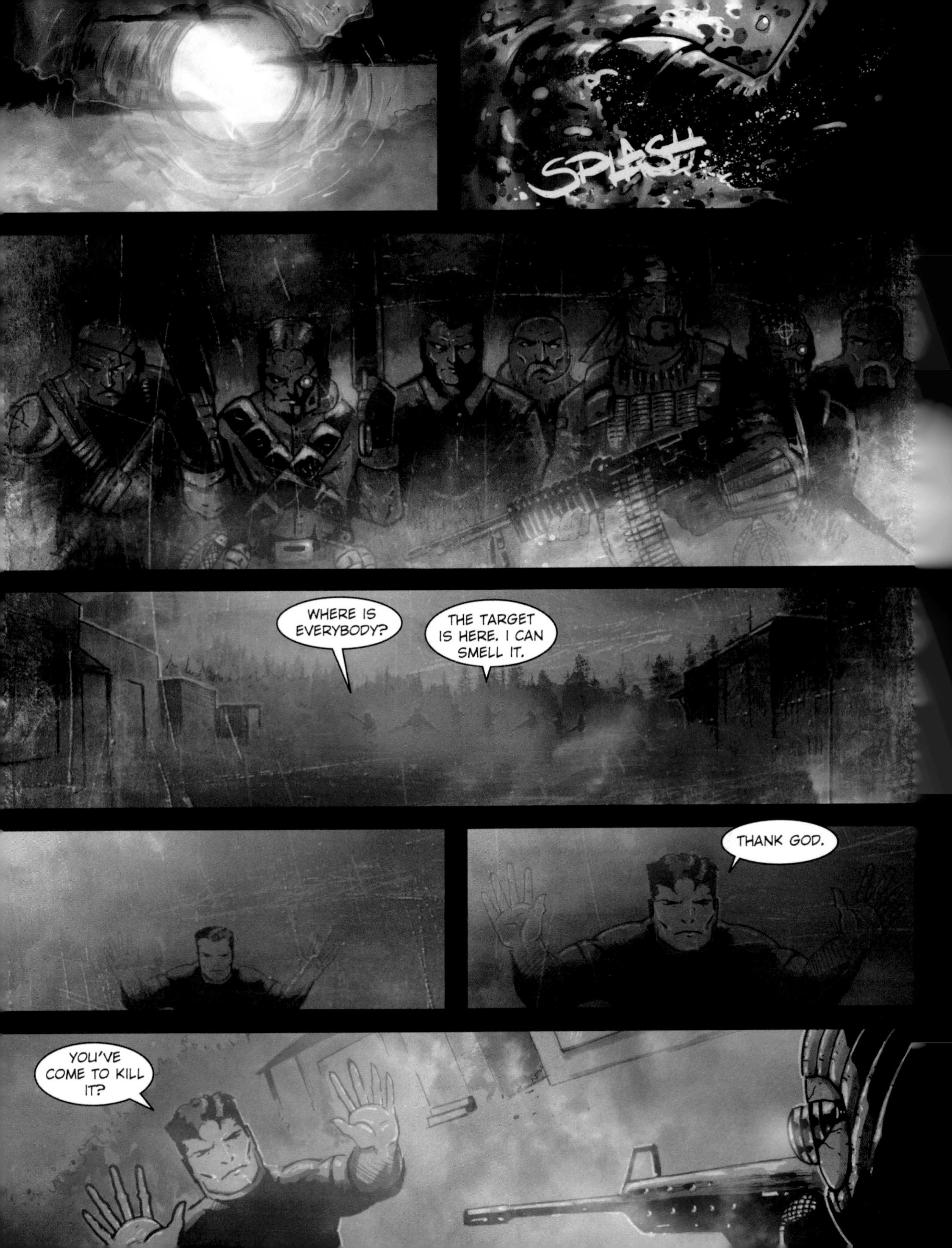
SPLASH
WHERE IS EVERYBODY?
THE TARGET IS HERE. I CAN SMELL IT.
THANK GOD.
YOU'VE COME TO KILL IT?

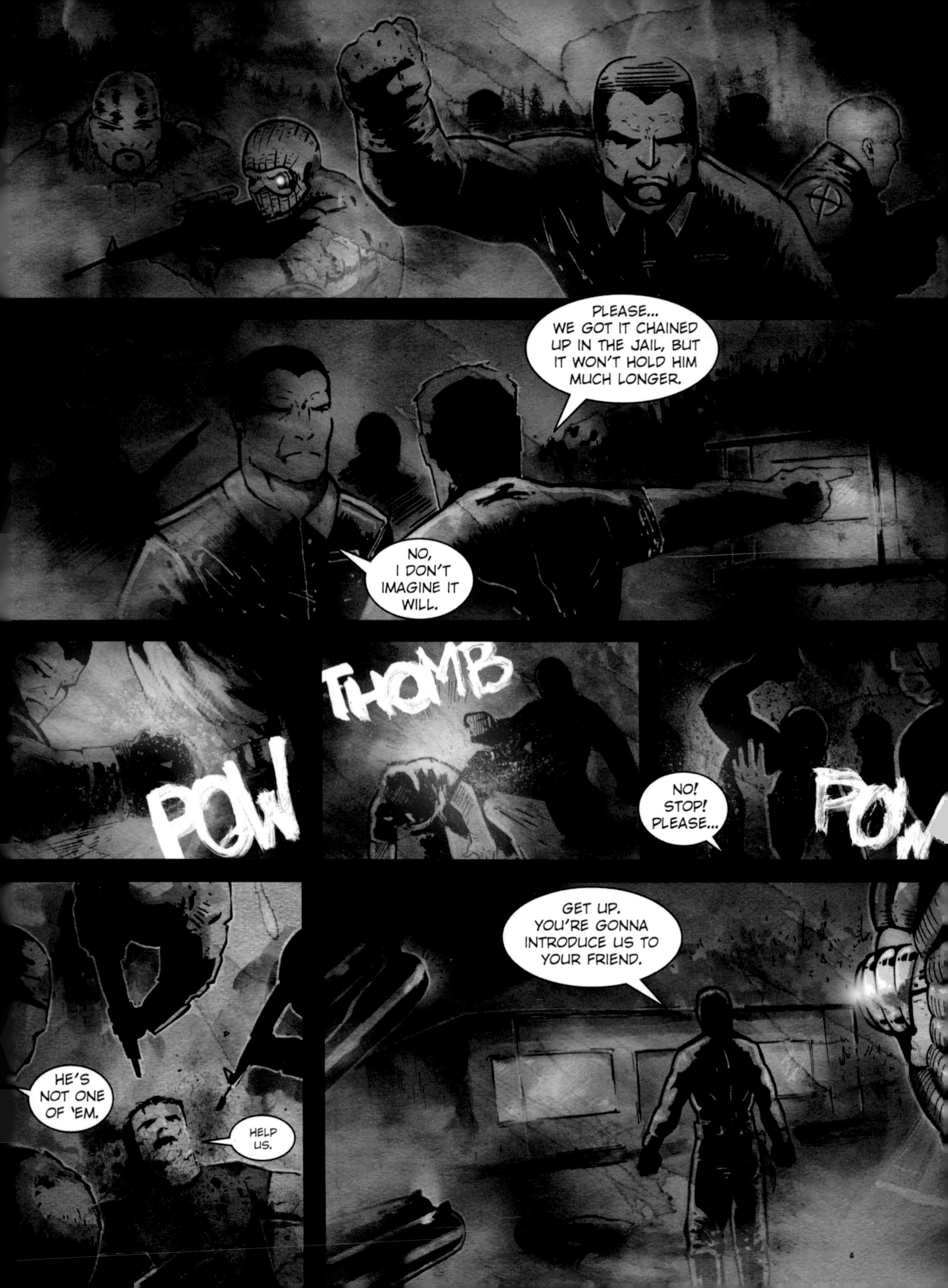
PLEASE... WE GOT IT CHAINED UP IN THE JAIL, BUT IT WON'T HOLD HIM MUCH LONGER.
NO, I DON'T IMAGINE IT WILL.
POW
THOMB
NO! STOP! PLEASE...
POW
HE'S NOT ONE OF 'EM.
HELP US.
GET UP. YOU'RE GONNA INTRODUCE US TO YOUR FRIEND.

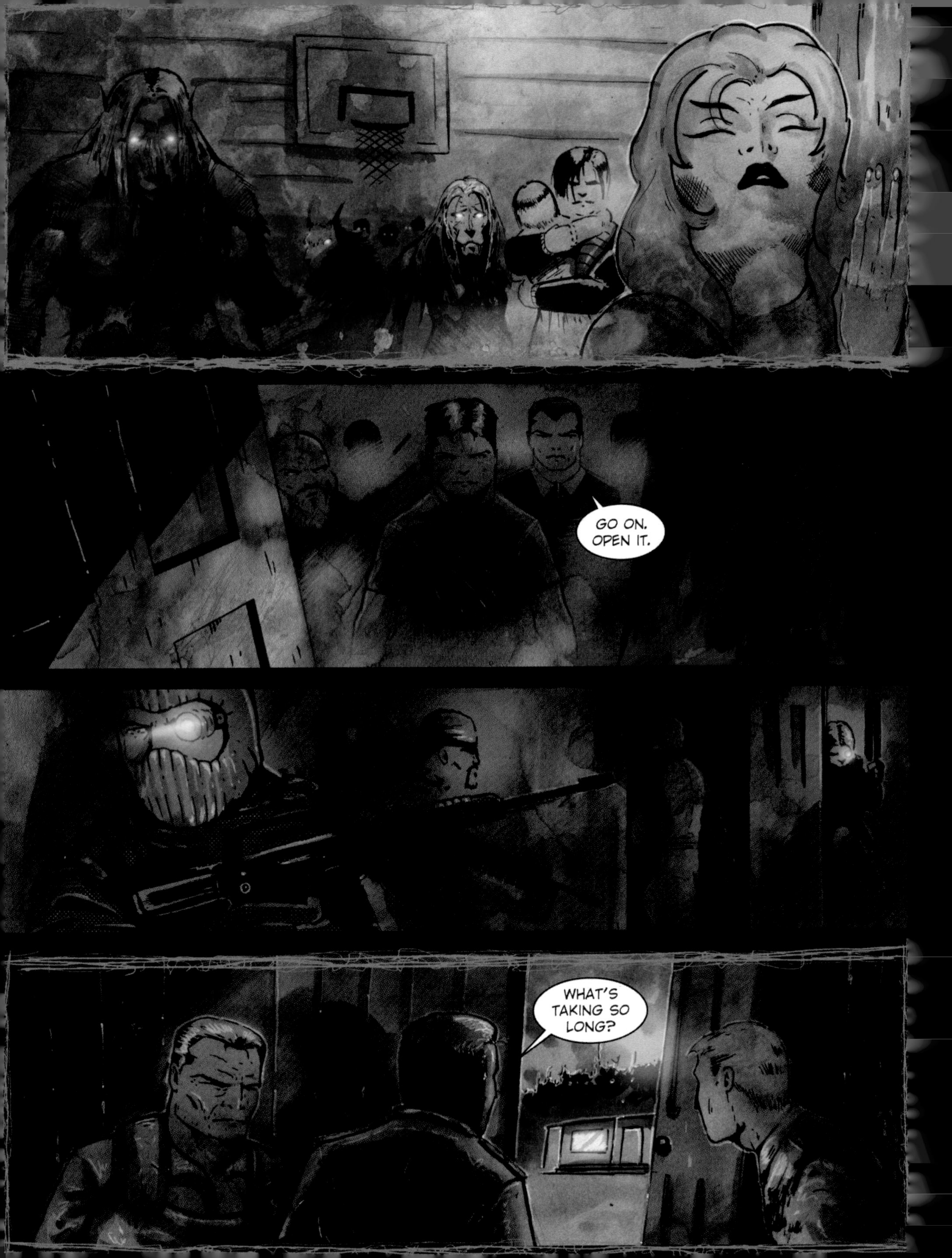
GO ON. OPEN IT.
WHAT'S TAKING SO LONG?

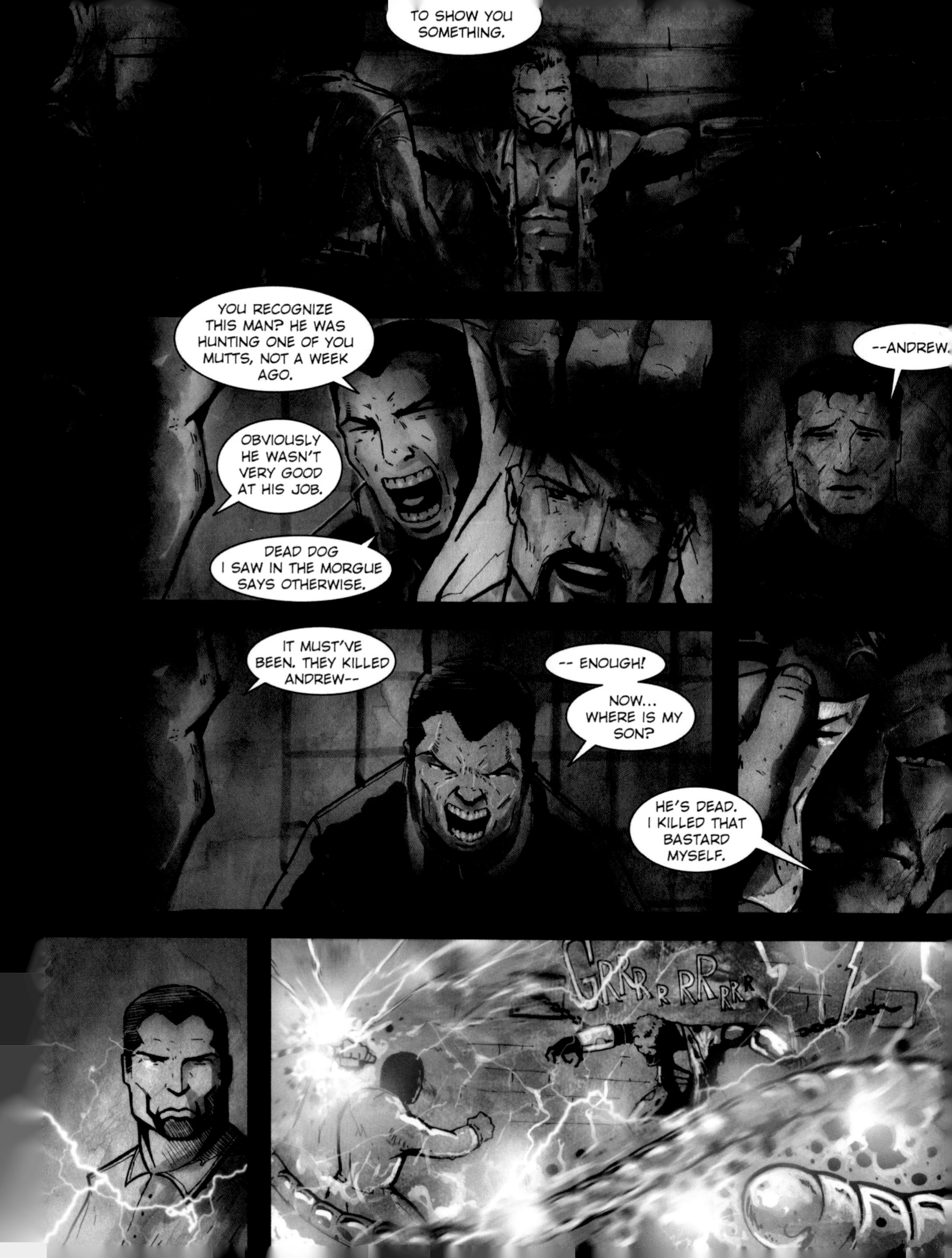
TO SHOW YOU SOMETHING.
YOU RECOGNIZE THIS MAN? HE WAS HUNTING ONE OF YOU MUTTS, NOT A WEEK AGO.
OBVIOUSLY HE WASN'T VERY GOOD AT HIS JOB.
DEAD DOG I SAW IN THE MORGUE SAYS OTHERWISE.
--ANDREW.
IT MUST'VE BEEN. THEY KILLED ANDREW--
-- ENOUGH!
NOW... WHERE IS MY SON?
HE'S DEAD. I KILLED THAT BASTARD MYSELF.
GRRRR RRRRR

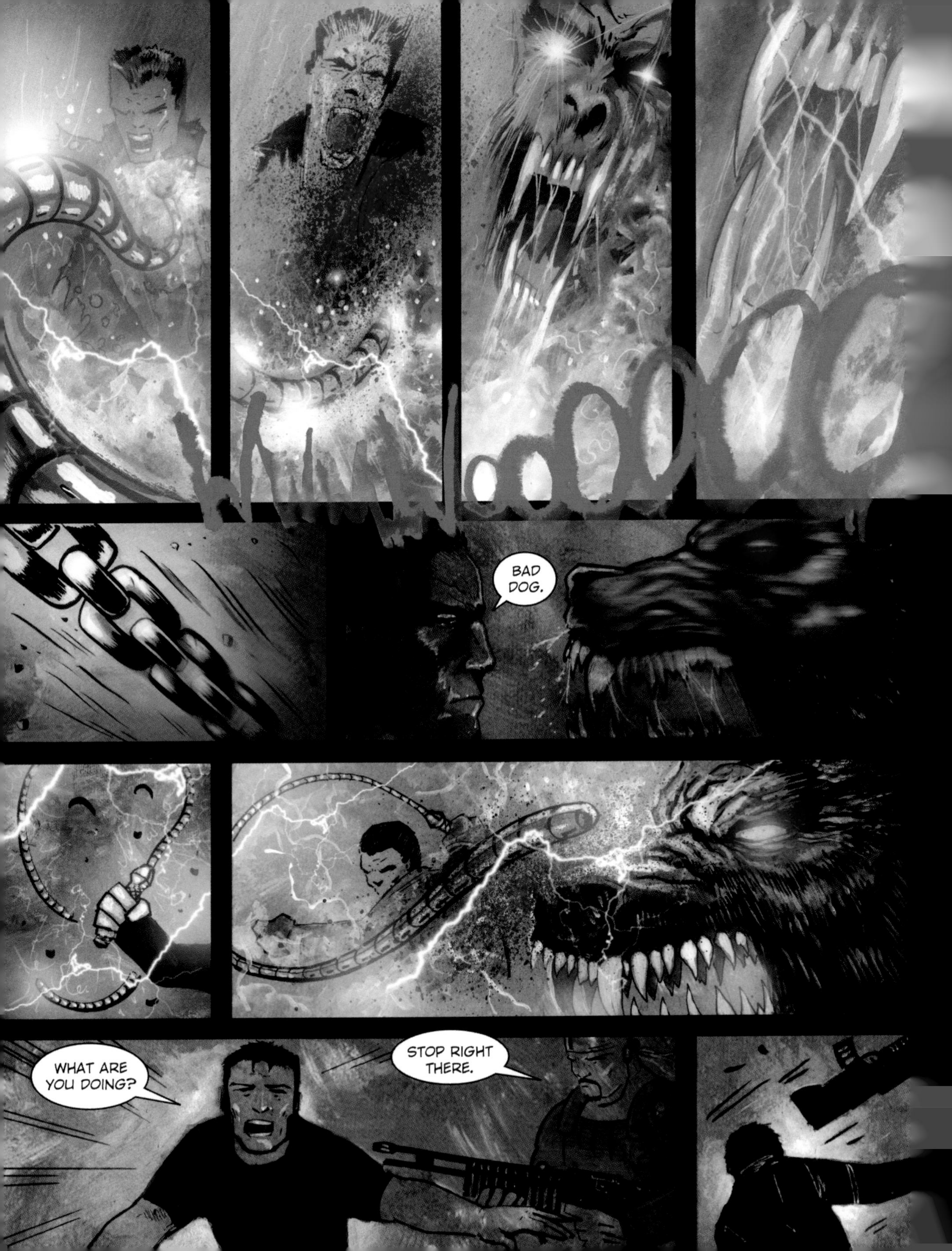
BAD DOG.
WHAT ARE YOU DOING?
STOP RIGHT THERE.

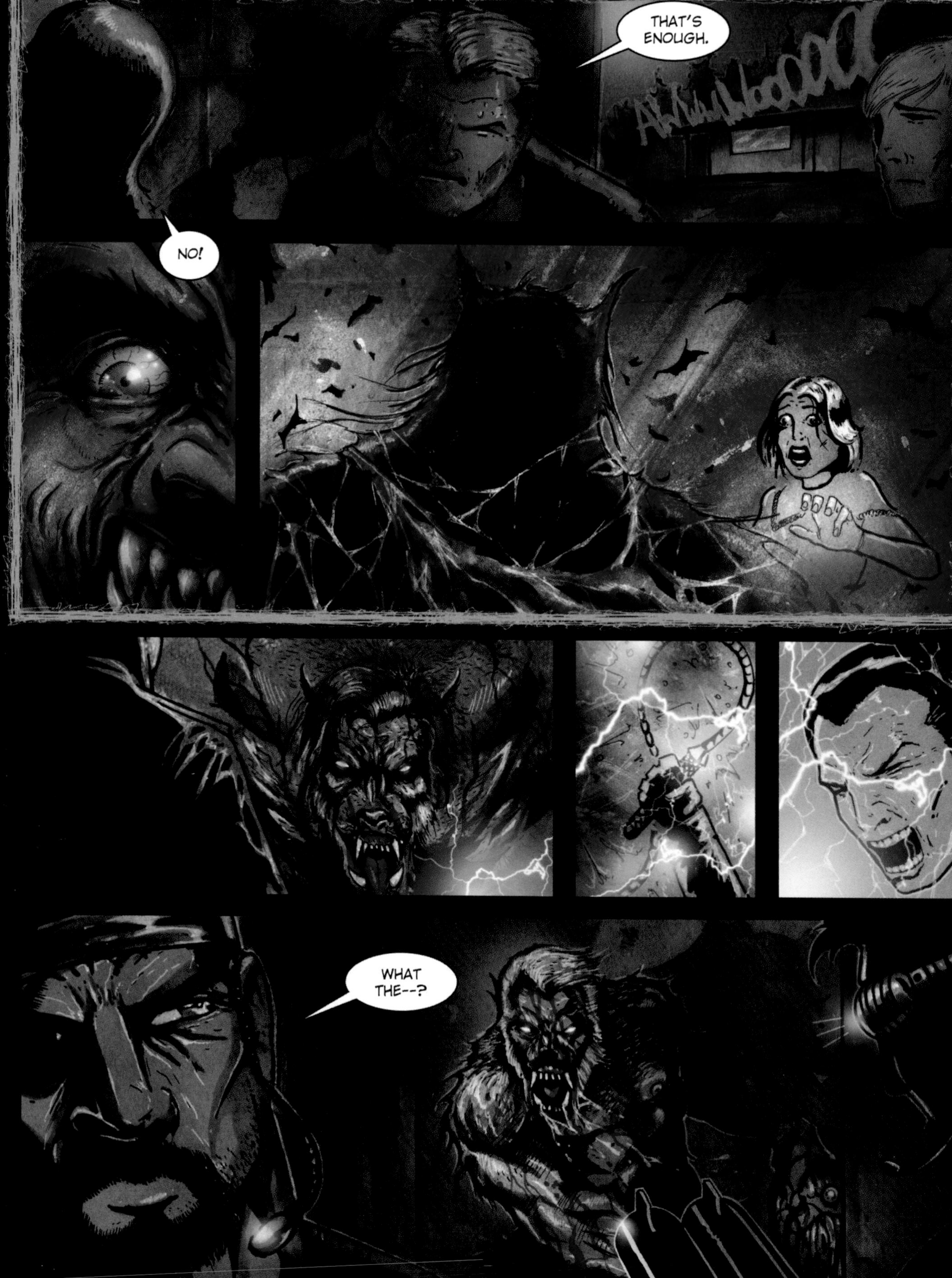
THAT'S ENOUGH.
AHHHWOOOO
NO!
WHAT THE--?

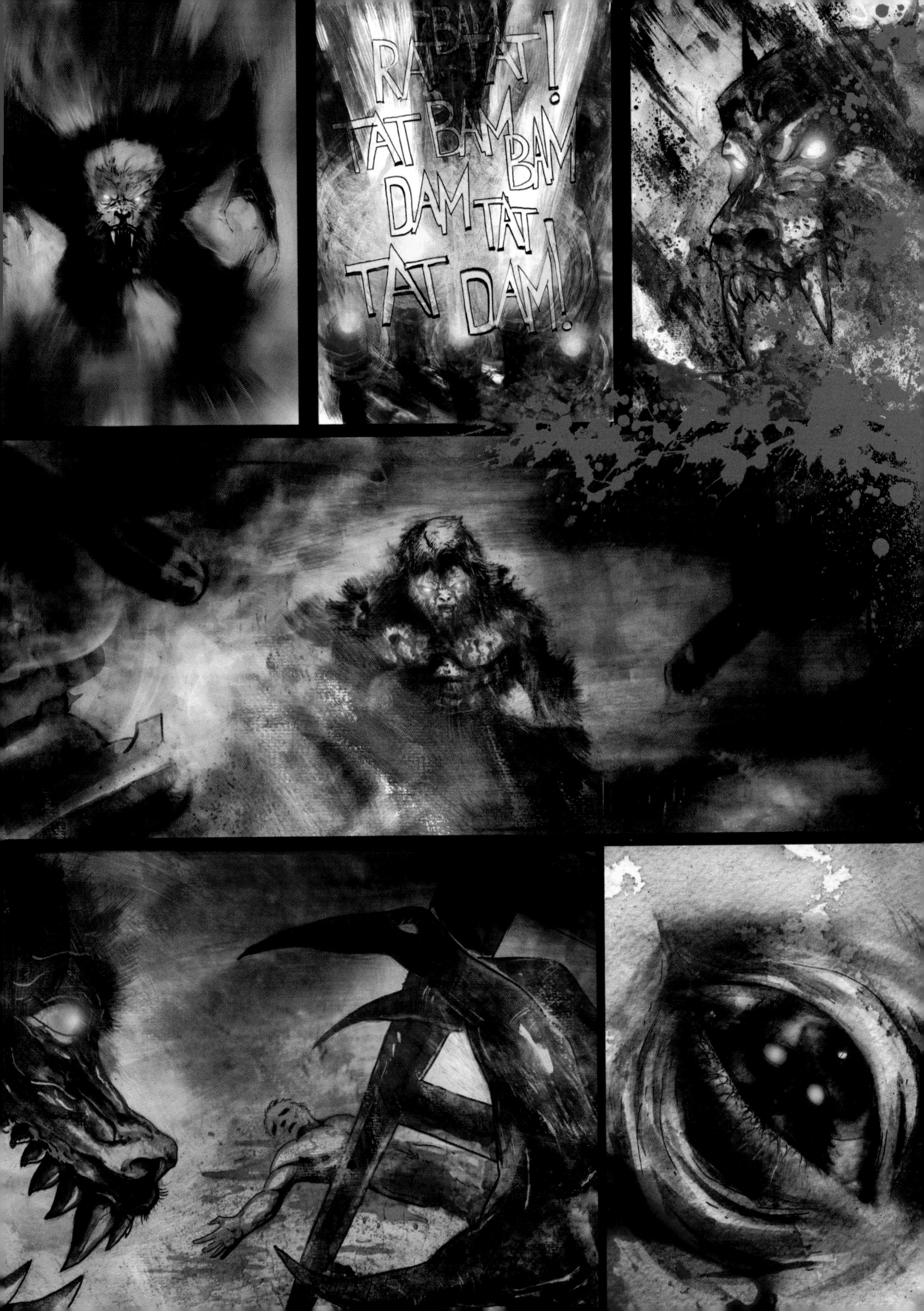
BAM
RAT TAT!
TAT BAM BAM
DAM TAT
TAT DAM!

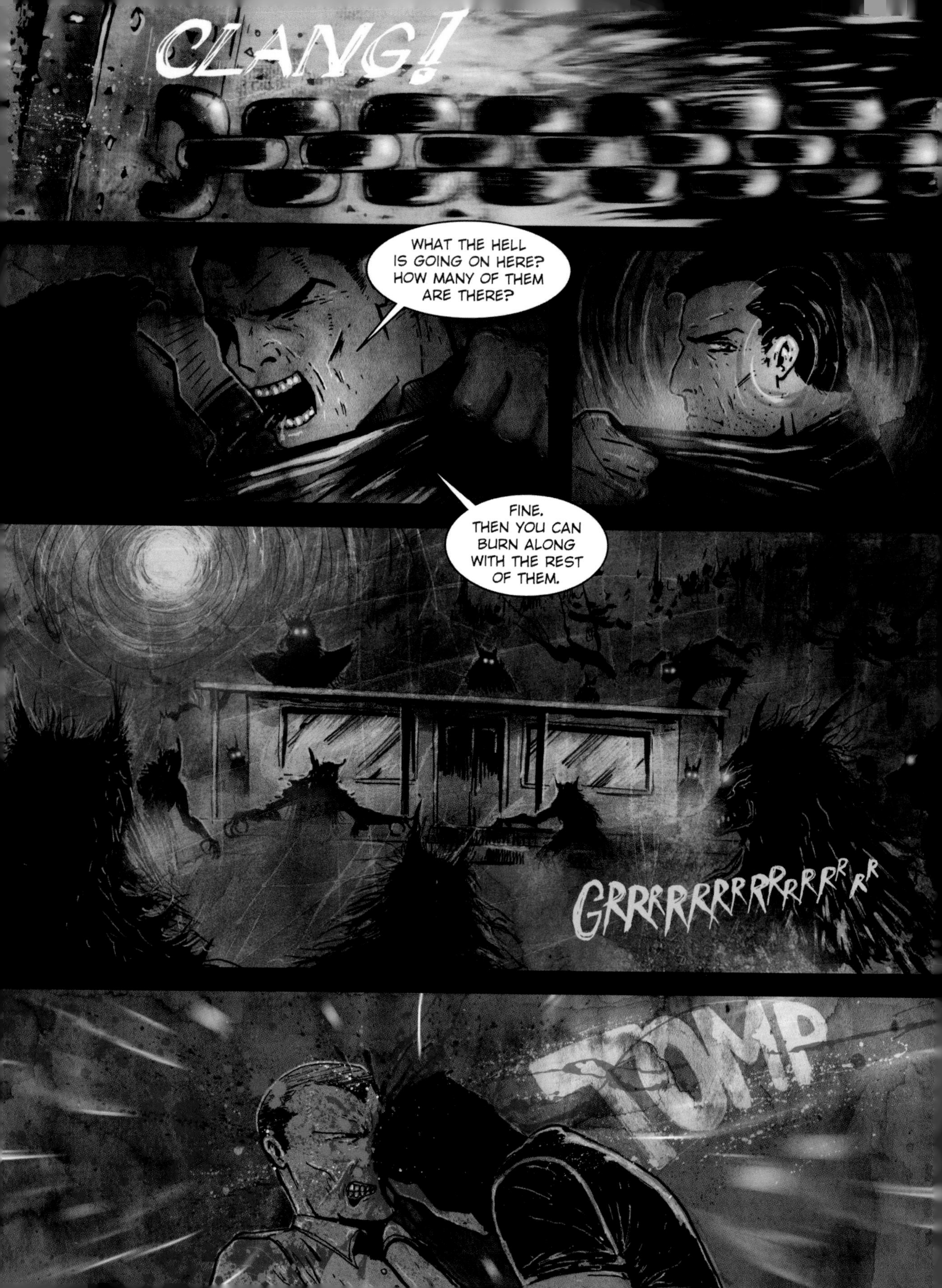
CLANG!
WHAT THE HELL IS GOING ON HERE? HOW MANY OF THEM ARE THERE?
FINE. THEN YOU CAN BURN ALONG WITH THE REST OF THEM.
GRRRRRRRRRRRRRRR
TOMP

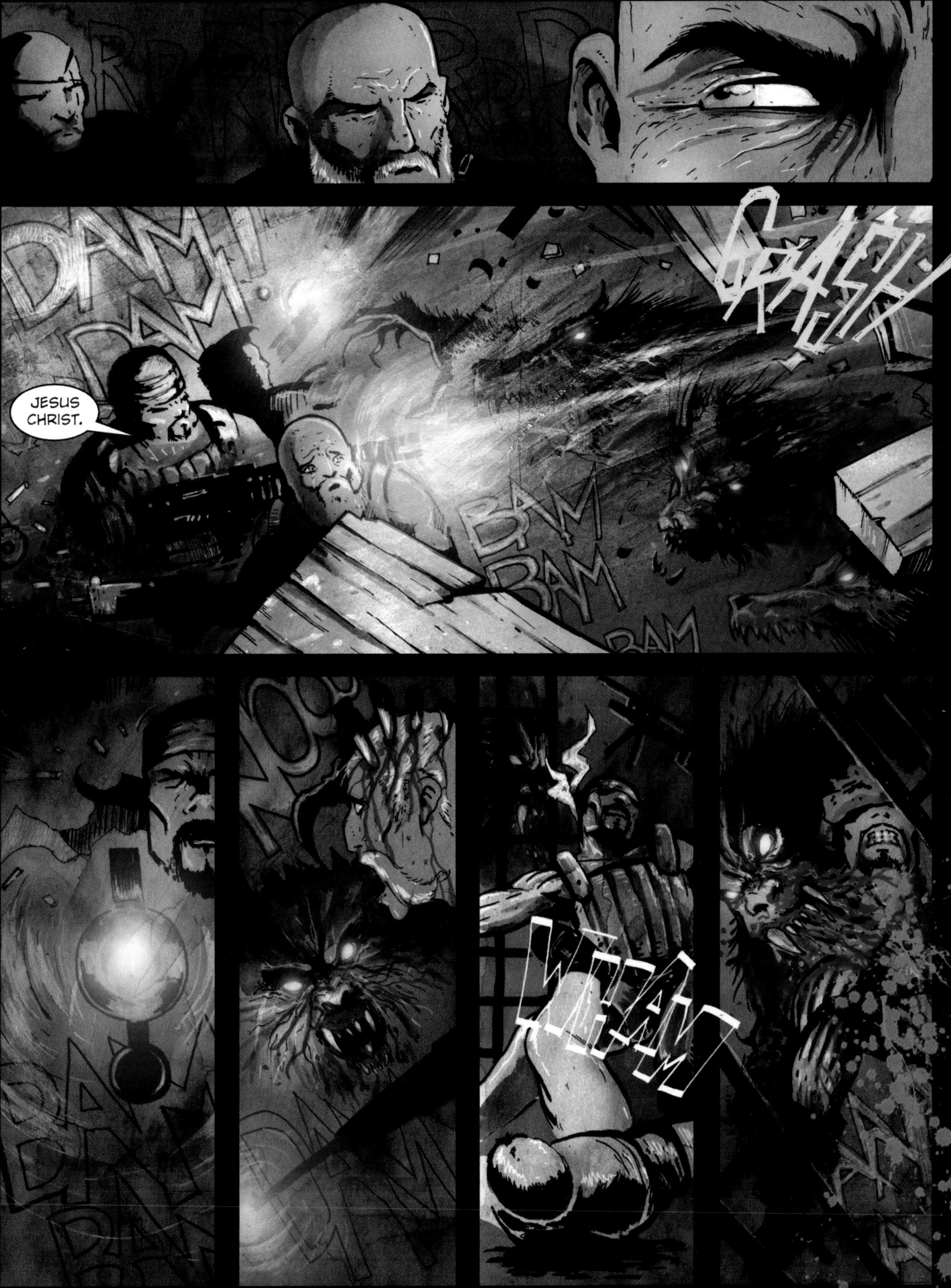
CRASH
JESUS CHRIST.
BAM
BAM
BAM
WHAM

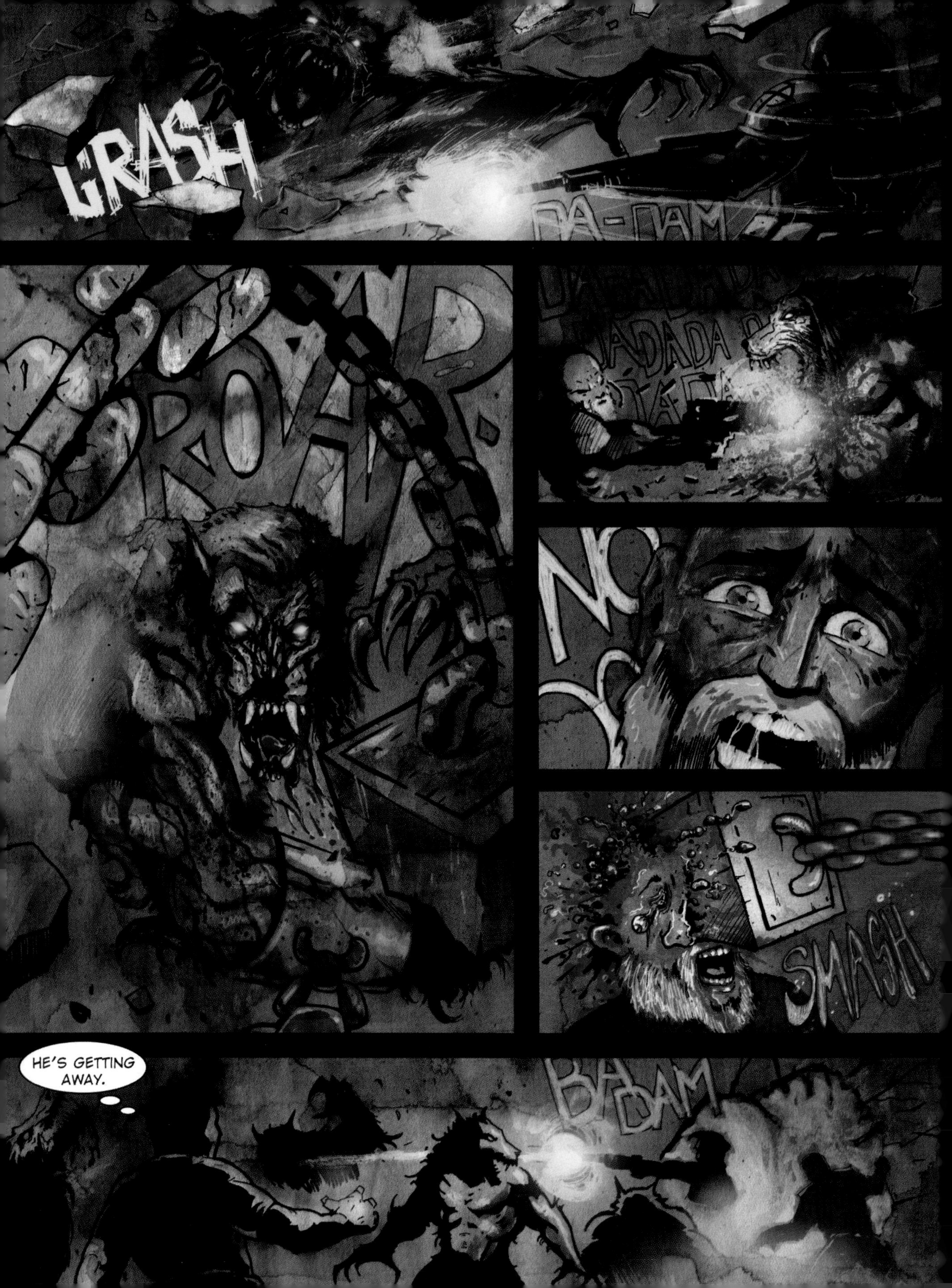

CRASH
DA-DAM
ROAR
DADADA
NO
SMASH
HE'S GETTING AWAY.
BA-DAM

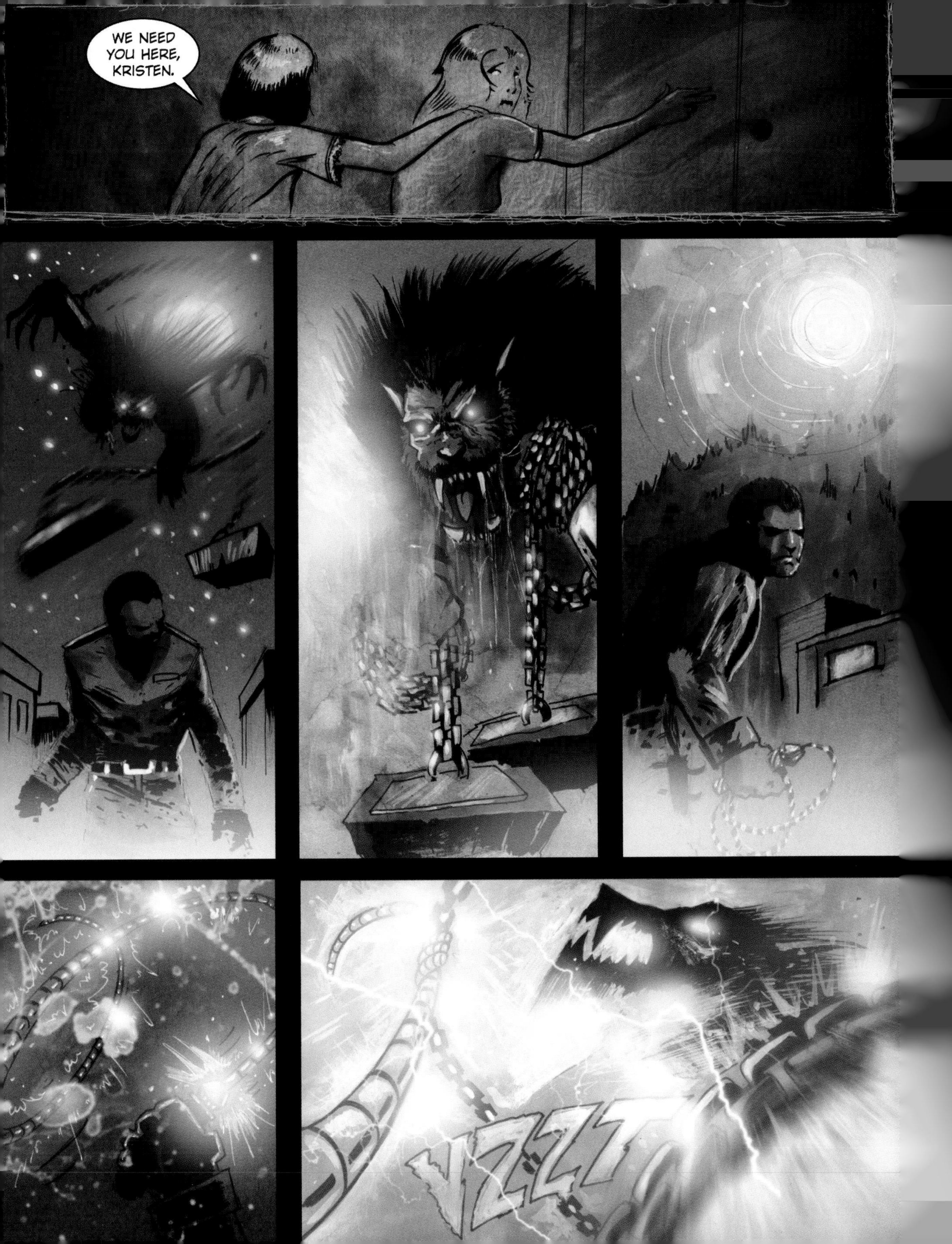
WE NEED YOU HERE, KRISTEN.
VZZZT

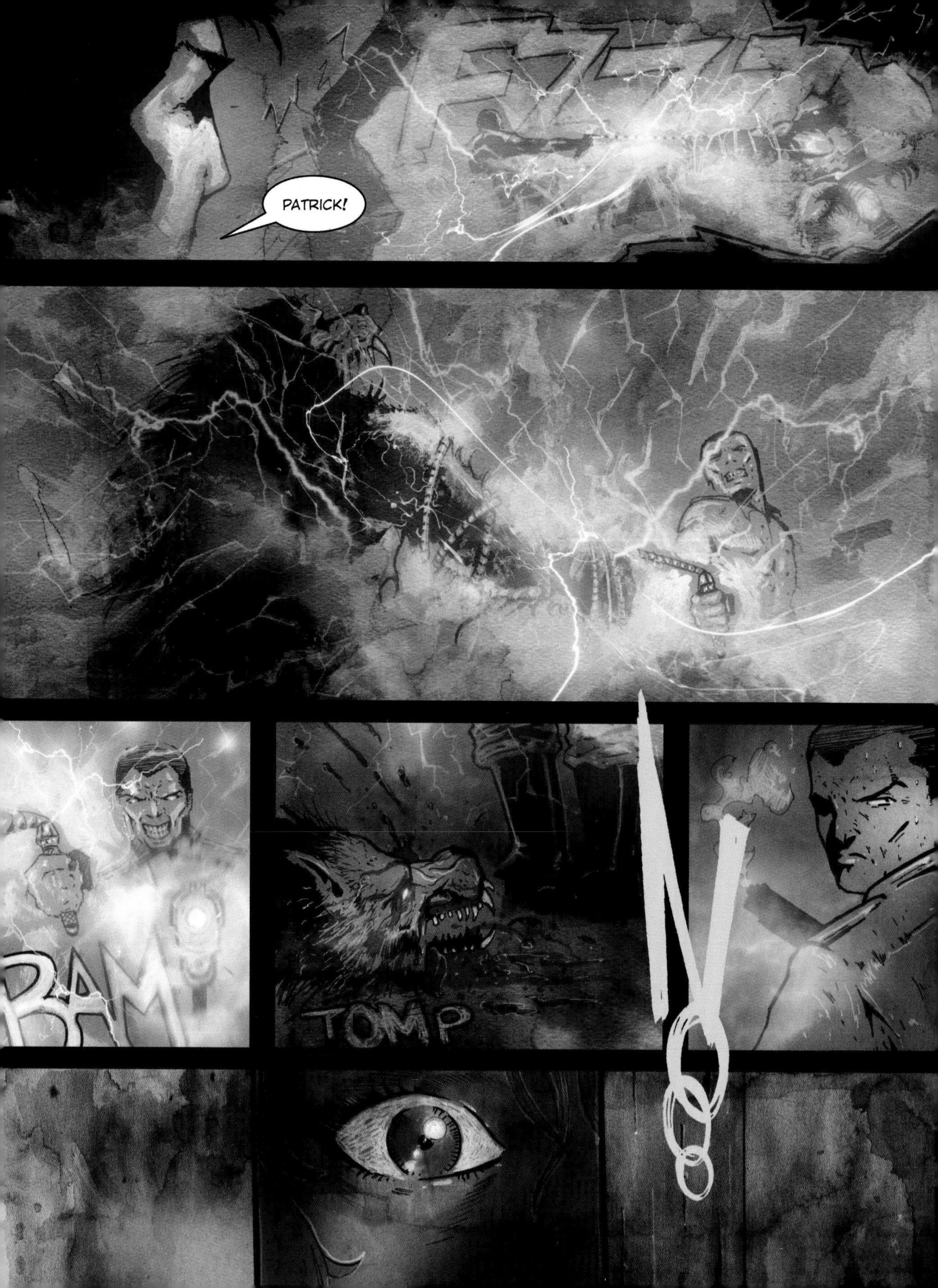
PATRICK!
BAM!
TOMP
NOOO

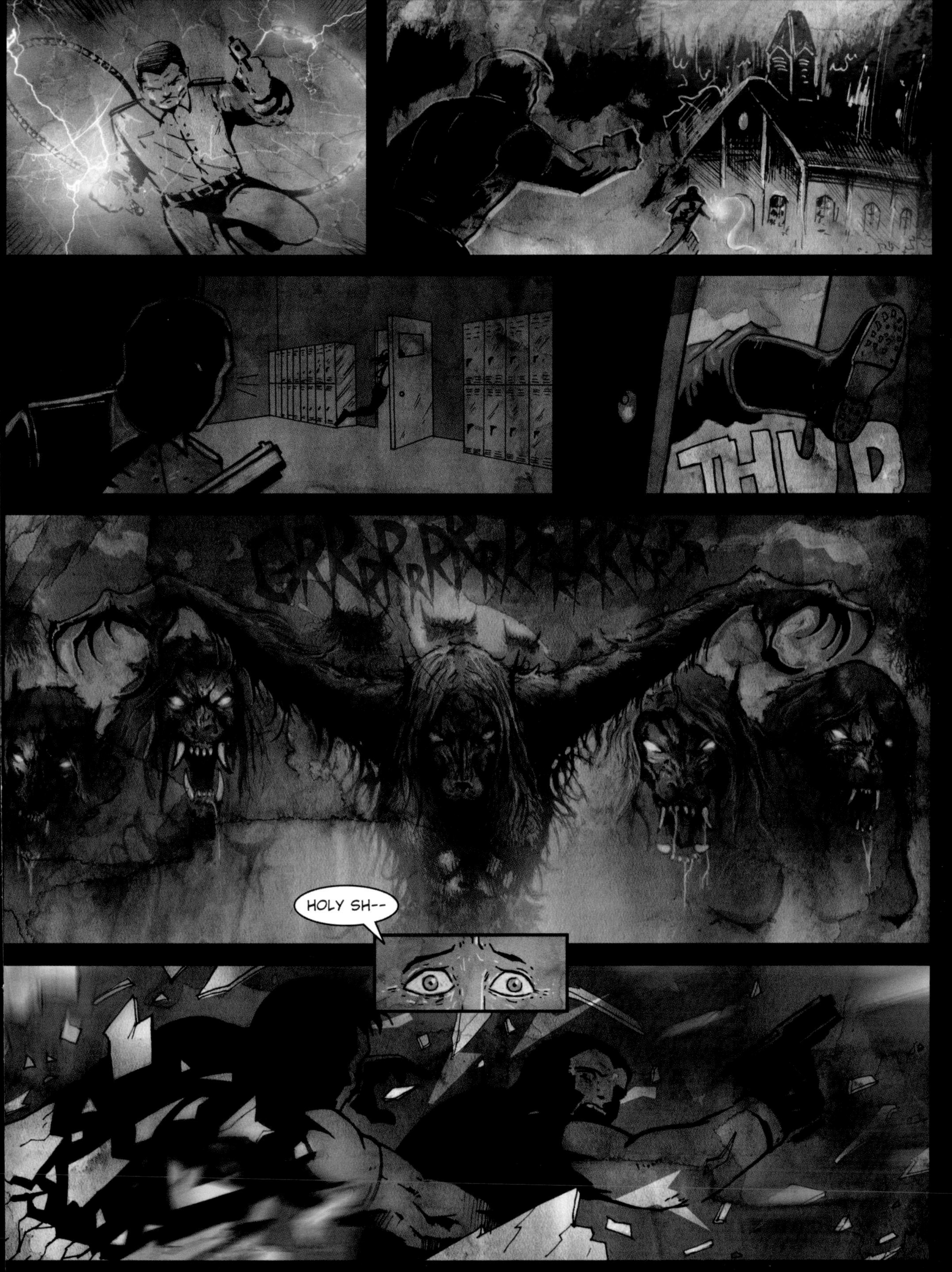
THUD
GRRRRRRRRRRRRRR
HOLY SH--

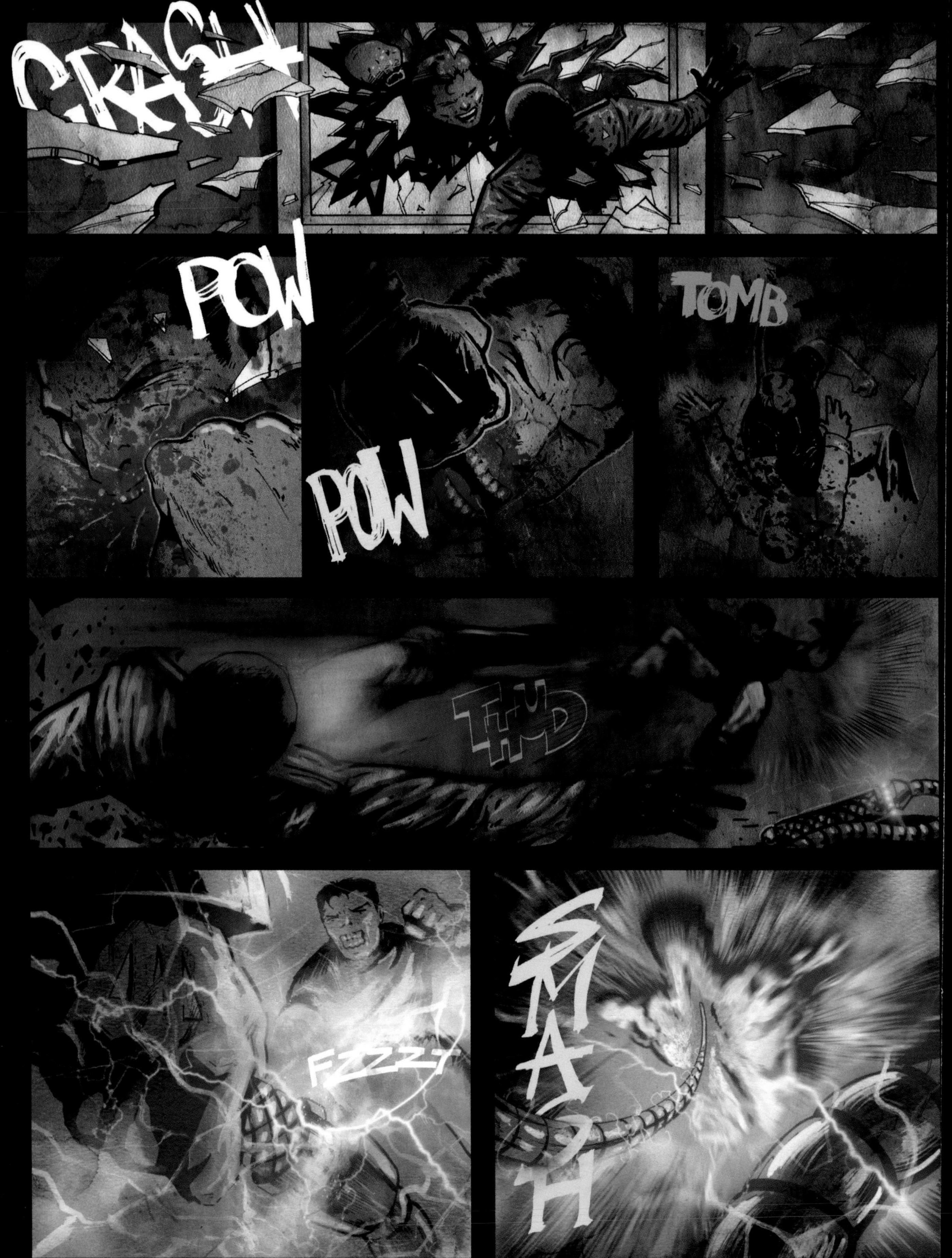
CRASH
POW
POW
TOMB
THUD
FZZZT
SMASH

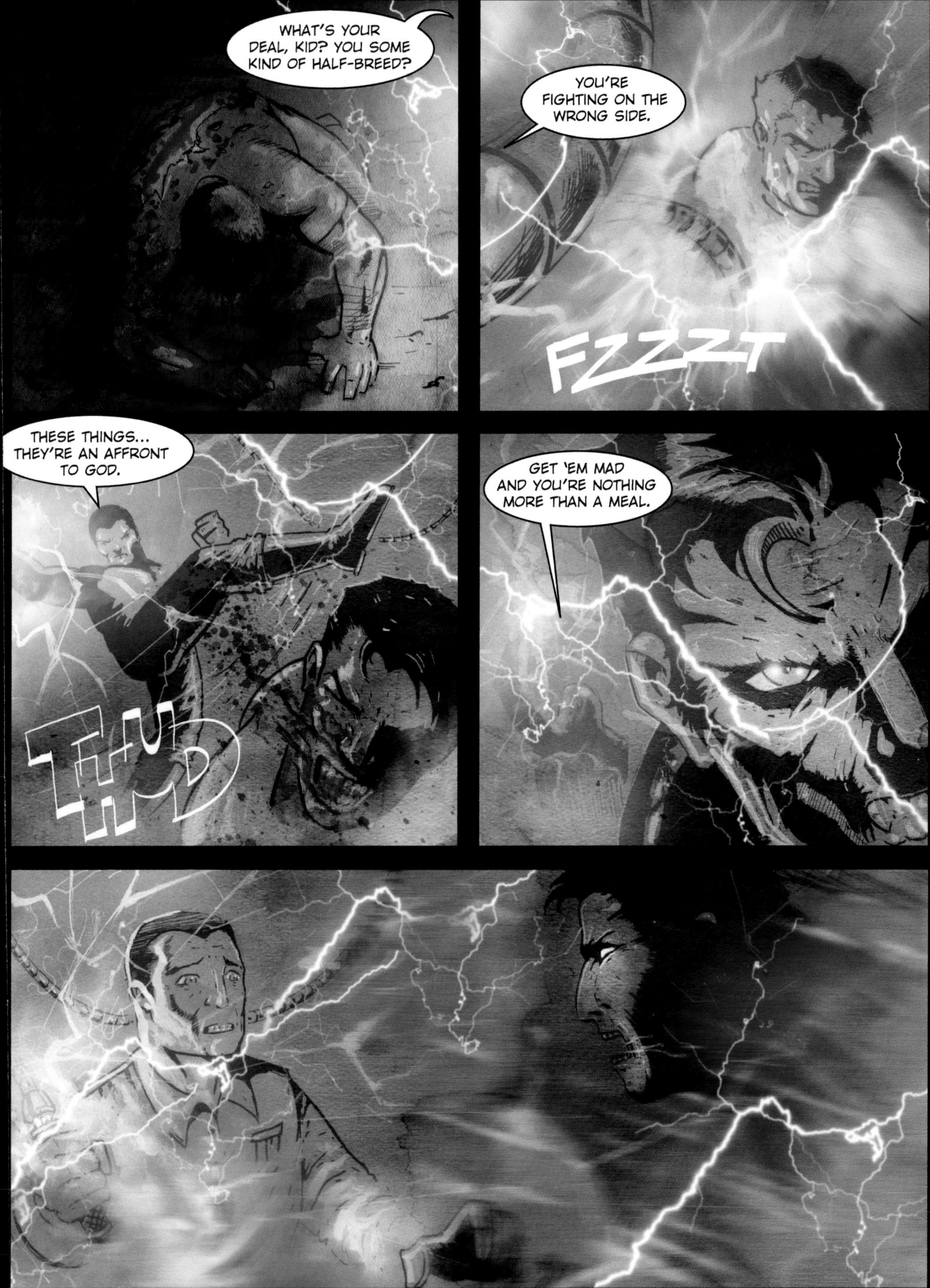
WHAT'S YOUR DEAL, KID? YOU SOME KIND OF HALF-BREED?
YOU'RE FIGHTING ON THE WRONG SIDE.
FZZZT
THESE THINGS... THEY'RE AN AFFRONT TO GOD.
THUD
GET 'EM MAD AND YOU'RE NOTHING MORE THAN A MEAL.

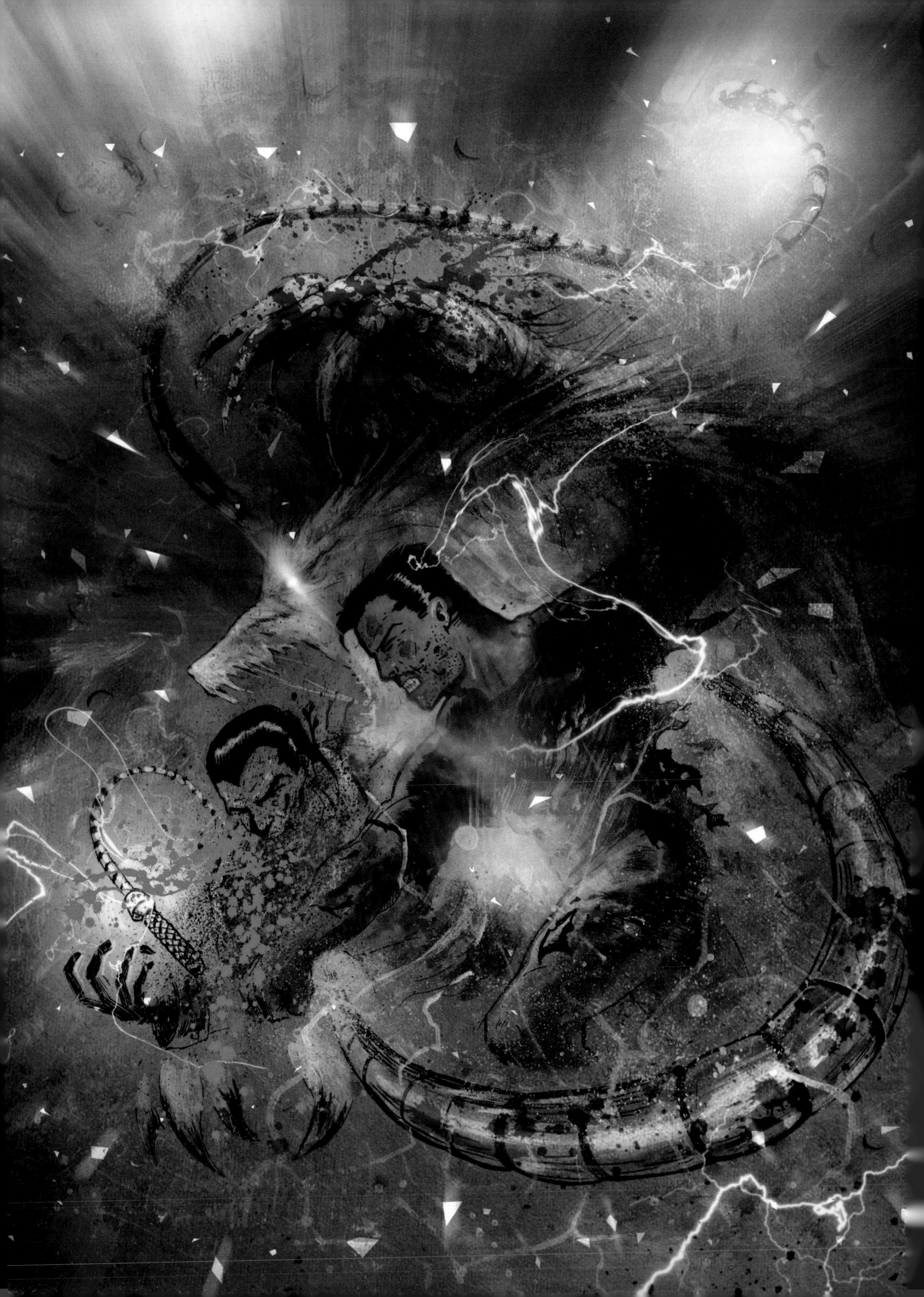

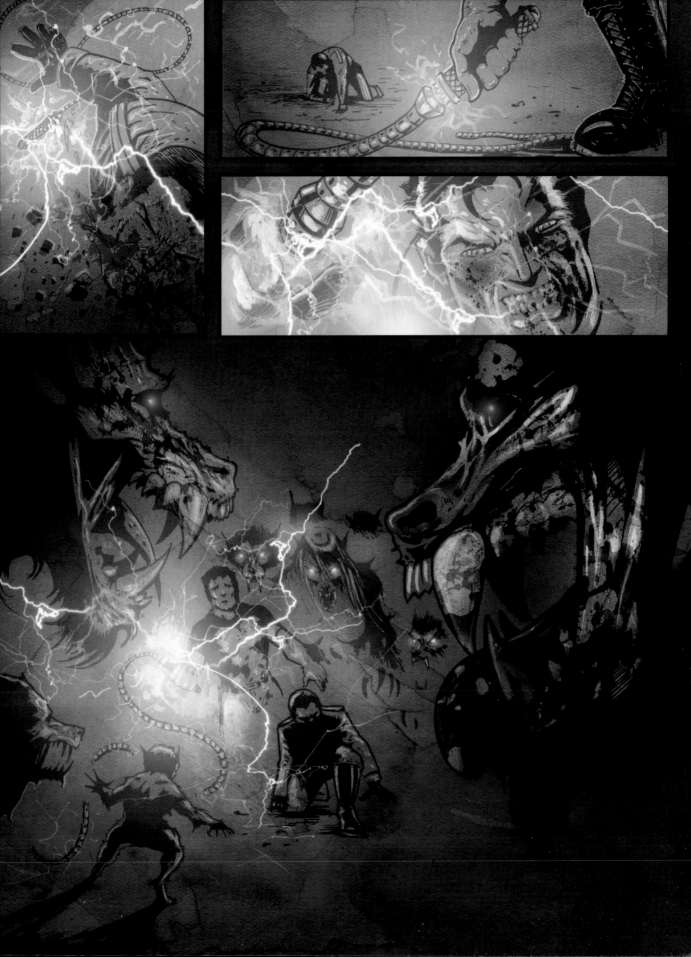

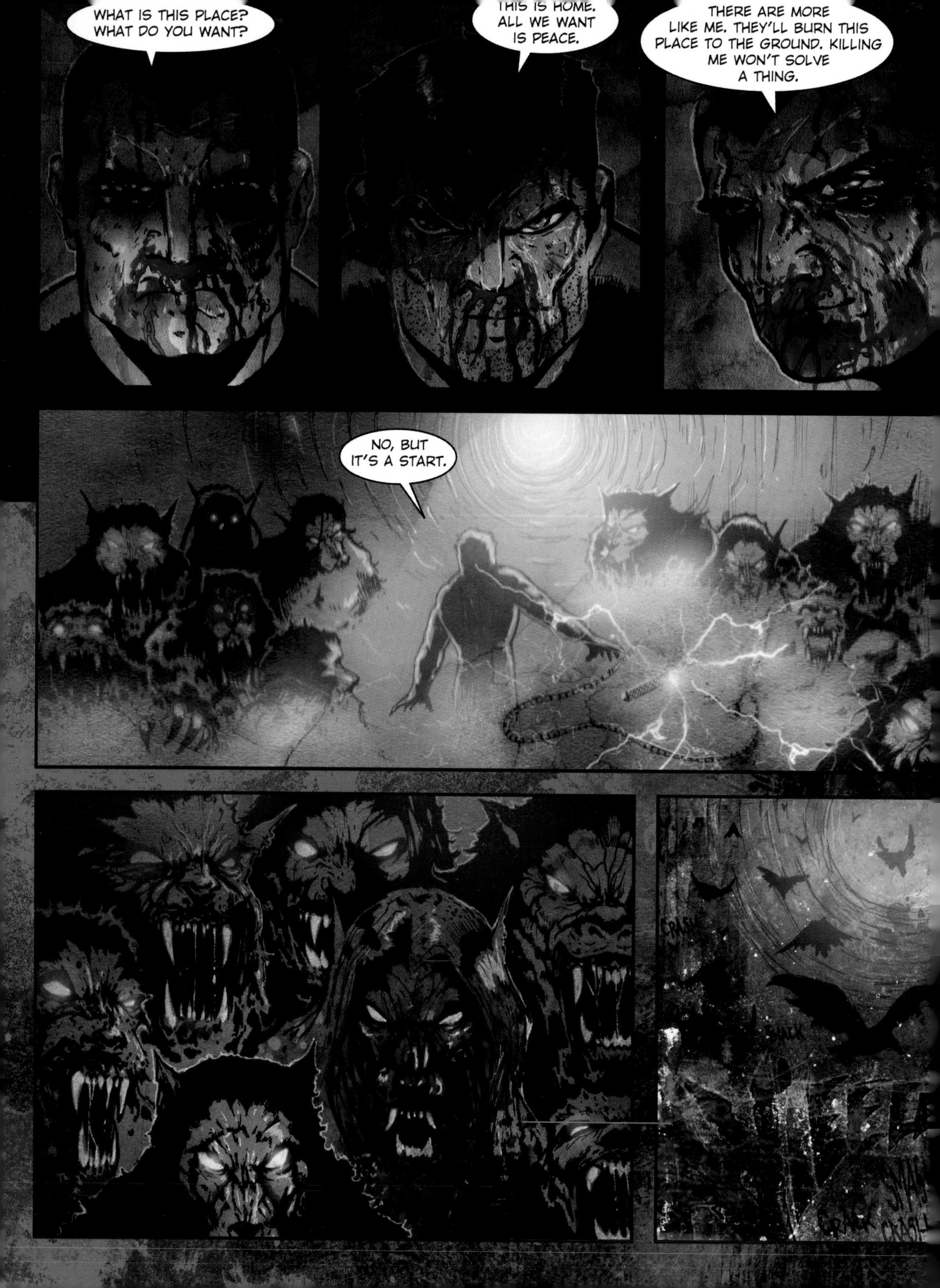
WHAT IS THIS PLACE? WHAT DO YOU WANT?
THIS IS HOME. ALL WE WANT IS PEACE.
THERE ARE MORE LIKE ME. THEY'LL BURN THIS PLACE TO THE GROUND. KILLING ME WON'T SOLVE A THING.
NO, BUT IT'S A START.

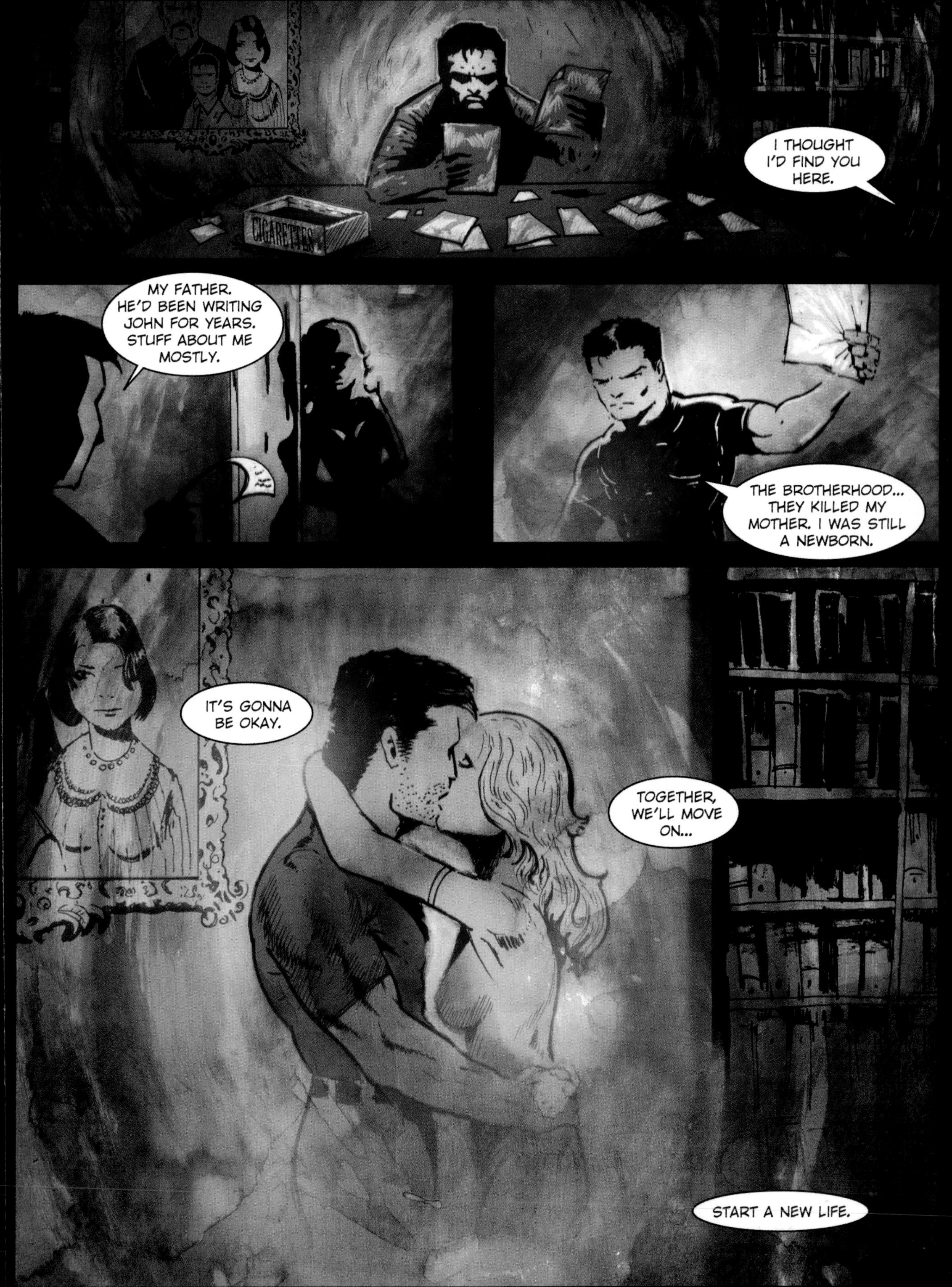
CIGARETTES
I THOUGHT I'D FIND YOU HERE.
MY FATHER. HE'D BEEN WRITING JOHN FOR YEARS. STUFF ABOUT ME MOSTLY.
THE BROTHERHOOD... THEY KILLED MY MOTHER. I WAS STILL A NEWBORN.
IT'S GONNA BE OKAY.
TOGETHER, WE'LL MOVE ON...
START A NEW LIFE.

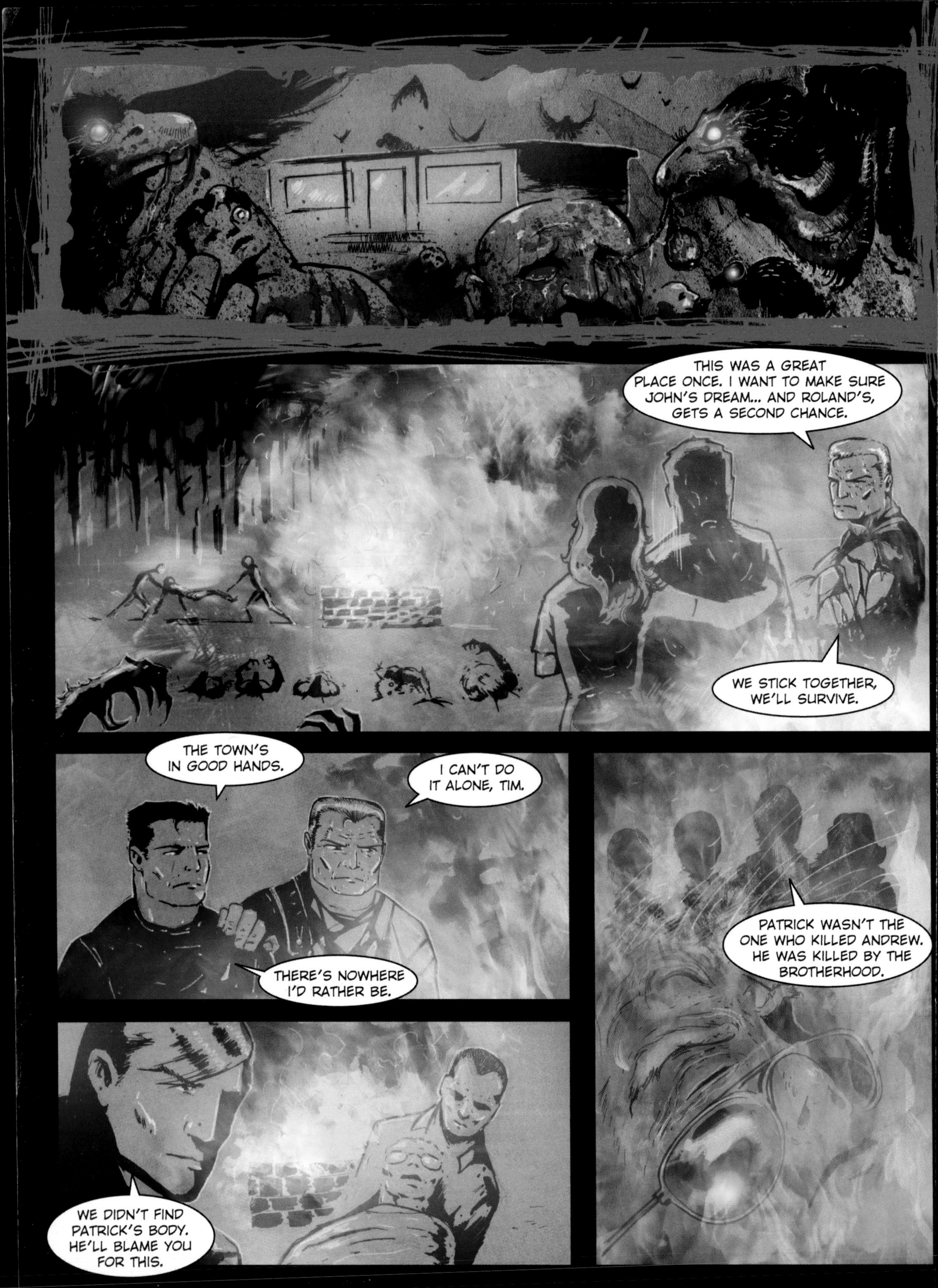
THIS WAS A GREAT PLACE ONCE. I WANT TO MAKE SURE JOHN'S DREAM... AND ROLAND'S, GETS A SECOND CHANCE.
WE STICK TOGETHER, WE'LL SURVIVE.
THE TOWN'S IN GOOD HANDS.
I CAN'T DO IT ALONE, TIM.
THERE'S NOWHERE I'D RATHER BE.
WE DIDN'T FIND PATRICK'S BODY. HE'LL BLAME YOU FOR THIS.
PATRICK WASN'T THE ONE WHO KILLED ANDREW. HE WAS KILLED BY THE BROTHERHOOD.

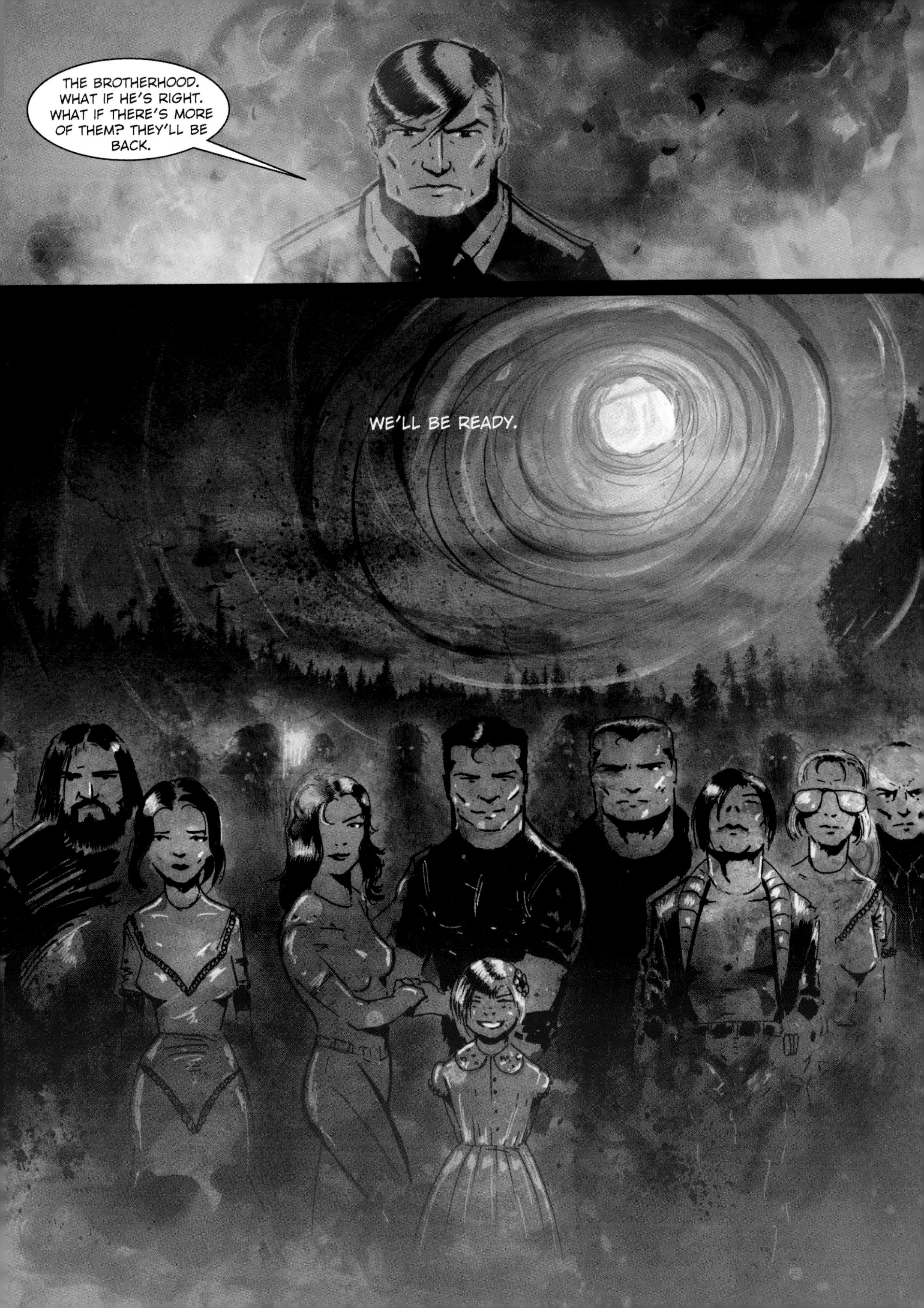
THE BROTHERHOOD. WHAT IF HE'S RIGHT. WHAT IF THERE'S MORE OF THEM? THEY'LL BE BACK.
WE'LL BE READY.

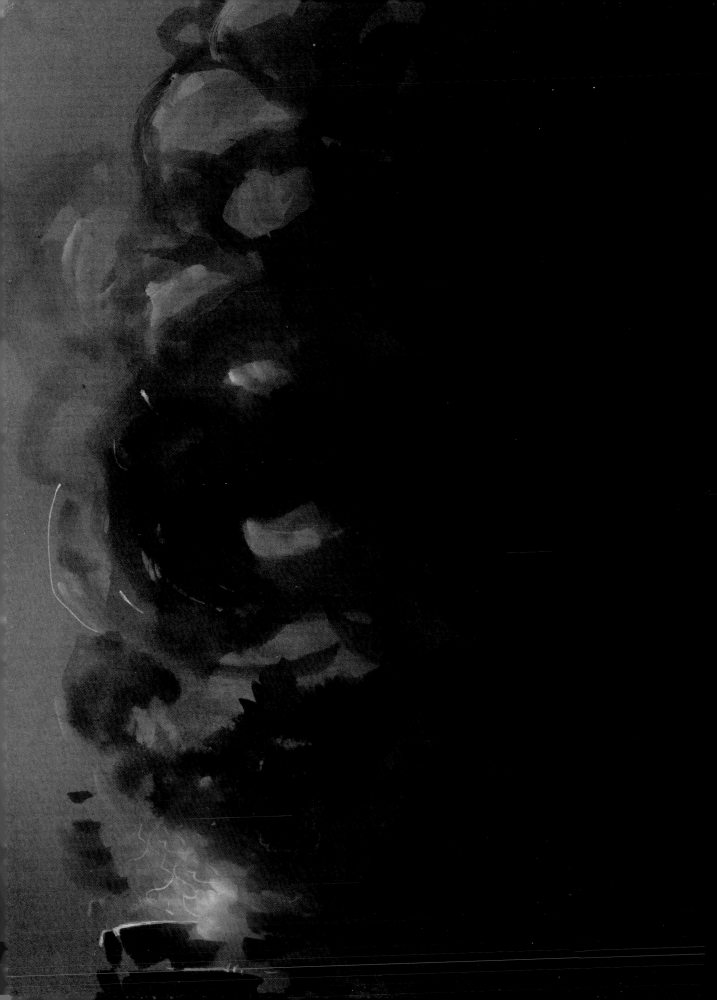